Retire
Inspired

It's Not an Age
It's a Financial Number

"For I know the plans I have for you . . .
plans to give you hope and a future."

JEREMIAH 29:11

Retire
Inspired

It's Not an Age
It's a Financial Number

CHRIS HOGAN

RAMSEY
PRESS

Published by Ramsey Press, The Lampo Group, Inc.
Brentwood, Tennessee 37027

Editors: Matt Litton, Allen Harris, Jen Gingerich
Cover Design: Tim Newton, Micah Kandros
Interior Design: Mandi Cofer

ISBN: 978-1-9370-7781-5

Printed in the United States of America
16 17 18 19 20 BVG 5 4 3 2 1

CONTENTS

DEDICATION

To Mama Hogan for all the love, prayers, and guidance you've given me all my life. Your wisdom and counsel have been instrumental! Thank you for being my mother and my friend. I've always remembered, and I will never forget!

To Melissa, my wife, cheerleader, and greatest supporter. Thank you for your constant encouragement and understanding. You are the catalyst for all this, and I am so honored to have you with me on this journey with our boys!

To the Hogan boys, Tyson, Brock, and Case. You are my greatest legacy. I'm proud to be your father and excited to see you continue to grow into great, godly men!

ACKNOWLEDGMENTS

When we started this project, I had no idea how hard it would be and how many people it would take to get a book off the ground! I now have a whole new respect for the incredible team of people I've been blessed to work with on this book. There's no way I could thank every single person who touched this project, but I definitely want to say a special word of thanks to:

> Dave Ramsey, my friend and mentor, for sharing your platform and pushing me to be better every day.
>
> Matt Litton, my editor, for helping me put countless hours' worth of coaching, teaching, and stories onto the page.

Allen Harris, friend and word master, thank you for steering and guiding this project from start to finish!

Preston Cannon for leading this project and blazing a trail!

Rick Prall and Jen Gingerich, for your incredible developmental and editorial support.

Luke LeFevre, Tim Newton, and Micah Kandros for overseeing all the design elements and cover art.

Beth Tallent and Meg Grunke, my publicity dream team.

Jeremy Breland, Suzanne Simms, Darrell Moore, Brent Driver, Dawn Medley, Jen Sievertsen, Brian Williams, Joel Rakes, and the rest of our Ramsey Solutions team for your time, prayers, leadership, and hard work throughout this entire project. We did it, guys!

FOREWORD

Dave Ramsey

I've been blessed to teach God's and Grandma's ways of handling money to people across the country for a few decades. Early on in my career, the people I looked up to, the ones who had paved the way in the area of biblical personal finance, were Larry Burkett, Howard Dayton, and Ron Blue. These guys were the masters, the dream team of biblical personal finance. It was an honor to come alongside them and carry the message of financial peace forward to a new generation.

But in all the years since I first started talking about money, I've felt like something—maybe *someone*—was missing. I believe that once in a generation, God sends a fresh, loud voice into the area of personal finance. A big voice to shake things up. A voice to get people's attention and get their financial plans on track. A voice to lead the way in a world full of confusing financial strategies, bad advice, and investing products that look like they were named with leftover Scrabble letters. I am excited to say that, after years of waiting, I've found that missing voice. In my opinion, Chris Hogan is the voice of retirement in America today.

Chris gets what so many other financial guys miss: Retirement isn't about math and interest rates; it's about your dreams. Sure, the math matters, but if you don't have your dreams at your back pushing you forward, you'll never be motivated to do the hard work of saving and investing over the course of several decades. You definitely need a tactical plan—and this book will give you that—but if you don't start with a dream of what your life will look like in that "someday world," you probably won't make it.

I don't hear a lot of so-called experts talk about dreaming as part of a healthy retirement plan. Maybe that's why when most people hear the word *retirement* they usually feel a sense of dread and despair. I hear those calls on my radio show every single day. So many of the people I talk to aren't working toward a dream; they're running into a nightmare! But when you follow the plan Chris outlines in this book, you won't just dream—you'll start *living* your dreams in high definition!

Ready to Invest?

But before you dive in to the incredible plan Chris lays out in this book, I want to make sure you're actually ready to invest. If you've read any of my books, listened to my radio show, or attended *Financial Peace University*, which Chris and I teach together, you already know about the Baby Steps. Just in case, though, let's take a minute to run through them. These seven steps show you exactly what to do and the order in which to do it. *Retire Inspired* is going to get you excited about saving for retirement, and that's great! But doing a good thing at the wrong time can lead to trouble. I want to help you avoid that.

Baby Step 1: $1,000 Beginner Emergency Fund

The first step to taking control of your money is to put a little buffer between you and the bumps in the road that often lead people into debt. Put a little starter emergency fund of $1,000 in the bank, and don't touch that money except for emergencies. If you have some money set aside for life's little hiccups, you won't be running to your credit card every time you get a flat tire. Believe it or not, a healthy retirement *later* actually begins with this little emergency fund *today*. You're starting a long journey, and this is the first step.

Baby Step 2: Get Out of Debt Using the Debt Snowball

Debt won't just add stress and regret to your life; it'll wreck your retirement dream. Chris will talk about that in detail in this book. For now, I want you to get mad and declare all-out war on your debt! List your debts (not including your home mortgage) from smallest to largest by balance, and then attack the smallest one. Throw every dollar you can at it and get it out of your life as quickly as possible. Once that is done, move on to the second one, then the third, and so on. As you pay one off, you free up more money to apply to the next debt. That's why I call it the Debt Snowball method: as the snowball rolls over, it picks up more "snow" or more money to put toward your debts.

Paying off your debt is your priority at this point, which means you won't be investing toward retirement yet. That may seem counterproductive in a book about retirement, but it works. The average American spends a huge percentage of their paycheck on consumer debts. Getting out of debt frees up your largest wealth-building tool: your income. When you're out of debt and ready to invest, you'll have a lot more money to put toward your retirement, and you won't be looking over your shoulder at your creditors because you won't have any!

Baby Step 3: Fully Funded Emergency Fund of Three to Six Months of Expenses

Once you're debt-free except your home, your next goal is to go back and beef up that emergency fund you started in Baby Step 1. A fully funded emergency fund of three to six months of expenses is a game changer. Just think about what life would feel like with zero debt except the mortgage and $10,000–15,000 sitting in the bank for emergencies! Do not skip this step. If you have no emergency fund but you do have a 401(k), guess what happens when a big emergency pops up? Your 401(k) *becomes* your emergency fund—and you'll lose up to 40 percent of your money to taxes and penalties in the process. That's a bad plan! Do the steps in order.

Baby Step 4: Save 15 Percent of Your Income for Retirement

Here we go! At this point, you are ready to start attacking your retirement dream with gusto! You'll use tax-favored plans to save 15 percent of your income for retirement. This is an exciting time, but don't go overboard. Unless retirement is right around the corner, you need to stick to 15 percent so you still have money to put toward the next couple of Baby Steps. That's all I'll say about Baby Step 4 here. Chris will tell you everything you need to know about how to put your money to work for your retirement dream.

Baby Step 5: Save for Your Children's College

If you have kids, the next step is to start saving for their college expenses in a good Education Savings Account, or ESA. Pay attention to the order here: you're investing 15 percent of your income into retirement, *then* you're working on college savings. Retirement is the higher priority. Your child may or may not go to college, and they will be able to help pay their own way. You, however, are definitely going to retire one day, and the income you have then depends entirely on what you are doing now. Don't shortchange your retirement by focusing on college first. Stick to the plan!

Baby Step 6: Pay Off the House

Baby Steps 4, 5, and 6 all happen at the same time, so any money you have left after you've contributed to your retirement and your children's college savings should go toward your mortgage. The home mortgage represents the last big hurdle in your financial journey. Don't lose your focus or energy yet! Climb that mountain, pay off the house, and then you'll be completely, totally, 100 percent debt-free! Can you even imagine what that would feel like? I've walked with hundreds of thousands of families through this process, and they all tell me the grass in the yard feels different under their bare feet when they actually own it.

Baby Step 7: Build Wealth and Give

At this point, you are a financial rock star. You don't owe a dime to anyone. You have a big emergency fund sitting in the bank just in case, you've been contributing to your 401(k) and other retirement accounts, and your children have college savings waiting on them. Now is the time to completely blow up your retirement savings. Now it's not just about reaching your retirement dream; it's about building wealth that can change your family, your community, and your legacy for generations to come.

But that's not all. Now it's time to practice incredible, outrageous generosity. When you can do whatever you want with every dime of your income, you might be surprised to discover that *giving* is absolutely your favorite thing to do with money. Being able to step in and intersect someone's life in a moment of crisis is the best thing in the world! I want you to dream about what life will be like at this point, and giving definitely needs to be part of that dream. Trust me on this one.

Chris will occasionally refer back to these Baby Steps in this book, so if they're new to you, be sure to bookmark these pages so you can flip back for a refresher whenever you need it.

This Book Is Your How-To Manual

I can't tell you how excited I am about Chris Hogan and about *Retire Inspired*! We at Ramsey Solutions are proud to have Chris on our team. I'm proud to have shared the stage with him. And I'm even prouder to call him my friend. When you hear Chris speak, attend one of his classes, or finish this book, you'll call him a friend too. You just can't help it! I've been helping people take control of their money for more than twenty-five years, but I've never had a rock-solid, comprehensive guide to retirement (that I trust) to put in their hands. Now I do. Once you're debt-free with a fully funded emergency fund, it's time to target your retirement dream with laser focus. This is the book that will show you how.

INTRODUCTION

"Well, right now I am doing whatever I want to."

The man sitting across the table from me delivered that line with a casual shrug of his shoulders. The "whatever I want to" part of his statement hit me hard because it was something I rarely heard when counseling people about their finances, and, frankly, I was a little confused by his response.

This gentleman wasn't Mark Cuban, and he certainly wasn't the CEO of some billion-dollar oil company. He hadn't gone to Vegas and hit it big playing blackjack, and he hadn't won the lottery. He hadn't inherited millions of dollars from a long-lost, rich relative. He was a faithful, blue-collar guy who had spent his early years serving the US military. He was in his early forties and had worked a nine-to-five job. He had stayed out of debt, worked, and saved.

I glanced down at the portfolio and back into the face of this guy who had come to me for financial advice. The numbers I was looking at on the paper didn't really match up with the age of the young man in front of me. And truthfully, most of the conversations I had with folks his age were filled with the familiar refrain of "I have to." I didn't hear "whatever I want to" very often.

Just to make sure I wasn't missing something obvious in the financial papers he had given me, I leaned a bit closer and asked, "I'm sorry, so what did you say you do for a living?" I guess I was fishing for his "have-to" explanation.

"Oh," he smiled, beginning to understand my confusion, "I'm retired now, so I pretty much do whatever I *want* to do for work."

His words hung in the air—"Whatever I *want* to do." It was a game-changing moment for me. You see, I was thinking the same thing you might've thought, because, up to that point in my career, I had worked with folks whose retirement was coming in their later years and closer to the "end" of their story. I had believed that retirement was an age. But this man was retired in his early forties. That didn't happen by accident. That happened because he had been working a smart, consistent plan from the time he started his first job in his twenties.

His life was no longer full of the "have-tos," and we were now getting ready to talk about the phase of his life where he could turn his attention to the "want-tos." We were going to discuss his dreams. And for a moment, I wondered if maybe he should be counseling me. In a culture of people with no investment in their own dreams and no plan for the future, I was inspired by his story.

I want you to be inspired by his story too. I need you to see that you can also move from the have-to stage of survival to the want-to stage of living!

Let's Begin a Retirement Revolution

I believe that *inspired* is an important word. In fact, inspired is exactly where we need to begin this retirement conversation. I could start this book by throwing out negative statistics. I could remind you that most people fail to invest in their dreams, but they willingly invest in $5 cups of coffee, $200 gym shoes, $300 jeans, $500 phones, $3,000 computers, and $50,000 cars that are all outdated within two years or used up in two minutes. I could explain the unnerving truth that over 60 percent of Americans have less than $25,000 saved for their own retirement.[1]

I could tell you about how I have traveled the country and talked with thousands and thousands of hardworking Americans who will be left almost completely broke, with no real hope of a financial future. But those statistics on debt and hopelessness are not just numbers to me anymore.

You see, behind every statistic are real people with real names, real faces, and real families. I've walked with them, laughed with them, and cried with them. I've seen the fear in their eyes—the distress of people who hit their senior years with no money and are suddenly unable to work. These stories are the real-life nightmares that keep me awake at night because, after years of working in the banking and finance business, after running the spreadsheets and playing with financial calculators for a million hours, I've realized something about retirement planning: It's not about the math. It's about people, and people matter.

I don't want to begin our conversation by scaring or depressing you with numbers and statistics or real-life stories about retirement in America. If you're like a lot of the people I've coached over the years, the very word *retirement* might give you the same shivers you'd get from watching a Stephen King movie. That fear might get your attention for a moment. And while fear can be a wake-up call, it is also a negative emotion. Fear doesn't create energy, and it doesn't really cause lasting change.

And, my friend, I want you to change. In fact, it is time for you to change.

I want to begin our conversation about retirement with inspiration. I want you to be inspired. I know from my own story and from working with thousands of people that inspiration is the fuel that will move you to action. I want you to remember that my friend who retired in his early forties wasn't a financial superhero. He was just like you and me. I want to start a retirement revolution with you, and it has to begin with you being inspired.

I began working with people and their finances more than twenty years ago. In those first years, I thought I was just working with money. It didn't take long for me to realize that I was doing something much bigger. I was helping people change their life stories. Like I told you, people matter to me. You matter to me. I am driven to help people make real and lasting change.

Now, let me tell you how I came to embrace the energy of inspiration and why I am so passionate about your retirement.

Educating, Encouraging, Empowering

I began my career after graduate school working as a lender and a collector. That's right. I was a bill collector. If you've ever met me or heard me speak, you may find this entertaining. I'm a pretty big guy, which served me well on the football field tackling opponents and winning a national championship. I also have an unusually deep voice. Think of the deepest voice you've ever heard (like Barry White deep), and then crank it down just a bit lower. That, plus my love of quoting lines from my favorite gangster movies, made me a pretty effective collector.

But what I saw early in my career was not entertaining at all. It was the reality of people living paycheck to paycheck and borrowing money to make ends meet. I was quickly promoted to manager, and eventually I was calling the shots on the "collecting crunch." I even trained people on how to collect "humanely but effectively."

After several grueling years, I transitioned to mainstream banking, where I watched the same depressing cycle: more people coming in to the bank to get loans that didn't help them. I knew they didn't need another loan. What they desperately needed was help from someone who could show them how to get out of debt for life. My wife and I had discovered Dave Ramsey and had worked through Dave's Baby Steps (which Dave covers in the foreword to this book), and we were getting our own finances in order. But going into work day after day and witnessing person after person in hopeless financial shape was really getting to me.

I longed to make a difference in the world, and it didn't seem that my current position would ever allow me the opportunity to do that. My wife knew that I was getting frustrated with the whole lending job, so she told me that I should go meet Dave Ramsey. "Sure, Dear," I joked. "Why don't I just hop in the car, roll up to his office, introduce myself, and sit in on his radio show too while I'm at it?"

But a year or so later, my wife and I attended a silent auction with some friends from our church. The event was held to benefit a nonprofit organization that helped families in need, and while we were there, my wife noticed an item marked "Dave's Chair." The chair represented a chance to sit in the studio with Dave Ramsey as a spectator during his national radio broadcast. Throughout the evening, I think my wife might've stalked this item like I used to stalk quarterbacks on the football field. I was eyeing some football tickets while my wife was on a mission to get me to meet Dave. Sure enough, when the auction closed, my wife handed me a framed picture of Dave and said, "Now, Chris, go meet this man!"

I went to the show and listened as Dave talked to millions of people on the radio. I was inspired by his heart for helping people. On commercial breaks we talked about the missional nature of his work and my own heart for helping folks get out of debt. The day after meeting him, I received an unexpected phone message from

Dave inviting me to lunch. I was pretty sure that it was a prank from one of my buddies who knew I was a big fan. But the following day, I received yet another message and realized it wasn't a prank at all. Dave wanted to get together with me to talk!

We met the next Monday, and I shared my heart for educating, encouraging, and empowering people. In a second meeting, we discussed ideas for bringing the message of financial peace to a broader audience. And after a third meeting, Dave asked me if I would be interested in joining his team. It was the beginning of a dream for me to be able to truly help people with their finances instead of watching them go deeper into debt. It was a chance to trade hopelessness for hope. I was all in!

By attending an event designed to assist people in need, I met a man who has devoted his life to helping people by sharing his financial knowledge. Now I use the experience I gained from working for credit companies and banks to help people avoid the same desperate situations I witnessed in my previous jobs. My professional journey has taught me that money and retirement are never just about money and retirement; they are about real-life, everyday people—and their dreams.

So we aren't simply talking about retirement. We are talking about making a real difference in your life, in your marriage, and in the lives of your children. I don't care how old you are or how much you have saved for retirement so far. My goal is to educate, encourage, and empower you to take the exact steps you need to take in order to experience not just any old retirement, but an inspired retirement—a dream retirement.

Moving from a Wish to a Dream

One of the first steps to take on the road to your dream retirement is to realize we're not just talking about the *end* of your life. When some people hear the word *retirement*, they immediately start thinking of death. Not me. I don't want to wait that long to enjoy what I'm working on. If we're talking about my dream, then I promise you I want to live in it for a while.

I'm all about putting in the hard work of making my dreams come true, but I really want them to come true sooner rather than later. To make that happen, though, I've got to get to work. I've got to put in the effort, make wise decisions, and make my dreams a reality. That won't happen by accident. I've met a lot of people who dream about their retirement, which is great. The problem is, most people don't turn their dreams into action. They never change their behaviors. They just hope for the best.

I heard former NFL head coach and ESPN analyst Herm Edwards speak at a conference once, and he explained that a dream without a plan isn't really a dream at all. It's a wish. I have spent time with plenty of people in my career who *wished* that their finances were in order. I have met with plenty of people who *wished* for a retirement. The problem with a wish is that it doesn't require any action. A wish isn't even as significant as a Hail Mary pass in a football game. A wish requires no follow-through, no discipline, and no action on your part at all. Wishes are as good as giving up! If you are going to have a real dream, you need a real plan.

Planning for a Dream

Since I began working with Dave, I have been a financial coach to some of the biggest names in Hollywood, professional sports, and entertainment. I have given guidance to complex financial decisions as well as fundamental money problems. These years of working "kneecap to kneecap" with people from all walks of life have taught me one fundamental truth: most of these folks lack a plan. The necessity of a plan sounds simple, but it is the one glaring omission that so many of us seem to overlook.

I have traveled the country enough to know that it is full of driven, honest, and hardworking people. But most of us are simply consumed with the task right in front of us. Think about it: We are raised to study hard, to do our best, and to get good grades in school. If we accomplish that, we get the opportunity to move forward to the next grade, maybe on to college, then into a good job. These principles of hard work may give you a chance to move up the ranks within your field or chosen profession. The goal as we move up the ladder is to gain more responsibility and have a chance to earn more money. We know the drill—it's the job, right? Wake up, show up, and work your way up!

The problem is that while we wake up, rinse, and repeat this process for our entire work career, we can actually forget that working is not the end result. We know *how* to work, we understand *how* to earn, but unless we are lucky enough to have someone teach us about the importance of having a plan for our retirement, the bigger picture is lost.

The reality is that the value of our work is truly savored only when we take the time to focus our effort and energy into a plan that leads us to a desired destination. Like the old Proverb says, "The plans of the diligent lead to profit."[2] Just working hard isn't going to do it (although it is a great place to start). Just wanting a retirement isn't good enough. Like Herm Edwards said, just wishing isn't going to get it done. I have found that people need to be reminded of their dream, and they need to have a plan in order to get there!

When you read the story of my friend who retired in his forties—the one who had left behind his have-tos and was living out his want-tos—you might've thought, *I wish I could be that guy.* If that crossed your mind, I want you to bite your tongue. Now, you need to understand that no matter your age, you can get to the want-to phase of your life. But it is going to take work. This is not a book about wishes; it's a book about your dreams. Dreams take some focus and some vision, but let me tell you, they are worth it!

What I Learned About Dreams from Russ

I learned many of these lessons about retirement from watching my good friend and mentor Russ Carroll. Russ was Dave Ramsey's first team member. He spent more than twenty years helping people understand how to apply biblically based financial principles to their lives. Russ coached people who were struggling with debt, helped them learn to build budgets, and taught them to responsibly enjoy their wealth.

Dave and Russ knew that it would be impossible to help everyone across the nation, so they needed to recruit more help for the cause. Russ began to train groups of new financial coaches from across the country in a seminar we used to call Counselor Training, which has now grown into our Financial Coach Master Series. Russ's job was to teach coaches the process of guiding and encouraging folks to take the necessary steps toward financial peace. In 2006, I joined Russ in teaching at the event. With my collections, banking, mortgage, and investing background and Russ's years as a pastor, counselor, and financial trainer, we made quite an effective team.

But Russ didn't just *teach* the principles of financial peace to others; he and his wife, Joy, *lived* those principles. They attacked debt and remained allergic to it over the years. I had the privilege of watching firsthand as Russ changed thousands of stories—including his own. He became my mentor for over a decade, and, over the last few years, I was able to witness how he and his wife earned the right to retire. And, after so many years helping others retire with dignity, it was time for Russ and Joy to retire themselves.

I took Russ out for lunch to celebrate his retirement, and I'll never forget that conversation. This man whom I had respected, who had become a mentor, whom I had admired for so many years was sitting across the table asking *me* questions about *his* retirement! The truth is that he didn't really need my input; he had done his work. But he wanted to bounce ideas off of me about the next step of his life.

Russ and Joy had done everything the right way. They hadn't wished; they had a dream and had stuck to a plan. He had at least a dozen options for his retirement. Russ and Joy believed that people matter. He and his wife wanted to pursue their dream of traveling the world to help people. I was able to sit back and enjoy watching my good friend's dreams become a reality. I had witnessed this talented man put in the work required of dreaming, and now he was going to be able to experience more of the want-tos. I left that lunch more inspired than ever about my own eventual retirement!

Russ and Joy are now focusing on helping others in need in a foreign country. Sure, they have faced some challenges in this new adventure, but money hasn't been one of them. In fact, money will never be a challenge for them the rest of their lives, and their daughter will receive not only a legacy of love from them one day, but also a financial legacy. And until that day comes, the people Russ and Joy are serving around the world are benefiting from the hard work and careful planning they put into their retirement. Everybody wins! That, to me, is what retirement is all about—living your dream.

You Can Do This!

Do you want a story like Russ's? Then make it happen. It's a choice, and it's a choice you can make this very moment. I want you to think about those moments that really make you come alive. We all have those moments. Maybe it is the birth of a child or marrying the girl whom you couldn't live without. Maybe it is secretly giving to people in need without anyone knowing, or maybe it is traveling the world. Maybe it is starting a new business, volunteering for a nonprofit, becoming a teacher, or simply sitting with your feet in the sand on a beautiful beach with nothing else to do but read a book or watch your children play! These moments, my friend, are glimpses of the dream. They are the want-tos of your life. If we are really going to change our story, if we are going to redefine the word *retirement*, then it has to begin with the dream.

But—and you knew one was coming—you and I have some work to do. We have to begin by casting a vision. I told you the story about my friend who retired in his forties because I need you to understand that you can do this too. This book must begin with that realization. You don't have to be the son or daughter of wealthy parents or the CEO of a million-dollar company in order to get to your dream. You don't have to wait until the last few pages of your story to do the things that you have always dreamed of doing!

Retire Inspired

I want you to take a few moments and think about what you want your retirement to look like. What is that one dream you have for your future? That one thing that would make you wake up every day and think, *I get to do this?* Casting a vision for yourself is the first step in this important process. Are you relaxing at the lake? Doing mission work? Traveling the world? I want you to take a moment and think about how good it would feel to do those things you have always dreamed of doing. Now, here is the real question: What are you willing to do to get to that place? What are you willing to sacrifice? What will you give up in order to make your dreams come true?

The thing that I learned from watching Russ is that he and his wife did things the right way. They started with a dream. They came up with a plan. They worked, they saved, they stayed allergic to debt, and now they are living out the best part of their story. They are living the life they deserve. You can do the same thing! You can write all of your dreams into the story. All you need to do is identify those dreams and follow through with a plan.

If you've already been working through the Baby Steps that Dave listed in the foreword to this book, or if you've attended our *Financial Peace University* class, you already have a plan in place.

Great! I'll show you how to make the most of Baby Step 4 and beyond. But if you're just now starting out, I'm going to walk you through the steps you need to take to get your financial act together and start working your way to a dream retirement.

So, let's figure out how you can retire inspired!

CHAPTER ONE

REDEFINING RETIREMENT

The Past, the Present, and the Truth

I can change the brakes on a pickup truck and tell you everything you need to know about planting a garden, thanks to my grandparents. But they didn't just teach me the simple how-tos of everyday life; they gifted me with the legacy of why-tos. They taught me the heart stuff behind the "work hard" mindset and the love-your-neighbor kind of faith that make my life so rich today.

When I was a kid, I was able to spend mornings gardening with my grandmother, afternoons working on cars with my grandfather, and evenings playing at their house. I spent every day talking with them, spending one-on-one time with them, and observing how they lived. My grandfather still worked because he enjoyed it and was wired that way, but my grandmother no longer had to work at all.

They never appeared stressed out, too busy, or in a hurry.

When I think back on it now, I understand that they had the

time, the space, the energy, and the financial ability to be present with me. My grandmother was always baking for someone in the neighborhood who was going through a tough time. I watched my grandfather fixing family members' or neighbors' cars or helping them with house repairs (and I never saw money change hands). My grandparents taught me through their example to have a deep concern for my neighbors. They showed me how to treat people. I wouldn't be the professional, the father, the husband, or the citizen I am today without that time with my grandparents.

If you had asked me back then, I would've described my time with them as "fun time," but they had a more grown-up word for it—*retirement*. I didn't know it when I was young, but they were showing me what it meant to live an inspired retirement. And it wasn't accidental. It was a result of their hard work and good planning. Because they focused on their retirement goal over many decades, they were able to live their dream in retirement—and that's exactly what I want for you.

You see, dreams are what this book is all about. Not just any dreams, but *your* dreams. Do you want to know what wakes me up in the morning, what really gets me excited about my work? It's simple: I get to help people make real and lasting change. My goal is to educate, encourage, and empower you to experience the same kind of joy and freedom in retirement that I saw in my grandparents. My joy comes in helping people achieve their dreams.

The first step in that process is to redefine what we mean by the word *retirement*. Too many people in their twenties, thirties, forties, and even fifties think that retirement is way off in the future and irrelevant to their lives today. Wrong! Others think that retirement is an age, something that magically happens on their sixty-fifth birthday. Wrong! Retirement is much, much bigger than any of that—and your retirement depends 100 percent on what you are doing today.

But before we begin the conversation about what retirement should mean in your life, let's see how we got here.

A QUICK HISTORY OF RETIREMENT

In the grand scope of world history, retirement is a fairly new concept. You won't read about too many retirees kicking back during the American Revolution. You can probably guess why. Before the 1900s, people rarely lived to be sixty-five years old. Think about it for a minute. In the 1800s, you could catch a cold out there on your covered wagon and die or get trampled by a stray buffalo! They didn't have antibiotics. Getting a simple infection in your arm or leg could have cost you a limb. Therefore, with so few people living long lives, there was really no need for retirement.

Pension Pinching

Workers near the end of the nineteenth century began to think about the idea of retirement, and one innovation that came out of that was the company-sponsored pension plan. One of the first pension plans was created by the Guinness beer company in Ireland in 1860. It was pretty revolutionary at the time, as Guinness chose to provide a pension not just for current employees, but also for those who were already retired and for the widows and children of deceased former employees.[1] The first pension plan in America came along fifteen years later and, believe it or not, was created by the American Express Company. More than a hundred years later, American Express has gone from funding retirements to helping people go so far into debt that they may never be able to retire.

These companies were motivated to create a stable, career-oriented workforce. Remember, back then most people would spend their entire careers with a single company. Things are definitely different today, when the average worker will have fifteen to twenty different jobs in their lifetime![2] Times have changed, and employer retirement plans have changed with them. By 2010, most companies had moved away from the idea of pensions and on to 401(k) options, which we'll discuss below, for their employees.[3] There are still a few businesses (and careers) out there that offer pensions, but they are few and far between.

Social Insecurity

Have you noticed that people kind of assume that retirement age is sixty-five? Ever wonder where that idea came from? I have two words for you: Social Security.

The Social Security Act of 1935 set up a type of government safety net for retired employees that provided some income at retirement. The Act recognized the age of sixty-five as the normal retirement age in the United States—and that probably made sense in the 1930s. Back then, the average life expectancy was around sixty years of age.[4] So, since the average life expectancy was sixty and Social Security benefits didn't kick in until sixty-five, the government was basically making a safe bet. By their estimations, workers who made it to sixty-five wouldn't live long enough to need those benefits for long.

Now, you may have heard that Social Security is in trouble today. Can you guess what the problem is? With things like modern medicine and technology, people are living much longer! The life span of the average American in 2011 was around seventy-eight years (eighty-one for women). So people retiring at sixty-five today could potentially draw Social Security benefits for twenty or thirty years! The system just wasn't built for that, and that's why it's breaking down. Plus, today Social Security represents a giant pool of money that Congress occasionally borrows from but never repays. Calling this a huge mess is a bit of an understatement, but we'll talk more about this later.

Enter the 401(k)

When we hear the word *retirement* today, most of us think of 401(k)s. But 401(k)s are actually fairly new in the world of retirement planning. The Employee Retirement Income Security Act of 1974 (ERISA) established guidelines, standards, and funding rules for retirement plans. Then the Revenue Act of 1978 established pretax deferred employee compensation plans. The guidelines for these plans were spelled out in section 401(k) of the tax code. That's where we get the name 401(k). Pretty clever, huh?

So, if you are like me—just a little north of forty years old—you are actually older than the 401(k). The interesting thing is that 401(k) plans for employees didn't really start growing in popularity until the 1980s. That means someone who got out of college around 1980 and went to work for a company that offered one of the very first 401(k) plans isn't even retired yet. They'd only be in their late fifties by now.

What's the difference between the old pension plan and a 401(k)? The big difference is that 401(k) plans are employee-funded retirement savings plans, meaning you have to save your own money, while pension plans are employer-subsidized plans, which means your employer made contributions into a retirement account for you. That was a pretty sweet deal, but those days are long gone.

The Lesson of History

So why bother with the quick history lesson? It is important to realize what was intended for retirement. I want you to understand that companies used to do it for you, but that almost never happens today. It's a nice thought that the government hoped to do it for you, but that just hasn't worked out well. So that brings us to the true point of our history lesson:

You are responsible for your own retirement.

You are responsible for your own pension plan. *You* have to be concerned. *You* have to be focused. *You* have to have a plan. Taking personal responsibility for your own retirement is the first step toward success.

THE RETIREMENT OBSTACLE COURSE

My boys will often drag stuff into the backyard and make up their own obstacle course to run through. Sometimes I'll look out the window and see them laughing and falling over deck chairs and tree stumps on their way to the finish line. An obstacle is something we have to climb over, crawl under, or figure out a way around. Sometimes, we just have to knock the obstacle over to get past it. An obstacle may get in our way, but it requires us to think and grow.

Obstacles require a little work, but there is usually a payoff at the end. That's definitely true when we're talking about the obstacles that stand in the way of you and a happy, fulfilling retirement. Here are four obstacles to look out for as you work your way to your dream retirement.

Obstacle #1: Misunderstanding Retirement

The first obstacle with retirement is our very perception of the word. I want to challenge you to reimagine the way you think about retirement. Most of us hear the word and think "the end." That may have been true(ish) in the 1930s, but it is not today!

We need to start by getting rid of all the negative feelings and assumptions we have attached to the word *retirement*: "dried up," "end of life," "insecure," "winding down," "broke," "disengaged," "worst years of my life," "afraid." Some of this has to do with the way we idolize youth and mistakenly attach age to the idea of retirement. Some of it has to do with how broke and stuck in debt many of us are. We need to take all this negativity and throw it in the trash can.

I need you to hear me and repeat these ideas until they become ingrained in your thinking: Retirement is *not* an end; it's a beginning! Retirement is not just the *rest* of your story; it can be the *best* of your story. Like I pointed out in the introduction, it should be the time when you stop worrying about the have-tos of life and start waking up every day focusing on the want-tos.

This whole idea of seeing retirement only as the conclusion or the final act is kind of crazy to me now because I have seen what it can be for people. I want it to start to sound crazy to you too! I have always loved how Gene Perret, the writer for Bob Hope and Carol Burnett, talked about retirement. He said that retirement means "no pressure, no stress, and no heartache—unless you play golf." I don't play golf regularly, so I plan on enjoying it! If you plan on that too, then it has to start today by changing the way you think about the whole concept of retirement.

Obstacle #2: Depending on Social Security

The second obstacle with retirement is this thing we call Social Security. Did you know that today, close to 35 percent of American retirees over the age of sixty-five rely almost entirely on Social Security payments? That's crazy! The average Social Security benefit is only around $1,194 a month.[5] That means a third of all retirees in this country are living on an average annual income of just over $14,000! It's hard to live your dream in your golden years when you're trying to make it on an income that's actually below the federal poverty line.[6]

The situation gets even worse when you start looking at the long-term feasibility of Social Security in general. Sixty percent of workers today do not believe that Social Security will be able to pay them benefits by the time they retire, and 56 percent of people who are already retired believe that the government will cut their current Social Security benefits.[7] But wait; it gets worse. The baby boomers are just now hitting their retirement years—and they're hitting hard. Between now and the year 2030, it is estimated that there will be ten thousand baby boomers retiring each and every day.[8] Where is all of the money going to come from? It sounds more like Social Insecurity to me!

My point is you can't really count on Social Security. Do you really want to place your financial well-being in the hands of a government that has proven over and over and over again that it can't do simple math? I've seen enough examples of the government making poor decisions to make me nervous about the long-term stability of Social Security. I will explain more about this in another chapter, but if you are going to take control of your own retirement, you need to begin to view Social Security as "extra." Anything you get from Social Security should be a fringe benefit. See it as the icing on the cake—not the whole cake. We just cannot afford to forget that we have no control over Social Security.

Obstacle #3: Acting Like Sheep

The third obstacle we need to address is our general attitude about retirement, and if you believe the statistics, our attitude about retirement stinks! Studies show that half of 401(k) participants have less than $10,000 saved for retirement—and those are the people who are actually doing something![9]

A third of the participants have less than $1,000 saved for retirement. Now, listen. If one root canal or automotive issue can completely wipe out your entire retirement account, you are in trouble. But here's where you really see the problem in our attitude about retirement: only 22 percent of 401(k) participants—that's just one in five—have more than $100,000 in their retirement account. That may be okay when you're thirty, but it's a potential train wreck if you're sixty. This is serious! These numbers show how distracted we've become. We have lost sight of what is really important. We have wandered off the path. We've started acting like sheep.

Let me tell you what I know about sheep. Sheep aren't the brightest animals on the planet. That's why they need shepherds. Sheep have a herd mentality. If one wanders off, then others might follow. We can be kind of like that in our lives, can't we? We can easily lose our direction and fall into following stupid! I say "we" because I have been there too. You know what I am talking about: Joe down the street just leased that new Mercedes, so I have to get one too. Judy just bought a $200 pair of jeans for the PTO bash, so I might run over to the boutique and buy my own pair. The person in front of us goes off a financial cliff, and we start making our way to the ledge too.

That is why shepherds carry those big staffs. The staffs have a big crook at the top so the shepherd can snag a sheep by the neck and keep it from wandering off. And that's what I want to do for you. I won't grab you by the neck, but I do want to pull you back onto the path. There is too much at stake for you to wander off the path that would lead to your dream retirement.

Obstacle #4: Not Having a Plan
The fourth obstacle is probably the biggest one. It's the one that keeps retirees dependent on Social Security. It's the one that turns the dream of retirement into a financial nightmare. Depending on your motivation, this obstacle can be the easiest one to get past, or it can be the hardest one to get past. What's this giant roadblock that stops us cold? It's simply not having a plan.

I've spent a good bit of my professional life working as a financial coach. I've seen people make huge mistakes with retirement and money—people who might've been better off with a shepherd there to grab them by the neck. But, I have also watched people win big-time with their money and with their retirement. There is a common theme among the people who are able to do retirement right, and it has nothing to do with intentions. It has everything to do with staying on the right path—with having and maintaining a plan.

Let me tell you a story about my friends James and Judy. This is a lesson about intentions. James had always been a fun-loving guy who enjoyed having a great time. Judy was the sweet wife who always helped others in the family and in the community. She was truly the glue that held the family together. They hit their sixties with decades of happy memories, a close-knit family and circle of friends, photo albums filled with snapshots of extravagant holidays, birthdays, and vacations, and a career history they were proud of. But you know what they didn't have? Money.

At nearly sixty-five years old, James and Judy looked up after a lifetime of good intentions, bad decisions, and not living with financial purpose to find that they had arrived at the edge of retirement with no money and no options. They had two incomes and made great salaries, but they never stuck to a plan or made sacrifices. They were carrying two mortgages, three car payments, and ten credit cards all maxed out to the hilt! Sounds crazy when you read it, right? But guess what: this is what "normal" looks like in America today. In fact, 76 percent of people in the United States are living paycheck to paycheck![10]

James and Judy had vacationed often, sometimes taking their three kids' entire families along, including spouses and grandkids. They didn't have the money, but Visa, MasterCard, American Express, and Discover were always more than happy to loan it to them. They spent what they didn't have to please people who really didn't understand the truth of their dire financial situation. They were what I call "fake rich," with a lot of stuff that looked shiny and nice to cover up how broke they really were.

Judy had heard about Dave Ramsey's *Financial Peace University* (FPU) class in her church and knew that James would be too prideful to attend. Every time an announcement was made about a new FPU class, she would nudge James and he would just nudge her back. I guess that was his way of saying "No, Dear!" He was sitting in a gorgeous house surrounded by beautiful furniture and decor with two luxury cars in the garage. Everything looked great! He simply didn't realize how broke he really was.

But Judy was a different story. She started to see the cracks in the façade they had built up around themselves. When Judy started thinking about retirement, she realized they had no money to live on if they stopped working. After receiving a few phone calls from various collectors about past-due credit card payments, she finally reached her breaking point. James came home from work to find her in the bedroom crying and upset. James was a proud man, but the sight of his wife weeping was more than he could bear. So James finally put his pride aside, and they reached out to me for some financial coaching.

I can remember our conversation like it was yesterday. I began to ask about their financial situation, and as they walked me through it, I could see that they were just now starting to realize how bad off they really were. They went through all of their debts, explained that they had no retirement savings, and talked about their lifestyle choices. Then they started telling me about their thirty-two-year-old son—who was still living with them! They were actually making the car payment on a new car their son had purchased before he had lost his job. He had been living with them off and on since he had graduated from college. The little safety net they thought they were providing turned out to be a pretty comfortable hammock that their son wasn't ready to climb out of.

The credit card debt was being used to bridge the gap between their income and their unpleasant reality. They were living beyond their means and knew something had to drastically change if they were ever going to be able to retire and travel the world like they had dreamed of doing back when they were newlyweds. They had always lived for the now. James and Judy believed car payments would always be part of life. Like most Americans, they never thought retirement would come to them. They believed the government would provide for them. They didn't make a plan for the best years of their lives.

So where are James and Judy now? Working—every single day. They will never travel the world like they dreamed of doing. You know why? Because they have no choice! They must work and will continue to work probably for the rest of their lives or until they physically can't work anymore. You may be in that same situation right now as you read this book—close to retirement but with little or no savings. I absolutely don't want to beat you up, but I do want to motivate you!

If you're getting started with your retirement planning late in the game, don't worry; I'm going to show you some strategies throughout this book to retire well. But, the truth is, stories like James and Judy's may keep you up at night. Pay attention: it is not okay for you to get to the end of your work life and have nothing to show for it but photo albums and credit card bills! James and Judy are wonderful people. They loved their family, they served their community, and they had the best intentions. But they had no plan, and it cost them their dream retirement.

GETTING MOTIVATED TO MAKE A CHANGE

Let me tell you another story about my friends Michael and Donna. I first sat down with them several years ago. I knew from the start of that meeting that they were not going to focus. Their minds were on everything except what we were there to talk about. Donna was playing with her phone, and Michael was literally staring at the clock. They weren't *trying* to be rude; they just weren't interested in being there. Sure, they'd answer direct questions, but I just could not get them to engage. As a coach, I knew the truth: They didn't care; it just did not matter enough to them. I tried to coach them, but they were stuck in their ways. When they left our meeting, I was sure I would never see them again.

Michael called me about two weeks after our appointment. I was skeptical. I said, "Michael, listen, you two weren't all that happy to be here the last time. Are you sure you want another meeting?"

He practically begged me for another session. I could tell that something was up, but I didn't want to waste another entire session on a couple who didn't want to be there, so I agreed to meet with them for thirty minutes—half the length of a normal session. I wasn't interested in trying to communicate through their blank stares for another hour!

From the start of that second meeting, I could tell that they were different this time around. Michael was focused, sitting forward, wired and ready. Donna put her phone away as soon as we sat down. They had each brought a pen and notepad to take notes. It was crazy! These were *not* the same two people I had met with a couple of weeks before.

Several minutes in, I just couldn't take it anymore. I had to know what turned them around so completely. Now, I've never been accused of being subtle in communicating with folks, so I hit the situation head-on: "Guys, you seem completely different. What's going on?"

Michael explained that, a few days after our initial financial coaching session, he had received a phone call from his favorite aunt. The person who normally cut her grass for free was off to college, and she was calling to see if he had time to do it that summer. Michael said he would be more than willing to help; this was the aunt who had always been special to him. She was one of those people who dedicated her life to helping others.

His aunt lived across town and, since getting married and having kids, Michael had not been able to spend as much time around her in the past few years. He got up early on Saturday and loaded up his mower into his truck. His aunt was going to attend a function at church, and after they chatted for a while, her ride came and she was on her way. Michael knew cutting the two-acre yard was going to be some work.

A couple of hours into the job, Michael decided to stop for lunch. However, he had been in a rush that morning, and he realized that he had forgotten to pack his lunch. So, sweaty and hungry, he thought he'd just go find something to eat in his aunt's kitchen. No big deal, right?

I could see Michael start to get a little emotional as he told me about his aunt's kitchen. He opened the fridge, but all he saw was some expired milk and a bottle of ketchup. He moved over to the cabinets but only found the dishes and cups. Finally, he checked the cupboard. That's when his heart sank. The cupboard was completely empty—except for seven cans of dog food. Michael reached in, picked up one of those cans, and held it in his hand for a moment as the truth of the situation began to sink in. Michael paused at this point of the story. He looked me square in my eyes, and his voice began to shake as he described the moment he realized the terrible reality this wonderful woman was living.

He said the words I will never forget: "Chris, my aunt doesn't own a dog."

The air left the room. Tears filled our eyes. Michael saw something that he could not "unsee." I had just heard something that I could never "unhear." I would never be able to erase it from my memory. This amazing woman, someone who had spent so many decades taking care of other people, was eating dog food. It was all she could afford.

And do you know what Michael and Donna's response was? It

was guilt and shame because they didn't have the money to step in and take care of this wonderful older woman who had taken care of those around her for so long. They were living out of control, and they realized they needed to get their own act together so they could take care of themselves and those close to them.

That story has stuck with me all these years. It drives me to help people, and when I think of it I want to scream, "That's not okay!"

I want you to remember these people's stories because I don't want you to end up there. It is not okay for anyone to end up there. But I want you to do far more than that. I want you to aspire to a great retirement. I want you to live your dream. And if you're starting later in the game, you may have to adjust your dream a bit. That's okay! You can still retire well. We'll talk about that throughout the book.

In order to get down to the business of dreaming, we have to begin to think about retirement in a different way. I want you to replace those old, tired, and depressing ideas attached to the word *retirement* with the truth. Retirement is a new chapter—some of your best years. It brings new opportunities. It's about your legacy. Retirement should mean wealth, peace, fun, satisfaction, security, and freedom! I want to remind you again that retirement shouldn't be defined any longer as an "old person thing." Retirement should be viewed as a "smart person thing." Retirement is a "focused person thing." It is the result of having a plan and making sacrifices to get there.

FACING THE EMOTIONS OF RETIREMENT (AND RETIREMENT PLANNING)

I've invited you into this new hope of what retirement can be for us. But that new vision, our hopeful vision, just doesn't match up with the realities of where we are as a nation when it comes to retirement. I gave you some of the numbers. They are depressing. What is the cause of the great divide between our hopes for retirement and the reality of our situation? There are some core emotions attached to retirement that we need to address before we can really move forward and make progress on our journey.

Guilt, Shame, and Cynicism

I believe that people really struggle with guilt when it comes to thinking about retirement. Guilt is a debilitating emotion. People carry guilt for making stupid decisions with their money when they were younger. They carry the shame of their bad financial choices, like credit card debt or the second mortgage. They feel the weight of shame for not doing the work to earn their time in retirement. They face the guilt and humiliation of not making their money do what they need it to do in order for them to become debt-free.

What happens to all of those guilty messages? They start to shift from "I *should*" and turn into "I *can't*." Our mistakes begin to convince us that we can't make a positive change. Guilt opens the door for cynicism to walk through, and cynicism can poison our dreams.

I want you to remember this when you are dealing with shame and guilt: a setback can be a set up for a comeback! You may, at times, waste a blessing or make a bad financial choice. But you must learn how to forgive yourself when you make mistakes. If you don't learn to let your mistakes go, your guilt and shame will grow into the monster of cynicism. In sports, my coaches would often say, "It's not about the *last* play, it's about the *next* play." It was a great life lesson in learning to let go of those mistakes and compete with freedom on the field. You might be telling yourself right now, *It's just not in my nature to handle money well.* That is a lie. It is cynicism. And it will only prevent you from achieving your dreams. It is time to let that monster go. You are writing a new story here.

Fear Not . . . Unless You Should

The second core emotion that we should address when it comes to retirement is fear. This is often the first sensation we feel when we start to take an honest look at our planning and dreams for retirement. We end up asking ourselves these questions based on fear:

- What if we outlive our money in retirement?
- What if we cannot find affordable housing?
- What about long-term health care?

A recent survey demonstrated that people over the age of forty-five (baby boomers) say that never being able to get out of debt is their biggest financial fear.[11] I understand this fear. As my company has worked with literally millions of families, we've found that debt (and misunderstandings about debt) is the biggest roadblock to financial security. We'll talk more about how to handle debt later in the book.

Another huge fear for many families is simply being able to pay their bills. I can understand this one too. Remember that statistic from earlier? Seventy-six percent of American households are living paycheck to paycheck. What happens in retirement when there is no paycheck? That can be terrifying to imagine.

Fear is a real thing. If we could go back in time to about twelve years ago, I would probably tell you there wasn't much in the world that truly made me afraid. But then something big happened in my life. Over a few years, my wife and I had these three beautiful, rambunctious boys. If you have children, you can probably relate. I now understand why my mom was always telling me to be safe. It seemed like a silly thing to tell me when I was young, but now I completely get it.

Right before we had children, my wife and I had the chance to be on the game show *Wheel of Fortune*. The show was taping right here in our hometown of Nashville. I was always a little bit of an experience junkie and had always wanted to have a motorcycle. We went on the show along with a really nice couple who had been public school teachers all of their lives. They won the big money. They ended up with over $60,000 that day—more money than the two of them made together in a year! I was really happy for them.

My wife and I also walked away with some prize money, and, as we went home that night, she made a deal with me. "Chris," she said, "I know you have always wanted a motorcycle, so I want you to take some of this money and go buy one for yourself. But, you have to promise me one thing." Oh, I was all in. At that point, I'd have agreed to pretty much anything she said. She finished, "Just promise me that you will sell it when we have kids. That's the deal." Done! I got a motorcycle—and it was great.

But then our first son was born, and guess what? I had made a promise. And many of the guys I was riding with agreed with my wife. I loved riding that bike, but I was too exposed to other people's driving mistakes. It was just an unnecessary risk. It wasn't the safest choice if I wanted to be there for my children. You may not feel this way at all, and I completely understand that. But for my wife and me, a motorcycle didn't make sense. It brought a level of fear into our family that just wasn't worth the reward, and that sense of fear led me to make a change in my life.

Sometimes fear can push us in a healthy direction because it means we have something we want to hold on to. But even though fear may be enough to prompt you to take action initially, it won't keep you motivated and focused over two, three, or four decades of working and saving. That kind of intensity requires inspiration! It calls for commitment and a big dream for a sweet retirement.

Fear may be an effective motivator, but it's a terrible master. Even if you're scared about your retirement prospects today, you can't make your decisions or plan your retirement based on fear. That's a recipe for disaster.

Regret and Rearview Mirrors

The final emotion we need to deal with on this journey toward your dreams is regret. Many of us deal with regret in relation to our current financial situation or to our inability to financially help out our children. But regret is a useless emotion unless you respond to it with action and a willingness to change.

I know something about the face of financial regret. It's really simple and something that maybe you can relate to. Car payments are the big, ugly face of regret. When I was young, I just had to have a Ford Expedition, so I took on a car payment of almost $600 a month. Was it cool? Yeah, I suppose. But you know what would have been cooler? My dreams.

Let me tell you what those five years of $600 car payments cost me. If I had invested that $600 a month for five years in my twenties instead of sending it to the loan company, I'd have more than $1 million extra sitting in my retirement account in my sixties. I would have been able to retire years earlier if I had done that, too, because I would have hit my retirement goal sooner. One car cost me more than a million dollars and a few years of my retirement! Talk about regret. I lost that opportunity, and I can't get it back. To this day, I still twitch whenever I drive by an Expedition. It's like a continual reminder for me to stay focused and not let my financial guard down.

How do we handle regret? When you make a mistake, you regret it, but if you continue to repeat that mistake over and over, it isn't a mistake anymore! That, my friend, is called a choice. Regret isn't all bad. It is that little reminder in our heads that we made a mistake and need to change our behavior. We cannot let regret weigh us down and keep us from our dreams though. I want you to glance back at regret in order to avoid those mistakes, but I also want you to look forward in hope. Think about regret like the rearview mirror in your car. You check it every once in a while to keep yourself from making terrible mistakes while you're driving. But why is that little mirror so small and the windshield of your car so big? Because you are supposed to look forward!

Regret can be your deterrent and your motivation, but I want you to train yourself to look out that big windshield toward hope. You need that regret as long as it stays where it belongs—in that little rearview mirror.

MOVING TOWARD A NEW VISION

I want you to be inspired to move forward in this process. We are chasing your dream here. Retirement can be something completely different from what you used to imagine it to be. There is a big emotional component in this process. The first major step here is to emotionally commit yourself to changing your retirement. The second step is to have a vision. What did retirement look like before you really understood what it was?

I told you how much my time with my grandparents meant to me. That was my first glimpse at what retirement could look like. They were the perfect example of retirement done the right way. They had a plan, they did their work, and they were able to spend years doing what they wanted to do instead of what they had to do. For the two of them, spending uninterrupted, unhurried time with me and the other grandchildren was just part of their dream.

No matter where you are right now, I want to assure you that it is never too late to get started working toward your dreams. I want you to take a minute and write down all the things that you would love to do if you had the financial freedom to do them—if money and debt were not a worry.

That is the substance of real dreams.

Don't Be a "Been Brother"

Look around at the people in your life who are doing retirement right, and let them inspire you. Maybe it is someone in your church? Maybe a coworker who recently retired well? Maybe it is a neighbor? Let the lives these people are living help you gather vision and motivation for your own dreams.

When I was growing up, Mama Hogan had these phrases she used to throw out at me. One time, she said, "Christopher, son, I need you to hear me, I don't ever want you to be a 'been brother!'"

I had no idea what she meant. She continued, "I don't want you to be a woulda-been, a coulda-been, or a shoulda-been." It was great advice. Her point was that I needed to be intentional with my plans, actions, and goals. She wanted me to realize my potential by taking the necessary actions. She wanted me to follow through. My mother's wisdom is even more applicable with the subject of retirement. I don't want to live my life and look back regretting that I didn't plan for retirement!

Let's look forward, move past our mistakes, and turn those lessons into action for a better future!

Retirement Isn't an Age

It is time that we started reclaiming the idea of retirement. Retirement is not the finish line; it is the new beginning. Retirement is not your last paragraph; it is the long, rich, rewarding final chapters of your own book—as many pages as you can dream up. Retirement is not the end of your life; it is the beginning of the *best years* of your life!

But if we are going to chase this new vision of retirement, we have to learn to plan the right way. Remember, this is a dream, not a wish. A dream that's ready to go to work is called a goal, and a goal requires a plan. If you do this the right way, you will have two things that you have never had at the same time before: time and money. You know what having time and money means? It means you have freedom. It means you have options—like my friend Joe.

I met Joe several years ago, and he was a relatively plain-looking man. He had come to me wanting to talk about wealth building and retirement. This guy had his act together. He had a budget and, as I looked at his portfolio, I asked him, "How much do you have saved up for retirement?" Of course, the numbers were on the piece of paper, but something didn't add up. Looking at this guy in front of me, it seemed like there were too many zeroes on the page.

But it wasn't a typo. Joe had saved $1.4 million—yet he had never earned more than $50,000 a year in his life. He had worked at his company for thirty-two years and had a little bit of pension money. He had stayed allergic to debt. He drove a truck that was over a decade old, and he lived in a paid-for home. He believed in being a good steward of the blessings in his life. He didn't have any sheep moments; advertisements had never really influenced Joe into the kind of behavior we call stupid. He had been generous with his giving. Now he had reached a point where he was going to have fun and enjoy life.

It was an amazing experience to look at what this man had accomplished and talk with him about his dreams and plans. It was one of those sessions that inspired me to do what I do today. He helped me understand the truth: Retirement is not an age; it's a financial number. It is the amount you need to live the life you've always dreamed of in retirement. I learned as much about retirement in my short time with Joe that day as he did from me. I learned that dreams are truly possible if you have a plan.

THE FIVE FUNDAMENTALS OF AN INSPIRED RETIREMENT

As we get started, I want to provide you with the fundamental steps that will help you work toward your retirement dream. I'm a big sports guy, so when I hear the word *fundamentals*, I think of the things you focus on every day, every hour, and every practice as you strive for excellence. Here are the Five Fundamentals that can help you stay on track as you begin to work toward retiring inspired:

Fundamental #1: Dreaming

Dreaming is an action, and it means that you must be able to see your retirement dreams clearly and that you need to own them. Dreaming is the process of discovering (or recovering) the things you have always wanted to do. It is the want-tos of your life. You need to remind yourself of your dreams every day. Remember, your dreams cannot be delegated to someone else; you must own them. We'll go into this in detail in the next chapter.

Fundamental #2: Planning

Planning is the strategic process of figuring out *how* to achieve your goals. If you are married, you and your spouse will get on the same page with plenty of discussion. If you are single, you will find an accountability partner who can hold your feet to the fire. Planning is the process where you connect your actions to your goals. So plan, and let the plan be your GPS to get you to your retirement dreams in style. A huge part of that plan will be your commitment to budgeting, which we will hit pretty hard in Chapter Three.

Fundamental #3: Execution

Execution means taking the right steps at the right time. It involves investing, budgeting, avoiding debt, working with your dream team, communicating with your family, maintaining healthy relationships, and, yes, even continuing to dream (because your dream will evolve). You are following through with a plan that is proven to work, and you understand that your actions matter and that focused attention brings results. Execution is the follow-through and attention to detail that you need to move your plans to reality. Throughout this book, I'll show you the action steps you need to take as you execute your plan.

Fundamental #4: Commitment

Commitment begins with the understanding that while this dream begins with you, it is not *just* about you. Commitment means embracing the sacrifices necessary to get you to your dream. It is the pledge to your spouse, your family, your community, your children, and your grandchildren (whom you may have not even met yet)! Commitment is the understanding that your health, wealth, work, and relationships are a blessing and that you have to embrace the responsibility of leaving a legacy. We'll talk more about legacy in Chapter Ten.

Fundamental #5: Vigilance

Vigilance means knowing that stupid is always lurking around the corner. It is the admission that someone is always trying to sell you something you really don't need. It is watching out for people trying to get you to invest in a risky, once-in-a-lifetime opportunity that will most likely leave you broke and embarrassed. Vigilance is a mindset that you are going to protect your dream and your legacy. It means you are going to ignore the Joneses and understand the temptation for pretending to be rich (even when you're not) is always present. It means that you will protect your retirement dreams and that you will stay focused on preserving the blessings of the legacy that you will leave.

We'll talk about a lot of different things throughout this book, but I want you to view all of it through the lens of these Five Fundamentals: dreaming, planning, execution, commitment, and vigilance. If you continue to stay on top of those five things, you'll be way ahead of the game with retirement.

RECLAIMING RETIREMENT

Do you remember accomplishing that one goal you had to put in years of hard work to reach? Climbing a mountain, winning a championship, or seeing your name on that office door for the first time? Maybe it was that feeling of finally meeting the kind of person you always wanted to marry? What about the birth of your first child? That moment when you get to experience the culmination of one of your dreams—that is what I want for you in retirement. I want you to understand that while you can't quite touch it right now, you can definitely experience some aspect of what it will feel like.

Think of those moments when you are on vacation with nowhere to be and nothing to do. Those moments when your kids are sleeping in or maybe you are just sitting there with your feet in the sand, not prepping for your next meeting or appointment, but just imagining what the day may hold for you. Those are all little pieces of this dream we call retirement. I want you to experience that moment in life of absolute freedom when you can do whatever you really want to do.

Like I said earlier, I experience that feeling often when I am on vacation with my family. I experience those moments on long weekends or when I take the family out of town, when I know I have put in the hard work and earned those vacation days. Retirement, in my mind, is that place where I spend more time with my family, where I give secretly to people in need, where I start a new business that I dreamed about trying out. That is just a glimpse of where I want you to go.

So how do we redefine retirement? By understanding that it is your dream and, more importantly, it is your choice. You are the one who gets to decide what it is going to be like. If your experience watching your parents and grandparents in retirement was a negative one, it doesn't mean that it has to be that way for you. You can make it positive. You are one decision away from making your retirement great. It's time to dream. It's time to make a plan. Let's get started!

CHAPTER TWO

DREAMING IN HIGH DEFINITION

Know Your R:IQ

When my friends from Texas came to see me for a counseling session, they began by telling me they had a little problem with their dream. It's most likely not the type of thing you would call a problem. It's not exactly what I was thinking before they explained the situation. They were both in their early fifties and had recently decided to retire. My friends weren't concerned with how they were going to pay the bills, where they were going to live, or how they were going to cover basic medical costs. They had been self-employed and were both successful in their careers. They had executed a plan and were now in the phase of life where they wanted to enjoy their success. They didn't need help with budgeting, and they didn't need my help with investing. So what was the issue?

They had come to talk with me because they wanted advice on how best to *give* their money away! What a problem! They were asking me questions like, "How can we *really* make an impact?" They were driven to be good stewards—a biblical word for "managers"—of the success they had earned. I sat and talked with them about establishing scholarship funds, giving to their church, funding some exciting ministries, and helping people in need. They were living what most would call a "dream retirement."

They had the means to travel the world if they wanted. In fact, they had the money to go sit on every beach on the planet, but they were driven by what they called the "responsibility that had come with success." They weren't confused about their wealth. Sure, they wanted to enjoy the fruit of all their hard work, but they didn't think that pile of money existed just for their own fun. They wanted to put that money to work to bless other people. You see, when you view money in its proper place, it changes your perspective and your behavior. They had lived with the responsibility of being good managers, practicing good stewardship of their finances for decades.

I was witnessing this couple live a dream retirement. They weren't only living out their dreams; they were enriching the lives of as many people as they could. And you know what? It was fun! They had earned the freedom to do that. Talking with them inspired me to ask what I could do for others. It caused me and my wife to start dreaming about what we could do if we were faithful to the plan and were good stewards of our money for ourselves, for our children, and for our communities. The dream retirement can have a serious ripple effect over several generations, changing the lives of folks much farther than our eyes can see.

Here's the thing: This kind of dream retirement is within your grasp. You have the choice. You get to decide if you can have the same type of "problems." You will get to decide the circumstances of your own retirement. I want you to understand that with some work, a change in attitude, and plugging into a plan that works, your retirement could be whatever you dream up—just like it is for my friends in Texas. And even if you are reading this book too late in the game to retire like this couple, you can still make a huge difference in what your retirement will look like!

RETIREMENT IS NOT AN OLD PERSON THING

I love the famous airline commercial slogan, "*Ding!* You are now free to move about the country." I want you to think of retirement every time you hear that commercial! I want you to experience that "ding." That is what my friends from Texas had put themselves in position to do. "*Ding!* You are now free to do whatever you want!" And they were free to choose a life of generosity and joy—and they did it when they hit their retirement savings goal, not when they hit some arbitrary age when people say you are "supposed" to retire.

I want you to say this with me one more time: Retirement is not an old person thing; it's a smart person thing. Before you move on to the next sentence of this book, I need you to let go of the myth that retirement is just for old people. Retirement is not only for people who are sixty, sixty-five, or seventy. Retirement is your chance to plug in and do that heart stuff, the things you have always wanted to do. And talking about retirement isn't just for seniors either. The earlier you talk about retirement and start working a plan for retirement, the more choices and opportunities you have to retire when, where, and how you want. But, as I've said before, that doesn't happen without a plan.

You Have to Have the Recipe

When I went off to graduate school in Pennsylvania, I knew one of the things I would miss about home was my grandmother's chili. My Nan was an unbelievable cook, and her chili was amazing! Fall arrived, the weather cooled, and I decided to stop on my way home from class to pick up what I thought I needed to make some chili. I ran through the grocery store and grabbed a basket full of ingredients, got to my apartment, and began cooking right away. I was boiling and stirring, and I thought everything was going just right. I couldn't wait to have some chili for dinner. A couple hours later, I poured some into a bowl. Man, I had been waiting for this all day. I took a big steaming spoonful, closed my eyes, and tasted it. Then I ran to the sink and spit it out. It didn't taste like chili at all! I might've invented a recipe for brown glue, but it sure wasn't chili.

I had to call my grandmother for some help. "Nan," I said when she answered the phone, "I tried to make your chili . . ." I could already hear the pity in her voice.

"What happened?" she asked.

"My chili is broke," I explained. "I mean, it's absolutely disgusting! I'm not even sure the dog would eat it." She thought this was hilarious. She must have chuckled over my "broken chili" for five minutes. Eventually, my grandmother asked me to get out a pen and paper, and she walked me step by step through her recipe.

As it turns out, I had missed a few really important ingredients—including the chili powder! Next time I went to the store, I had that list of ingredients I needed to make chili. And when I came home to cook, I had a better idea of the process I needed to mix those ingredients together. I knew when to add each one, how long to boil, how long to simmer, how long to keep it covered. My next attempt to make chili didn't come out perfect; it wasn't exactly my grandmother's chili, but it still tasted pretty good. You know why? Because I had a recipe. I had a plan. Retirement is a lot like Nan's chili in that way.

Failing to Plan or Planning to Fail?

Before we talk about a plan, let's take a moment to examine what retirement looks like for most people today. The current average retirement age is around sixty-two years old—and you aren't even eligible for your full Social Security benefit at that age. For those who haven't yet retired but are edging closer, the projected average age is sixty-six.[1]

Too many people immediately jump to Social Security in their minds when the word *retirement* comes up. So what is happening with the good ol' "Social Insecurity" system that we touched on earlier? I explained that ten thousand people are hitting retirement every single day, and most of them will be drawing money from Social Security.[2] That is worth a second mention. I'm not saying Social Security isn't going to be there; I'm saying that ten thousand straws a day are being added to that lonely, underfed camel's back—and his knees are wobbling. It's a good enough reason not to completely count on Social Security to be there for you the same way that it may have been for your parents.

Social Security is really only meant to replace 40 percent of your paycheck.[3] Think about that for a minute. Can you live your dream on 40 percent of what you are currently making? When is the last time you were pleased with 40 percent of anything? Do you go to the steakhouse and order 40 percent of the sirloin? What if the waiter only fills up your tea glass 40 percent of the way? What if your team at work only puts 40 percent effort into a big project? And even if you think you can make it on that number, do you really want to trust a government that can't seem to add or subtract to be the principal funder of your dream?

The current speculation about the system won't make you feel any better. Some believe that by the year 2030, Social Security will only be able to cover 30 percent of your working salary. That, at least, should make you think twice. So here's my advice when it comes to Social Security: If it's still around when you retire, then be thankful and definitely take advantage of it. But don't make that your only plan. Again, like I've said before, think of your Social Security income as the icing on the cake—not the cake itself. We will get into the details of how to handle Social Security later in the book.

There's an old saying that goes, "If you fail to plan, you're planning to fail." I'm afraid that's what too many people are doing with their retirement. By ignoring it or putting it off, or by assuming Social Security will take care of them, they aren't just making a mess for themselves, but they're making a mess for their children as well.

The "Choose Your Own Retirement" Adventure

When I was in high school, I would rejoice when I heard that a test was going to be multiple-choice (or "multiple-guess" as some of my friends called it). A multiple-choice test gives you several answers to choose from, but only one is considered correct. So, if you knew the material like you were supposed to, the correct answer would jump out when you saw it, and the incorrect answers would fade away.

Retirement is a lot like those multiple-choice tests. The question you have to answer is, "What kind of retirement do I want to have?" I believe there are four options to choose from, and, assuming you still have some time to work and to save between now and retirement, you can pick only one. Which would you choose?

Option 1: The Nightmare Retirement

The Nightmare Retirement option sounds ominous and scary —because it *is* ominous and scary. People retiring in the Nightmare scenario have no money saved and no options for income. They may be physically incapable of working, have no relatives to care for them, and have to depend entirely on Social Security and other government programs.

This option means you will face the realities of poverty from housing to health care and will struggle to meet your basic needs. Choosing this type of retirement means that welfare might be your only option.

Option 2: The Burden Retirement

The next option is called The Burden Retirement. Like The Nightmare Retirement, in the Burden option you have no savings and you're unable to work, meaning you won't be able to make it on your own. However, things are a little easier here because you have others—probably your adult children—who will help support you.

We all have to lean on somebody from time to time, right? There is nothing wrong with that! But when you have to lean or completely rely on other people to help you financially, you are placing a stress on their financial well-being as well as that of their children.

I will never forget sitting down with three adult siblings who were trying to figure out how to help their aging parents. Mom and Dad had done absolutely nothing to prepare for retirement and now found themselves physically unable to keep working. Only one of the three adult kids was financially able to help, so I sat down with them all to figure out how to fairly divide the responsibility for their parents' care between the three of them. It was a heartbreaking conversation because not only were these grown children concerned about their parents, but they were angry with them too. Why? Their parents had not planned to support themselves in retirement, and they had placed a huge burden of stress and financial strain on their children. I've seen it more times than I can count, and this is a sad and scary retirement option.

People willfully going into retirement with this "they'll take care of me" mindset often never think about the true cost of their decision. I once talked to a couple who was getting ready to stop working, and as we began to talk about their finances for the next phase of their life, they sat confidently across from me and explained, "We took care of our children when they were growing up, and now it is their turn to take care of us."

I had to rest my hand on my chin to keep my jaw from hitting the floor. It was one of the strangest interactions I've ever experienced as a financial counselor. I sat there speechless for a minute hoping they were being sarcastic or funny, but they were dead serious. You know what broke my heart about this? In the same conversation, they talked about how much they adored their grandchildren. They never considered how this "now it's their turn" attitude might dramatically impact the lives of those grandkids. How might the financial burden they were imposing on their children affect the direction of the grandchildren they adored so much?

Now, if you're currently retired and living with an adult child out of financial necessity, I certainly don't want you to feel guilty about it. That's a reality in many, many families, and I'm sure your child is happy to bless you in this way. My goal here is not to make some of you feel bad about where you are *now,* but to encourage others to think about where they want to be *later.* This is about setting goals for the future.

The first two options look pretty grim, don't they? If this were a multiple-choice test, I don't think those would be the two options that would immediately leap off the page for most of us, right?

Option 3: The Normal Retirement

With those two options out of the way, let's take a good, long look at where most people will stand at the end of their working days. We can call this The Normal Retirement. People in this category usually have some retirement savings, but not enough to fully live on. That means they will have to keep working after the age of sixty-five in order to support themselves. Think about that for a moment: they may not *want* to work, but they will always *have* to work—at least as long as they're physically able. Americans living The Normal Retirement can't really focus on their dreams because they're too focused on their necessities.

How does this happen? Because most people only half think about their retirement, they get only half the results. Remember, it's not that we don't work hard; it's that we don't have a plan for the results of our hard work. We don't come close to maximizing our retirement.

You can classify The Normal Retirement people into two groups: the sheep (that I discussed earlier) and the ostriches. We've talked about how easy it is to go into "sheep mode," where you get distracted and wander off the path after one shiny thing or another. I've also talked about how we need a shepherd on this retirement journey—a guide who can help us put together a plan and stick to it. I want to help you with that. I don't have a big staff, but I want to shepherd you in the right direction to help you stay on a path and move beyond just The Normal Retirement.

The second group heading into The Normal Retirement are the folks who choose to live in what I call "ostrich mode." You know what ostriches like to do, don't you? They bury their heads in the sand. So when it comes to retirement, these people know it's coming and they know they *should* do something, but they just hide their heads in a hole and pretend that there will not be consequences for the way they manage their money.

These folks are what I call "fake rich." Remember James and Judy from the previous chapter? They were surrounded by luxuries, but it was all a mask hiding the fact that they'd never be able to stop working. Ostrich-like people think they can carry mortgages and car loans into retirement, have no security plan, and live only for today.

Did you know that fewer than one in ten workers say they expect to retire before age sixty? The reality is that 36 percent of retirees had to stop working *before* they turned sixty. Comparatively, only 29 percent of workers retired between the ages of sixty and sixty-four, and only 9 percent retired at the traditional age of sixty-five. And well over a quarter of people believe that they can work until age seventy, but only 6 percent are able to work for that long![4] The problem with this ostrich mode is that the end of your work life is inevitable—like death and taxes. It will arrive whether you are ready for it or not.

I know they say sixty is the new forty, but let me tell you, friend, a day will arrive when you can no longer work. You cannot play "fake rich," and you cannot just put your head in the sand and live as if retirement will never happen to you. Don't settle for normal! There's a much, much better option for those who dare to dream it.

Option 4: The Dream Retirement

I am a positive guy, and I want to point you in the right direction, so I've saved the best choice for last. I have told you some great stories about people living out what I call The Dream Retirement. The Dream Retirement means that you are able to do *what* you want to do *when* you want to do it!

Remember my friend Russ Carroll? He lives with an amount of freedom that most of us can only glimpse in little moments (like when we're on vacation). He and his wife can pick their want-tos because they no longer live under the tyranny of have-tos! Why? Because they were focused. They had a plan, and that plan led them right where they wanted to be!

Russ dedicated his life to helping others. Let me tell you one of the many reasons why I love this man and his family. Do you know what Russ is doing in retirement? He is still giving! Because he can. Because that's what he chooses to do.

If you are intentional about helping others right now and you understand the deep joy and the blessings that you receive from dedicating yourself to the betterment of others, then you need to plan for retirement even more. The world needs you to have a plan so that you can continue to live that way on an even greater level after you finish your have-to phase of life!

Remember, failing to plan is the same as planning to fail. You'll never get where you want to go if you don't plan your route; that's true for road trips and retirement! I want you to experience The Dream Retirement. But you need a plan to get there, right? That's why I put together my R:IQ tool for you.

THE R:IQ: YOUR RETIREMENT ROAD MAP

R:IQ stands for "Retire Inspired Quotient." It is an assessment tool I created to help you see where you are today, dream of where you want to go in retirement, and make a plan to get there. I'm giving you the best way to begin that process—and it's free! I'll tell you what to do and where to find it in a minute. For now, let me touch on what working through the R:IQ will look like for you. You shouldn't be surprised by now that I think your dream is the most important starting point. So, the R:IQ starts with you defining your dream for retirement! You must first visualize what you want retirement to look like for you.

Dreaming in High Definition

My wife and I were out on a date recently, and on the way home we stopped by the big electronics store. She wanted to take a look at some of those new washers and dryers that do everything but fold the clothes and put them away for you. She went off in that direction in the store, and you probably don't have to guess where I was going. It was Saturday evening, and there was a football game on TV!

I walked back toward the TVs like a mosquito drawn to a backyard bug light. I could see it from thirty yards away, and it was drawing me closer. Every man in the store was standing there mesmerized. All of us stood with our mouths open in awe before the football game on that eighty-five-inch, flat-screen, high-definition television. I have good eyesight, but I don't think football was that clear when I was playing on the field in college! I mean, the picture was so vivid that you could see sweat dripping off the quarterback's eyebrow as he looked over the offensive line to call an audible. You could see the blades of grass swaying in the breeze and the bloodstains on the players' jerseys. I was lost in the amazing clarity of it all when my wife interrupted me. "Honey?" I think it actually took her a couple minutes to break me out of my trance. She even stood there with me for a few minutes to check out the incredible clarity of high definition!

When I think of that TV, it reminds me how important it is to see our dreams with the same type of clarity. We need to see our dreams in high definition! Because if you can really own that vivid picture, if you can see your dream in every detail, if you can fix your eyes on it, then I know you can muster the effort you need to hit your R:IQ numbers.

The R:IQ will help you begin to get more clarity on the financial figures you need. It will help you really plug into a plan. If you are going to be successful, you have to put your money to work. R:IQ will help you take a look at what you have invested and understand how to grow it the right way. It will move retirement from this ethereal thing to something vivid, practical, and part of your everyday behavior.

It will also help you avoid the terrible mistakes that could derail your dream. The R:IQ tool makes you fully aware of how much you will need to retire and live the dream that you want to live. Do you have a target? The R:IQ tool will help you aim your actions. It will help you understand how to be intentional, how to make the sacrifices you need to make, and how to stay allergic to debt.

R:IQ will help you make sure that you have enough money to

enjoy the retirement lifestyle that you dream about. It will show you how you can live comfortably, travel, enjoy your family, help others, and give like crazy! Your R:IQ is going to help you think bigger so that you can do better. It is going to be your GPS, your recipe, and your plan!

Three Emotional Reactions to the R:IQ Tool

I have had the chance to work with plenty of folks as they sat down with the R:IQ assessment tool for the first time. Using the R:IQ tool generally leads to three emotional responses. Once we get into the tool, we will lay out some clear strategies to move forward no matter where you are today. But to start, it's good to have some awareness going into this process of what you may feel when you begin to plug in the numbers.

"Oh, crap!"

First, there is the "Oh, crap!" response. It is the realization that you are in pretty bad shape. It is also the recognition that something has to change—and change *fast*. It means it is time to get radical. Some tough decisions are on the table, and you cannot waste another day! "Oh, crap!" means that your actions need to be refined immediately.

"Oh, boy!"

You might be in the category of folks who start to plug numbers in and say, "Oh, boy, I still have some work to do." If you're in this group, you've been saving here and there, and those savings are starting to grow. However, unless something changes, you definitely won't have enough to fund your dreams in retirement. That means some sacrifices are going to be necessary. You are coming face to face with the truth that you still have some work to do if you are going to get where you want to go. It might mean picking up some extra jobs or creating some other type of income, but, most importantly, it means understanding that those changes can't wait. You've got to start today.

"Oh, yeah!"

Last, you may be one of the few who plug numbers into the R:IQ tool and say, "Oh, yeah, things are looking pretty sweet!" Maybe there are some high fives, maybe a few fist bumps. This response comes from the recognition that you are on track toward your dreams and everything looks good—so far. This group has already been budgeting and saving for retirement. These are the people who have been on a plan. But, this is also the group that needs to remember that it isn't time to pop the cork on the champagne just yet! The "Oh, yeah!" group has to stay focused and recognize that it only takes one bad financial decision to derail your dreams.

A New Way of Thinking

It is time to start thinking differently about retirement. I want you to understand that, if you have kids, you'll probably spend more time in retirement than you spent raising your children. I know that sounds crazy, but it is true! I've said it over and over: Retirement is not the end of your life; it's the start of what could be the last third of your life. If you're going to live a few decades without working, your only income *then* depends on what you are doing *now*.

Retirement is not an age; it's a number—a *financial* number. It's the amount you'll need to fund your dreams in retirement. Maybe it will help if I explain what that means in my life. Let me tell you about *my* number. I'm on track to hit my number in my mid-fifties. Now that doesn't mean I will quit my job or disappear at age fifty-five, but it definitely means that I will be able to choose what I want to do. You see, I do a little bit of traveling right now because I want to get out there and speak to people about the importance of saving for their dreams. So I miss some occasional weekends with my family. I miss some evenings with my boys. But I plan to get that time back when I hit my number. I have specific things that I want to do when I get there. I want to travel with my family for *fun* instead of for work. I never want my boys to be spoiled, but I do want them to have some experiences. I want them to see the world and gain a bit of perspective and appreciation. I also want to live without any burdens and give generously when I see a need. That is what my number represents: my dream.

Right on Target for Your Dream

I keep coming back to the importance of having a dream because it is the vital jumping-off point. Let me tell another story to explain why. My first year in college, I was one of the few freshman starters on my football team. I was so new that the coach didn't even know my name. In our defensive meetings he sometimes called me "Curtis." Coach Ernie Horning was really into motivational tactics and would go to conferences and bring back new ideas. He was always trying to find new ways to get us to push harder and be better.

One Monday, we came into the defensive meeting to talk about a really big game ahead on Saturday. He looked around the room and picked on me, the lone freshman starter, asking, "What are we going to do this weekend, Curtis?" I sat for a moment, thought about it, and responded, "Coach, we are going to play some football."

He shook his head. "No, gentlemen, that is *not* the correct answer." He then began to pass out notecards to everyone in the room. He told us that we were to write down specific goals for the big game on Saturday. He wanted to know how many tackles, assisted tackles, and sacks we would have in the game. I wrote on my notecard: "nine tackles, one forced fumble, and two quarterback sacks." I turned the card facedown on the table and Coach collected it.

You know, I thought about my goals all week. Saturday, when the first half of our game ended, I knew I only had four tackles so far. Not enough. See, I had written a specific goal on that notecard. There was a number I needed, and I hadn't hit it yet. I was striving to live up to those numbers. I had a good second half because I was determined to meet the goals I had written out for myself. We won the game and, sure enough, Monday morning in our defensive meeting, Coach handed our notecards back to us. He called on me to read my goals to the entire team.

Coach asked me, "So, Curtis, what were your numbers in the game?" I had finished the game with seven tackles and two quarterback sacks. I responded honestly, "I didn't meet my goals, Coach." But Coach shook his head and explained, "No, you are seeing it all wrong!" He looked at me and then to the team and said, "You didn't come up short; you came in right on target."

I will never forget the lesson he was teaching us. Coach eventually got my name right, and his positive thinking and goal-setting sessions have definitely made a lasting impact on my life. If you set those lofty goals for yourself, you might not get to your exact numbers, but you will come in right where you need to in order to be successful. That is why visualizing your dream is so vital! It is the same way with setting our R:IQ goals. Dream big and you won't be disappointed.

Your R:IQ Homework

We must dream our dreams, but we also must own the obligation to work them into reality. These aspects of responsibility and accountability are required for *anyone* to reach and retain success. So all of this talk about the R:IQ tool doesn't mean a thing if you don't stop and figure out your own R:IQ number. This isn't just a theory; it's a formula for your own retirement goals and planning. You can read this book a hundred times, but if you don't stop to figure out your own number, none of this will matter. This is the point where you have to decide if you want to read some theories about retirement or if you want to build a game plan to live the life of your dreams in retirement.

Still with me? Good. Here's your homework. We've built a free R:IQ assessment tool that will show you exactly how much you need to fund your dreams in retirement. You enter in how much you have saved already, how long you have to save before retirement, and what kind of income you think you'll need to fund your dreams. The tool takes all that information, throws in some math and magic, and then tells you exactly how much money you'll need to retire (your number) and how much you need to save each month between now and then to make that number a reality.

Your retirement is all about your number. There's no point moving forward until you clearly identify your goal. Stop and do that right now. Visit chrishogan360.com to take the free assessment. It'll only take a couple of minutes, and then we can move forward.

LIVING FOR NOW AND LATER

Okay, so I'm trusting that you actually did what I told you to do and that you've got your number in front of you now. That's good. I want you to keep that number in front of you for the rest of your working life! That's your goal. That's where we're heading.

But now that you have a number to shoot for, you might be thinking, *How do I ignite a fire to save toward retirement but still give myself permission to live in the now?* That's a great question, and it's one all successful savers have to deal with. You need to stay focused on your retirement goals, but you still need to have a little fun. I'm all about delaying gratification, but you can't delay all of your fun to some later date that may never come.

Saving Doesn't Mean Putting Life on Hold

A friend of mine told me that his father-in-law had spent his whole life staying allergic to debt. He had retired from the phone company but continued to work, saving for retirement well into his sixties. For years, he never went on vacation and rarely did much to enjoy the hard work and saving he had practiced his entire life. Instead of living a fun, full life while working toward a dream, he had always been a bit of a miser. He pretty much just worked all the time and never stopped to let off any steam.

He finally stopped working at age sixty-five and officially retired in March of that year. A month later, he was diagnosed with a crippling form of dementia that left him hospitalized in full-time care. Now, keep in mind, he wasn't a burden to anyone because he had put in the work, but he also had put his whole life on hold waiting for retirement. And now that retirement had arrived, he wasn't able to enjoy it.

There must be a balance. You definitely don't want to borrow from American Express to take your kids on vacation—because that kind of vacation follows you home and shows up in your mailbox—but that doesn't mean you can't take a vacation. As we talk about having a game plan and saving for retirement, I am not asking you to stop living your life. I want you to live your life *while* investing in your future! You absolutely can do both if you make a plan.

Fun Doesn't Equal Money

Don't forget that fun doesn't require money. If money is tight, you can stay focused on your retirement goals while still enjoying time and freedom with your family. I counseled a single mother who was working her way out of some pretty significant debt. She was in such bad financial shape that she couldn't spend the money to take her children on vacation someplace nice. You know what they did? They had a "staycation." They baked homemade pizzas, watched movies, and played games. She recently became debt free and told me that of all the vacations she has taken with her children, none has topped their "staycation." The children remembered that vacation more fondly than any beach or even their trip to see the famous mouse. You know what a "nice" vacation really means for kids? It means spending quality time with them. Unplug the phones, power everything down, and just be present with them. It is as simple as that.

However, if you're living on a plan and have some money to go toward a nice trip, then do it! Just do it on purpose—with savings—instead of on impulse with a credit card. Figure out how much the trip will cost, divide that by how many months you have before the trip, and save that much money every month. When it's time to leave, you'll have the money, you won't need debt, and your retirement savings will still be safe and sound.

My wife and I visited that big park in Orlando to see the mouse with our kids, and we had cash envelopes for everything! We had ice cream envelopes, dinner envelopes, mouse-shirt envelopes, and souvenir envelopes. We paid cash for the whole trip, and that vacation was actually built into our plan. It was an ingredient in the grand recipe. But it didn't steal from what we are working for: to keep the have-tos shrinking and the want-tos growing.

You Can Do This!

Before we move on to more specific directions, we need to take some time and look at what you have right now. What is your starting point? What do you have saved at this moment for your retirement? As we've discussed, each dream is going to have a little bit different price tag. But, believe me, I need you to understand that you *can* save for retirement.

Beginning today, you can do it! No excuses. Try this: just save $5 a day. Five bucks a day could mean just one latte at that high-priced coffee joint or three to four cups of coffee at your favorite gas station down the street. Just saving $5 a day during the work-week can add up to $100 a month! So what would a $100-a-month investment look like? Just as an example, if you used a 10 percent rate of return (and that is not a stretch), you could have $76,275 after twenty years! If you stuck to this plan for thirty years, you would have $218,315! After forty years of saving that little bit of pocket change a day, you could end up with $588,748!

Doesn't that sound possible? And hey, if you're twenty-five and reading this, let me ask you something. Which tastes better: a $5 cup of coffee today or a cool half-million at retirement?

Let's take it just a little bit further and bump your savings up to $150 a month. That is just $2.50 more per workday—the cost of dry-cleaning one shirt. By using the same 10 percent rate of return, you could have $114,413 after twenty years, $328,315 after thirty, and after forty years, $883,122!

And let's take a moment to get a little bit crazy. (That's what people will think when you start working toward your dreams any-way!) What if you could sacrifice a little more and pull off $20 a day? Maybe you fire the lawn guy and cut the grass yourself? Maybe you cut that car payment and drive something older and paid for? That would mean $400 per month toward your retirement. After twenty years with interest, it would add up to $305,103! After thirty years, $875,508! And after forty years, it would mean $2,355,992! Yes, you read that correctly, but go back and read it one more time: $2,355,992! You would be a millionaire a couple of times over, and all it cost you were some cups of gourmet coffee, ironing a few of your own shirts, and cutting your own grass every now and then. That's not bad!

I want you to take a deep breath and pretend you are look-ing at your dreams for retirement on that eighty-five-inch, high-definition television for just a moment. I want you to see the blades of grass swaying in the wind—the want-tos all over that screen in vivid detail. You have that beautiful vision? Now, I have one simple question for you:

Do you think you might be able to retire on $2.3 million?

The answer, of course, is yes! But keep in mind, you are only one bad decision from giving away this plan to save for retirement. Think about it with me one more time. Four hundred dollars a month is less than the average car payment. That means you can keep the coffee and yard guy and still become a double millionaire if you simply get out and stay out of debt. You can do this!

Never Too Early, Never Too Late

I want to encourage you that it is never too late to start saving for retirement, and it is definitely never too early to start the process. Let me tell you a couple of quick stories to explain my point.

I met a lady in Denver who was in her late sixties. Her age and health told her it was time to retire, but her numbers weren't there. I've had this kind of conversation hundreds of times, talking with people who realized pretty late in the game that they needed to do something for retirement. But you know what? There are still things most of those people can do.

This lady was sixty-eight years old and hadn't saved for retirement at all. She had, however, stayed allergic to debt and had even paid off her home. After we talked, she began to view her paid-off house as a financial resource. She would have to sacrifice the sentimentality wrapped up in that home; it was the place where her kids had grown up. She would have to find a reasonable place to rent, and she'd probably rent the rest of her life. However, her home was worth over $400,000, and that decision would enable her to fund the retirement that she wanted.

She wrote me a three-page thank-you letter for taking the time to speak with her and helping her see that she had options. In reality, she had done all the work herself by paying off her home. I just helped her see her home as a resource.

It is never too late to find your dream! It is never too late to see retirement in a different way and take action. But it is also never too early. I met a young man who was only nineteen years old, yet he had already saved quite a bit of money by working through high school and college. He was paying cash for his college classes, he was driving an old, paid-for '87 Datsun, and he was ferocious about staying away from car payments and debt. He explained that he was also already beginning to save for retirement. I talked with him about staying the course and staying away from stupid. We discussed making good financial decisions and even being sure to marry someone who had the same values about life and money that he held.

After spending a little time with him, I told his parents, "Your son is going to be a millionaire by the age of thirty." And if he sticks to the recipe, he certainly will. His want-tos, his heart-moments, will come way earlier than for you or me and most folks we know. I might beat you down with this phrase, but it is vital for you to remember: Retirement is not an age; it's a number! It isn't about getting *old*; it's about being *free* to do those things that really make you come alive!

Ask yourself for a moment: what could you do with $1 million or $2 million in retirement? You see, regardless of your number or of where you are now, the key to this dream is learning to manage what you have. The recipe involves understanding how to be responsible with what you have been given. So where can you find the means to invest for your dreams? It starts with a budget. The budget is the recipe. Learning to place a name on every dollar is the one thing that can help you plan for your dream, and, at the same time, it can empower you to enjoy your life right now.

If you haven't taken the R:IQ assessment yet, do it now! Take it for free at chrishogan360.com.

CHAPTER THREE

BUDGETING

Be the Boss of Your Money

D o you want the GPS upgrade on your car, Mr. Hogan?"
I had just landed for my first speaking engagement in Arizona.
The venue was a couple of hours from the airport, and the nice little
lady at the car rental place was going through all the fancy upgrades
they usually try to tack on to the rental agreement.

Now, keep in mind, this was back in the day before we had all this
stuff on our phones. I shook my head when she asked and thought,
No, I've got this. I definitely don't need a GPS. She peered over her
glasses a little concerned. "Are you sure?" It was one of those "You're
not from around here, are you?" kind of looks.

I responded with an air of irrational confidence the way too many
other men can relate to. "Yes, ma'am, I'm sure. I don't need the GPS,
but thanks!"

After two hours of driving, and right about the time I was supposed to be pulling into my hotel, I came to my senses and looked around. You know what I saw? Nothing. Nothing but desert and cacti. I'm pretty sure I saw some tumbleweeds blowing around ahead of me too. I was completely lost!

I drove a little farther until I finally found a gas station and walked inside to ask for directions. And the directions they gave me sent me forty-five minutes back the way I had just driven. I was almost three hours into a trip that should've taken two. I could just imagine that nice little lady at the rental car counter peering over her glasses, shaking her head at me, and thinking, *Bless his heart!*

I got back in the car and thought, *Okay, I got this!* I knew where I was heading. But I drove another forty-five minutes and wasn't seeing any of the landmarks they had told me to watch for. Once again, I realized I was completely lost. I found a convenience store, but this time I walked in with a pen and some paper. I was going to write these directions down, draw my own map, pay someone to go with me, whatever it took to get where I needed to be!

I looked pitiful when I asked the clerk for help. "Ma'am, I have been driving for almost four hours, but I still don't know where I am. Can you help?" We looked up the address together and she explained that I was only twenty minutes away from where I was supposed to go. But, she cautioned me, there was one tricky turn ahead. She told me that I had to be careful because if I missed that one right turn, it would take me another forty-five minutes out of my way. Needless to say, I followed each specific direction to the letter and it took me twenty minutes to get there. When I finally pulled up at my hotel, I wanted to hug the valet!

I know what you're thinking: *he should've taken the GPS.* Right? I could've arrived on time. I would've saved myself a lot of headache, frustration, and wasted energy. I knew where I *wanted* to go, but I didn't have a written plan—a map—for getting there.

The same thing happens in our retirement planning. We have a dream for what we want to accomplish, but we never make a plan to get there. We just hope we somehow arrive at retirement's door. That's just not going to happen. You need a map. You need a GPS to safely arrive at your destination. And when it comes to your retirement, that GPS is called a *budget*. The budget is our tool that provides us with the precise directions we need to get to our dream!

BUDGET BASICS

First off, it is important to understand that, no matter what phase of life you are in, you will never outgrow the need for a budget. Budgeting is and always will be your road map to financial success, no matter how much or how little money you have.

If you're just starting out, now is the perfect time to start budgeting. If you develop the habit early, you'll be blown away at how quickly you'll build wealth. It's never too early to start.

But it is also never too *late* to begin using a budget, even if you've already hit your retirement goal. Let's say you're sixty-five years old and have $3 million in investments. At that level, budgeting becomes more important than ever! It's like John Maxwell says, "A budget is simply telling your money where to go instead of wondering where it went." If I have $3 million, you better believe I want to know where it's all going!

Find Those Dollars and Give Them a Name

When my wife and I first heard Dave Ramsey talk about finances, we immediately began working to get out of debt. The first thing we needed was a budget. We didn't have kids yet, and we were both making decent money. We sat down together and began looking through our bank statements to track each category and find where our money was going.

The first thing that jumped out was how much we were spending at the grocery store. Now, keep in mind, it was just the two of us, but we were sparing no expense when we went shopping for food. I began to add up what we were spending and just shook my head. My first thought was, *That can't be right!* As we began to look back through our account records, we discovered that we had spent even more on our groceries the month before! We were spending way too much for a family of two.

My wife and I sat down and took a good look at what we could do to cut that expense back, to actually set a budget for our monthly groceries. We ultimately decided that we could cut our monthly grocery bill in half.

We even took it one step further. We began to look at the groceries we already had. We took everything from the pantry, set it out, and began laughing because it appeared we had enough canned food to feed a small city. Then we took inventory of everything in our deep freezer. The food covered all the counters and our kitchen table. We began to plan meals right there. We didn't need to go grocery shopping for at least a month! We were just in the habit of going to the store and spending.

Once we realized that our money could be directed where it *needed* to go, we were able to use that money to attack credit card debt and get our financial lives back under control. Without sitting down and examining our monthly spending, we would've never realized how much money we were carelessly wasting at the grocery store. We found that, by budgeting, we could name those dollars for a better purpose.

The Three Key Steps of Budgeting
I want you to keep in mind the key steps of a budget:

1. Start with your income.

You have to begin with what you earn. All of it: the side projects, bonus money, every single penny. There is no such thing as "found money" when it comes to the budget!

2. Separate needs from wants.

Take a good, long look at what you actually *need*. Just like my grocery overspending, there is a big difference between what we *want* and what we actually *need*, and sometimes we don't even realize the difference until we step back and think critically about it.

3. Make a plan for your money.

The final element of the budget is to understand exactly where your money needs to go. You may want to take a look at your bank statement and assess your spending. The only way to wrangle those dollars is to put them on a plan.

Budgeting Can Protect Your Dream

Having a budget is going to help you get to the Baby Steps that Dave talked about at the beginning of the book. And the greatest thing about putting together a budget is the sense of taking control of your money. The budget will help you understand that you can actually afford to do the Baby Steps! The budget will also give you hope that you can retire with dignity.

Not only is learning to budget essential for getting to your dream retirement, but it is also going to be an essential practice to maintain your dream in retirement. Let me say that one more time: budgeting will become even more important in retirement! Without a regular paycheck, your monthly income will be completely up to you. That makes it more important than ever to make sure you are living well within your means. If your nest egg is going to fund your life for twenty or more years, you can't blow half of it the first year of retirement. You have to plan for it to last.

The other thing to remember about a budget is that it will give you the freedom to actually *enjoy* spending your income. Once you dig into your spending habits, you are going to find that many of your dollars are sneaking off to places that they don't need to go. Once you name them and send them in the right direction, you'll most likely realize that you have some extra money to enjoy. Most people go into the budgeting process feeling like it's going to be a straitjacket, but they end up feeling like they got a raise! And it's just because they stopped the careless flow of money through their fingers.

A budget also puts some guardrails on your money, giving you some boundaries that will keep you out of trouble. In other words, it will keep you from those sheep or ostrich moments. It'll keep you on the path and away from that one stupid decision that might derail your progress.

Building the Habit of Budgeting

From working closely with people who have tackled budgeting, I can tell you that the first several months are the toughest. You may have heard or read somewhere that it takes twenty-one days to build a new habit. Recent studies show that it actually takes a little bit longer. They say it requires around sixty-six days to build a new practice or habit.[1] That means the first two months are going to be especially tough, but by the third time you sit down to do a monthly budget, it will have become a habit.

Early on, budgeting was a tough process—especially with the grocery shopping. I still remember that first trip to the store once we got on a plan. I went in there with my calculator and an envelope filled with exactly $150 in cash. That's all the grocery money we had for the week, and I didn't have the option of going over.

It was the slowest shopping trip of my life because I stopped to keep the tab on my calculator every time I put something in the cart. About halfway through, I ran into one of my friends. We began talking and laughing and, right in the middle of our conversation, I accidently hit "clear" on my calculator. With all the talking, I had lost focus and lost the number! My friend walked away, I looked back into my full cart of groceries, and I had no idea what I had spent so far.

But I didn't reach for my debit card and risk it. I didn't give up. Instead, I went back up and down the aisles and I put everything back in its place and I started all over again. Finally, I rolled up to the checkout line and took out my cash envelope. I watched carefully as the clerk scanned each item and the tally appeared on the register. $132.59 . . . $135 . . . $140 . . . Finally it hit $143.02, and I was starting to sweat! I looked at the conveyer belt and grabbed a couple small items and set them off to the side. When all was said and done, my total came in safely at $148.06! I rolled that cart out to my car with a sense of accomplishment. I had gone to the grocery store and paid cash for my groceries. I had followed my game plan and come in under budget.

That first month was tough. There were funny moments like that one, but, over time, it became second nature. As my wife and I flexed our budgeting muscles, they became stronger and stronger. And we didn't realize it in the moment, but we were cutting miles off of our drive to retirement. The truth I want you to remember is that your first two months of budgeting will feel a little uncomfortable, somewhat difficult, and maybe even a little stressful. That's because change isn't easy; if it were, everyone would do it. But, I also promise you that budgeting will get easier by the third month!

Budget Committee Meetings

Remember this rule: from now on and for the rest of your life, you have to prepare a written budget every month—before the month begins. I guarantee that by the time you hit month six of budgeting, it will take way less time than it does at first. It will become second nature.

If you are married, you should schedule budget committee meetings. Now, you might be thinking that sounds a little formal. But let me ask you this: how successful would a business be that never had budget meetings? I know the federal government seems to operate that way, but for the rest of the world who actually has to pay their debts, operating without a budget means disaster. We need to think of our homes in the same way we think about our businesses. You and your spouse, if you're married, are the CEOs of your own little operation—the most important operation in your life!

I shouldn't have to tell you how important this is. I am not a marriage counselor, but all you have to do is a quick Internet search to understand that finances are one of the most common reasons for divorce. So not only will it get you on track toward retirement, but also it is important to your relationship that you and your spouse sit down and talk about your finances. I tell people to set aside thirty minutes together for these budget meetings. I want people to take thirty minutes because it gives them the time and space to really engage the topic with each other and not just fly over it quickly.

My wife and I keep that thirty minutes sacred, but after several years of practice, we knock out the budget quickly and then cover other important family business: What's going on? Where am I traveling this week? What's happening with the kids? It is a great time for both of you to come together and do a status report on where the family is going. It is our official board meeting to keep everyone moving in the right direction.

If you're single, accountability can be a little trickier. Married people have a built-in accountability system because there's always someone waiting at home to see how much they spent! But single people can fall into a trap of isolation, making all kinds of mistakes just because there's no one around to keep them in check. That's why I always tell single people to find an accountability partner to help them stay on track. Just make sure it's someone who loves you enough to be honest when you need a reality check and who is willing to hurt your feelings for your own good.

Row Your Boat Together!

Throughout this process, you will learn how to agree on a monthly budget, make a spending plan together, and stick to it. Having a budget committee meeting with your partner will help both of you know what is going on and help you to stay on track financially. It will also ensure that if something terrible happens to either of you, the other would be prepared to take over and keep things moving. You may be thinking, *That will never happen to us.* That is the ostrich mode talking.

I once worked with a couple named Jim and Lisa. Jim was a financial executive and Lisa was a painter. Despite my insistence, they really didn't come together and work on finances. Handling money was right in Jim's wheelhouse, and Lisa was artistic, free-spirited, and not interested in learning how to deal with the family finances.

But then Jim got sick. He was on dialysis, his energy was really low, and it was all he could do to make it through the requirements of his job. They came to me for help. Lisa was in her forties and had never touched the household finances. But now it was game on. She had to learn quickly. There was a lot of anxiety and confusion on her part. She was a bright woman, but it was difficult for her to jump right in to handling the finances after being disengaged for so long.

She knew she had to step up to the plate and get it done. I helped her to understand what was going on and to see where the dollars were going. Did Lisa do things just like her husband? Nope. Jim liked to handle everything online. He had a system set up that he understood. It was easier for Lisa to write actual checks. So she and I worked on setting up a system that worked for her. Over time, Lisa became more confident throughout this process. She learned quickly and was putting her new skills to work. She handled their finances not just effectively but beautifully throughout the family's time of crisis.

The best part of the story is that Jim recovered. The two of them now work on the money stuff together. There was a little bit of power struggle when Jim got healthy because he had given up control, and handling the family's finances was something that he liked doing. He had to learn to be okay with his wife's process as well.

One of their first arguments happened because he felt they needed to go back to paying things online, and she had gotten into the habit of writing physical checks. I'll never forget that coaching session. It was a real moment of tension between the two. I watched as they talked the same way you watch a tennis match: looking back and forth and back and forth. Finally, I helped them work out an arrangement where she handled some aspects by writing checks and he handled the other parts by paying online. But the beautiful thing about the whole experience was that they were both growing together. Regardless of what life threw at them now, they were both equipped to handle what was necessary for their children and to continue to work toward their retirement dream. The finances became a point of unity for them instead of a point of conflict.

Working together on the budget over the course of many years sets you up to work together in retirement. We said earlier that you'll have two things in retirement that you've never had at the same time before: time and money. But, if you're married, you will have an abundance of something else, maybe for the first time—togetherness.

You spend forty years working separately in two jobs or with one spouse at work and the other one at home with the kids. But the day's coming when no one goes to work and you both have to figure out what to do with each other all day. With years of budgeting together behind you, you'll be a perfect team in planning all the time, money, and togetherness you'll have to enjoy. Remember, you're in this boat together, so row it together!

GETTING STARTED WITH BUDGETING

When it comes to retirement, the *why* is really where we need to begin. The *why* is that high-definition dream. It is your target, your destination, and the budget is the vehicle that is going to help get you there. I need you to understand how essential budgeting can be to finding that extra $200 or $400 that will help get you to your retirement dreams.

Budgeting Builds Momentum

Money does exactly what you tell it to do—every time. So when you start to budget, you immediately feel and see this sense of progress. It gives you momentum. Our eyes are on this high-definition retirement dream and we begin to ask ourselves, *How can we do better? How can we move faster?* When you begin to feel traction or forward motion, you get excited and find even more ways to make your money work harder.

Once my wife and I got our money under control, we realized we could make more sacrifices. We cut out some unnecessary things in the budget, like that landline phone no one ever called us on. Every one of those little cuts gave us more money to put into retirement, and we got the power of momentum on our side.

And then the fun really started. We began looking at some

things that we thought might hurt a little. We didn't go to restaurants as much. Our vacations started looking a little different. And then, the big hit came. One day, my wife suggested that we could save over a hundred bucks a month by ditching the cable TV. I thought, *What? What about sports? What about Shark Week? I can't do this!*

My wife didn't push, but she was smart. She simply said, "Honey, it's over $100 a month that we could save. Just think about it." So I did. I realized there were plenty of games I could get on network TV with an antenna. If there was a really big sporting event that I wanted to see, I was sure I could find someplace to watch it. I started to really crunch the numbers and look at things. I calculated how much we'd earn in just five years if I invested that $100 a month, and that's all it took.

Over time, I began to understand the value of making those sacrifices, and I no longer felt like I was having things *taken away*. It was a *sacrifice* that became a worthy investment. I didn't lose much by cutting the cable and, in return, I'll get to retire a little sooner if I want to. That's not much of a sacrifice at all!

Get the F.A.C.T.s

So, as your coach, let me give you some quick fundamentals about budgeting. Let's use the acronym F.A.C.T. I call it that because it is an absolute *fact* that if you do not budget, every single dime you have will slip through your fingers! Whether you are young and just starting out or much older, these basic budgeting principles can help you tremendously.

F: Four Walls

The first priority in your budget should always be protecting what I call the Four Walls. These are the absolute necessities, the things you cannot skip or get behind on. These include food, shelter and utilities, clothing (I'm not talking about Gucci or Prada), and reasonable transportation. Don't let anything—not even your retirement goals—get between you and the basic necessities your family needs to survive.

A: Awareness

Awareness means that you have an understanding of your own income, expenses, and habits. Awareness also includes knowing where your money is going because every dollar has a name and you have a plan!

C: Connected

You have to stay connected to your finances. You should know where you stand financially on any given day. Connected means you don't have any surprises in your budget or bank account.

T: Tamed

What must be tamed? You. Tamed means you have the self-control to not do something that will set you back, like signing a stupid car note that will steal precious retirement dollars from you every single month. Tamed means that you can tell yourself no. We have to learn how to be grown-ups and tell a want that it has to wait.

Begin with the F.A.C.T.s and I promise that you will be on your way to a successful budget.

Zero-Based Budgeting

The best budgeting method I know is the zero-based budget. No, that doesn't mean letting your bank account hit zero! It just means that you are making a plan for every single dollar you bring home. To put it simply, your income minus your expenses should equal zero. When you create your budget before the month begins—meaning before you bring the money home—your dollars know exactly what to do and where to go, and you don't have any surprises. Here's how it works:

> **First, write your expected monthly income at the top of the page.** That means every dollar coming in that month—no exceptions.

> **Second, list all of your planned expenses.** Everything from giving to savings to gasoline to food to debt (if you have any). If you're going to spend money on anything for that month, it has to be on the list. Use the Baby Steps from the foreword of this book or Dave's *The Total Money Makeover* book to set the priority.

Be sure your expenses include things we often miss, like club dues or birthday gifts. If you have any irregularly occurring expenses (like a semiannual insurance premium), divide that expense into monthly chunks and stick that into your budget every month. So, if you have a $600 expense that hits twice a year, you should save $100 a month for it so the money's there when the bill is due.

There's a lot more I could say about the mechanics of budgeting, but I think the best thing I can do is point you to the site with the best budgeting tool in the world: EveryDollar.com. It's a free tool that you can use to create a zero-based budget every month, and it walks you right through the Baby Steps. You can also download our free e-book *Chris Hogan's Guide to Budgeting for Retirement* at chrishogan360.com/budget. That will answer pretty much any question you have about how to build a budget that works.

YOUR RETIREMENT IS UP TO YOU
AND YOUR BUDGET

So how do we use budgeting to get us to retirement? Well, for starters, after you eliminate all debt except your home and build up a fully funded emergency fund, you should budget to invest 15 percent of your income into your retirement plans. Remember that we said you are never too young and you are never too old to begin planning your retirement. We'll talk about the specifics of investing in a later chapter. For now, though, let me remind you that this journey toward your dream, your retirement, is completely up to you. You cannot depend on winning the lottery. You cannot depend on the government. You cannot depend on your children. You shouldn't depend on some big inheritance from a parent or distant relative. It is 100 percent in your hands.

Don't Count On What You Don't Have

I've worked with many people who weren't actively contributing to their retirement because they were expecting a big inheritance from their parents. Their attitude was, "Why should I worry about it? My parents did a great job with their money, so I'll get theirs when they're gone!"

Counting on something like an inheritance is a recipe for disaster. This is something my friend Andy learned recently. He and his wife just got a great deal on a new home. It was a sweet custom job with a ton of upgrades in a new neighborhood. I'm talking granite countertops, a stone fireplace on the outside patio, and a bathroom that was bigger than his room in college. It was beautiful! You'd have thought he and his wife had meticulously picked out every option, but they hadn't. It had actually been sitting brand-new on the market for months when they found it. The builder was stuck with it after the original buyer fell through.

The couple who had originally built the home had been counting on an inheritance from an ailing parent. They had nothing to put down on the home other than the expectation of a sudden windfall. But guess what? The other family members figured out what they were doing and all heck broke loose! After a lot of family drama, the couple had to back out of the deal. They hadn't taken anything into their own hands. They thought a potential inheritance was their own retirement plan, and it didn't work out so well for them.

The interesting thing was that my friend, who had been budgeting, saving, and doing things the right way, was able to capitalize on this opportunity. They put an offer on the house that was tens of thousands less than the original asking price, and the builder took it just to be free of it!

The original couple lost out on their dream home because they were spending money before they even had it. The inheritance never came, and now someone else is enjoying their dream house at a steep discount. One of the many lessons from this nightmare story is that those types of blessings are risky and unexpected. An inheritance is great if you are blessed with one, but you can't count on it as part of your plan.

Budgeting for Windfalls

So how exactly do you handle budgeting windfalls such as an inheritance or an unexpected sum of money? I counseled a guy once who had received a $150,000 inheritance from his grandparents. This isn't that uncommon, but it's a pretty dangerous situation. As many as 70 percent of people who receive some type of financial windfall end up broke within a few years![2] That is what I call a total waste of a financial blessing!

As we talked, I told this guy what I always tell people in this situation. The first thing you should do is just take a big, long, deep breath. The second thing you should do is take that money and put it in a money market account for three to six months and leave it alone until you come up with—you guessed it—a plan. You see, if you don't have a plan, you know what will happen? You'll take a $500 weekend trip here and make a $2,000 purchase there, and then take a once-in-a-lifetime vacation. In no time, that huge blessing is completely gone, and you don't have anything to show for it. I didn't want that to happen to this young man I was coaching.

We talked about all of the ways that he could make some real progress with it. He left the meeting, and I felt pretty good about what we had discussed. But then, he missed our next meeting. Months went by and I never heard from him. Then, five months later, he called and asked for an appointment.

I will never forget the look on his face when he got back to my office. I glanced at his portfolio for a moment and noticed that he only had $5,000 in his account. I looked up and said, "Is this it? Where's the rest?"

He looked up with the saddest expression I'd ever seen and said, "Chris, this is all I have left."

In five short months, he had spent $145,000! He only had $5,000 left of that amazing gift his grandparents had left him. I sat back and looked down at the table in total shock. I wanted to grab him by the shoulders and shake him a little bit! I am sure his grandparents would've felt the same way. Did all that money buy him a home? Did he invest it all, pretty much guaranteeing he'd be a multimillionaire in retirement? No. He spent the money on some clothes, some furniture, a new car, and vacations. Plus, he had bought not one but two Rolex watches—and he had already lost one of them.

I remember listening to him talk and thinking to myself, *This young man just squandered a legacy.* He completely misused the money that his grandparents had worked for and left him—and he had done it in less than six months. I could see the regret on his face. I knew that if he could go back in time and fix it, he would. He had learned two lessons about inheritance the hard way: First, you have to have a plan for the money. And second, you shouldn't try to soothe the grief of losing a parent or grandparent by spending money. If you will stick to a plan and a budget, it will actually empower you to go out and enjoy some of that windfall without squandering the legacy.

Remember, if you receive any type of inheritance, I want you to proceed with caution. Slow way down and be extremely intentional with the money. If you are married, talk about it together. Inheritance money can cause anxiety, bitterness, and jealousy if a couple is not fully united on how to handle money. I worked with a couple who was receiving a large inheritance—almost $400,000. They had been struggling financially, and I knew the money could either be a great blessing or a huge curse for their marriage. I encouraged them to always remember where this money came from and how they received it.

You see, remembering that the money was intended as a blessing brings a level of responsibility and accountability to the receivers. That couple took my advice, parked the money in a money market account, and agreed not to touch it until they were in complete agreement about what to do with it. They brainstormed how to best use the money, had patience, and, as my grandmother used to say, "were prayerful and careful" with their actions.

Eventually, they used my "pie graph approach," which is to set up various ways of using the money as if it were slices of a pie. They devoted an amount toward giving, some toward debt elimination, and some of it was dedicated to paying off their home and boosting their retirement savings. But they also allocated a certain dollar amount for some fun stuff, like a vacation. They also established a small scholarship fund in the name of her parents for a local university. Being intentional ensures that an inheritance will be the kind of blessing it was meant to be.

BUDGETING IN RETIREMENT

Clearly, budgeting is the GPS that gets you to that high-definition dream of retirement we've been talking about. But once you arrive at your destination, do you stop budgeting? Is the highlight of your retirement party a ceremonial burning of the final monthly budget? No!

I remember one couple I worked with many years ago. They had been on fire throughout their working years. They had a target. They knew how to get there. The budget was a staple for this couple, and they never started a new month without a new budget to go along with it. It was impressive.

However, right after retirement, this couple got off track. They got sloppy with the budget, and they eventually gave it up altogether. They didn't stick to the plan. These two had a beautiful 3,000-square-foot house, but once they retired, they got hit with house fever out of the blue. They looked at the pile of money in their retirement accounts and started to think, *We deserve a nicer, bigger place.* So they upgraded their home.

Yes, retired folks are still susceptible to sheep-mode thinking. They went out and purchased a 4,500-square-foot home in a high-end neighborhood. The budget that they had worked out and planned for was now completely thrown out the window. All of the work they had put into their retirement was made obsolete with one stupid decision.

The paint was still drying on their retirement dream when they had to scrap the whole thing. They both had to go back to work in order to maintain this new lifestyle. Bottom line: they had to "un-retire." So at a time when they should've been simplifying life, they actually complicated everything with one bad financial decision. I like to think of it in football lingo: When pursuing your dreams is the play that you have called, remember that you must play both offense and defense to reach that goal. Offense is budgeting and being intentional. Defense is deleting debt and keeping dumb decisions sitting on the bench so you don't get sidetracked. We will focus more on specific offensive and defensive strategies later in the book.

This is where your R:IQ is so important. Look at that number and remember it, because that number represents your plan. Remember, retirement isn't an age; it's a financial number—how much you will need to live your dream retirement. Your budget will have to line up with that number. There is an R:IQ formula that fits every family situation. You have to decide what works best for your own family.

Bills Don't Stop at Retirement

Now let me put a little healthy fear in you about retirement. You still have to consider the wants and needs and understand the difference between the two. Remember that your dream still comes with bills to pay. You need to remember to view your retirement as a source of income, not a nest egg. So, as you retire, you actually want to set a salary for yourself, and you must develop a monthly budget based on this amount. No exceptions!

Yes, if you did your work, your home may be paid for, but you'll still be on the hook for homeowners insurance and property taxes, not to mention general upkeep to make sure your home outlives you. And don't get me started about health care costs. Managing the cost of health care can become a huge financial burden because way too many retirees completely forget to include health care costs in their monthly budget. Statistically, the average retiree spends about $5,000 per year out of pocket for health care. But experts—including me—actually suggest playing it safe by budgeting $11,000 per year for health care costs in retirement.[3] That's more than $900 a month that needs to be accounted for somewhere in your budget.

It's also important to account for giving in retirement, whether it's to a church or another charity. Charitable giving and grace giving shouldn't end when you retire. In fact, if you have planned the right way, retirement can be your best opportunity to share the blessings that you've received throughout your own life.

And don't forget about budgeting for big expenses. Your cars are going to keep aging just like you are, so take care of them and have a plan for replacing them that doesn't include a new car loan or lease. Then there are the big-budget events to consider such as traveling. Traveling is a big part of my wife's retirement dream, so I imagine we'll always have a "Travel" line on our budget—especially when we actually have the time to take those trips in retirement. Or maybe you will want to pay for your grandchildren's college? That's an awesome goal. Just make sure that is also in the budget.

Here's the deal: You cannot base your budget on the $50,000 a year you think you'll need to live on, but then spend $30,000 more than that on cars, trips, giving, helping with college, and so on. If you base your long-range budget on $50,000 a year, then that must include *everything* you want to do. Of course there will be exceptions from time to time, but the exceptions cannot be the rule.

I want you to enjoy the work you have put in. If you've done a great job, then absolutely celebrate and have a blast. That's the whole point, right? The goal is to live the life of your dreams in retirement. Just always remember that the budget is the tool that makes that possible—today *and* tomorrow.

Some Early Retirement Considerations

I've told you over and over that retirement isn't an age, but there are definitely some considerations when talking about retiring early. You have to realize that there are certain investments that you may not be able to access early on in your retirement. For instance, if you are retiring at fifty-nine years old or younger, you should meet with your investment professional to fully understand what funds can and cannot be accessed and when they can be used. Taking money out of an IRA looks a lot different at sixty than it does at fifty-eight. Don't make a mistake that could cost you tens or hundreds of thousands of dollars at retirement! You need to make sure the income you expect at retirement will actually be accessible to you before you pull the trigger and leave work behind.

Budgeting shouldn't be a *sometime* skill; it should be a *for-all-time* skill. What I mean is that while you have to have a budget to get to retirement, it is just as important to maintain a budget during retirement. And there are plenty of things you need to ask yourself if you are going to budget effectively in retirement. How much will you be able to pull from investments? How much cash flow will you need? Will you have to beef up your emergency fund? How can you increase your income by deferring your Social Security payments? These are all things you need to consider when you look at early retirement.

Don't Forget to Get the Professionals Involved

I reluctantly signed up to play flag football at work. Now, I don't have a lot of time for that sort of thing these days. My wife and kids and a few persistent coworkers actually talked me into it. My wife said, "It's only Saturday mornings, and you are always going to see the kids play their games. I bet they would enjoy seeing you play."

The hard truth is, I'm not getting any younger. But hey, I played on a national championship football team, and I thought it would be fun. Plus, the idea of my boys watching me play was a big push to get me out there and relive the glory days. I had a blast! The boys were both proud and excited to be cheering for their dad. Well, one Saturday, four weeks into the company league, I really messed up my knee in a game. Did I go to the doctor? Nope. It hurt, but I kept toughing it out. In fact, I went an entire month just trying to power through it until I just couldn't ignore the pain anymore.

My wife finally talked me into setting up an appointment with a specialist. The doctor did the MRI, and it was clear I needed surgery. I recall the doctor telling me that I must have an unusually high pain threshold because my knee was a mess.

I had a torn meniscus and a microfracture. I had the surgery, went through physical therapy, and eventually I got healthy again. But the lesson, besides the fact that my football days are over, is that I should've gone to the doctor sooner instead of trying to tough it out. I actually did more damage to my knee and experienced a lot of unnecessary pain by not bringing in the experts earlier. My story is a perfect cautionary tale for people looking toward retirement.

That story reminds me of how important it is that we don't go it alone with retirement. There are things that we just shouldn't tough out by ourselves. There are problems we shouldn't just ignore and hope they go away. It is important to engage with someone who knows what they are doing. I didn't go out for coffee with my friend in real estate and ask him what he thought of my knee. I actually went in to talk with someone who specializes in knees. He knew what to look for. He knew what tests to run. That's what you want when you start building a team of experts. It is the same common-sense philosophy that I want you to use with your investments. If you are going to get to your dream, you will need a team of people who will help you make the best decisions when it comes to your investments, insurance, real estate, taxes, and estate planning. We'll talk more about how important that team is in Chapter Nine.

Embrace Budgeting as a Lifetime Skill

Every retirement success story I could ever share with you involves one common practice: budgeting. We have talked about many of the strategies that can get you to retirement, but the truth is that budgeting is a daily practice we have to adopt as a way of life. Think of it in terms of physical health. I grew up around athletes and still work with many of them today. The healthiest people I meet are not the ones who binge on a fad diet or jump in to a month of temporary workouts. No, for them eating healthy and exercising has become a lifestyle. If we are going to enjoy our high-definition dreams, we have to embrace budgeting as a way of life.

So much of our retirement conversation requires you to see things in a different light, and I am going to ask you to do the same with budgeting. I want you to remember that budgeting is a life-long skill. Budgeting is like the basic training for our retirement journey, but as we have pointed out, it is a discipline that will also keep you financially healthy long into retirement. Yes, it may be difficult when you first get started, but after some practice it will become a vital life skill. It will help you get to retirement, and it will keep you there, living out your want-tos. Budgeting is essential to getting where we want to go.

For the best budgeting software I've seen, visit EveryDollar.com.

Chapter Four

DEBT

Your Dreams Deferred

Sailboats make me think of freedom. I'm not an expert on boats, but from my seat on the shore, it looks like you just throw that big ol' sail up and just kind of go wherever the wind takes you, right?

I once worked with a couple who wanted to sail around the world. How is that for a dream? If you're going to have a high-definition retirement dream, that one is as good as any. They had an interesting story too. It was a second marriage for both, and they had each come out of divorces carrying a ton of debt. They had heard Dave's message and had worked really hard to pay everything off. They both worked overtime and second jobs to earn extra income, and they cut their lifestyle and spending back drastically. I mean, they got radical and paid off everything in just eight years—including their home mortgage. They were completely debt-free, and they were ready to focus fully on retirement.

It was a great story—until they told me the punch line. You know how they celebrated becoming completely debt free? They went out and financed a $100,000, thirty-eight-foot sailboat! Now, think about this for a moment. They had absolutely busted it for eight years to dig themselves out of financial ruin. And they "celebrated" by making one decision that "sunk" them right back into debt! I was in shock.

The most ironic part of the story was that they named the new six-figure toy Free Spirit. Now you and I both know there was nothing free-spirited about making the payments on that boat. If I could have spoken to them before they signed the loan documents, I would have said, "Stay focused! Take your time. Pay cash for the boat. It will sail much better without a payment attached to it." But they didn't ask me first because they knew what I would have said. And, of course, the boat salesperson was all too willing to help them adopt a payment. They had to spend the next seven years—that should've been devoted to saving for their retirement dream—working to pay off Free Spirit.

WHAT'S THE BIG DEAL WITH DEBT?

This couple was just a few years away from retiring. Their plan was to pay off the boat by the time they stopped working. I get that people have different views of debt, and maybe you don't see what the big deal was in this situation. Let me explain it to you. First, they celebrated freedom by going right back into debt. They got away from the plan. They worked for eight long years to get out from under the chains of debt, and the first thing they did when they got there was pick up a pile of shiny new chains and an anchor to go with it. That just doesn't make any sense.

Second, this couple took on an incredible degree of risk when they were right at the door to retirement. You may be thinking, *What's the big deal? This was their dream!* But what if something happened to one of them before they paid off the boat? What if one of them had lost a job or gotten really sick? Do you think those boat payments would've stopped showing up each month? No! Remember, 60 percent of retirees report having to retire earlier than planned for one reason or another.[1] What would happen to this couple if one of them—or even both of them—had to unexpectedly stop working? They'd be completely crushed by this debt, and their whole retirement plan would be wrecked. That's way too much risk that late in the game.

Third, this couple didn't factor in opportunity cost. That's a fancy financial term that basically means this: if you spend your money on *this*, you can't spend it on *that*. Every dollar they spent paying off that boat, along with every dollar they wasted on interest and finance charges, was a dollar they didn't have to invest toward retirement. Sailboats are great, but they won't feed you in retirement! This is a classic case of putting your *wants* ahead of your *needs*, and that's always a bad plan.

It Takes Just an Hour of Stupid

This couple represents something I've seen hundreds of times in my coaching. People will work so hard to put themselves in a fantastic financial position. They will do whatever it takes to get ahead of the game. But then, just when it looks like they're winning, it's like their brains take a coffee break and their impulses take over. That's when people fall into stupid temporarily—just long enough to finance a boat, or an unreasonable new home, or a convertible, or some fancy jewelry, or even a vacation around the world.

That hour of stupid can unravel decades of hard work in your past, and it can steal decades of future joy in your retirement. That's why I always say that debt is a thief. No matter where you are in your planning or career, you have to remember that you are just one bad decision away from derailing your retirement dream. You have to stay focused, vigilant, and ready to stick to the plan! The truth is that the opportunity for debt may look and sound good. Heck, sometimes it can even *smell* good (new car smell, anyone?). The problem is that it never *feels* good—especially when you are making those payments.

I don't want you to steal from your dream, so let me be very clear about something: Debt is never a good idea. It will always cause problems for your retirement plan. And what is worse, if you have no urgency to pay off your debt, that debt is going to lead you into major problems in retirement. Debt will always defer your dream. It will always delay your arrival or take you in the wrong direction. We can't stay motivated if the dream keeps moving further and further out of reach. The Bible says, "Hope deferred makes the heart sick."[2] That's what debt does; it defers our hope and makes us sick.

Opportunity Costs and Risk

Let's take a look at the opportunity cost and risk involved when you're living in debt. I've already said that opportunity comes down to this: If you spend your money on *this*, you can't spend it on *that*. Once it's gone, it's gone. You lose the opportunity to do something else with those dollars.

Take a new car, for example. That's something that most Americans can identify with. If you're thinking about financing a car, I want you to consider what else you might be able to do with that money every month. Since we're talking about retirement, let's say you could make a $500 monthly car payment or you could choose to make a $500 monthly contribution to your retirement plan.

Ten years later, if you had chosen the car, you would have lost the earning potential of tens of thousands of dollars, and the car (if you still had it) would need to be replaced. If you had invested the money instead, you'd be sitting on an extra $105,000 or more in your retirement account after those same ten years. By choosing the car, you're missing out on $105,000 in ten years. Different people have different priorities, but I can't imagine choosing *not* to have $105,000.

It is easy for people to get so caught up in having their wants that they are actually able to convince themselves that those wants are needs. And when you begin to feel that you *need* something, you are more willing to do whatever it takes to get it. This takes us back to the whole idea of being intentional with what you earn. If you are not intentional with your money, you will always spend more than you earn. You will always find a way to rationalize that car payment as a need. It's easy to *rationalize* stupid, but you'll never be able to *out-earn* stupid.

I remember working with one gentleman who had an $850 monthly car payment. That probably meant he also had terrible credit and was likely in a subprime loan. That's bad enough, but when I looked at his budget, I realized that his home mortgage was only $700 a month. I remember calling him out, "Do you realize that your car payment is bigger than your house payment?" He needed to hear another human being put that fact into words so he could think about it!

When did it become okay to pay more for what you drive than for where you live? According to him, he was working hard. He was putting in fifty-plus hours a week, and he felt like he deserved it. That word *deserve* puts you on the fast track to stupid. It is so dangerous. You can justify anything in your mind when you start to use that word.

"I work hard, so I *deserve*..." or "I've paid some stuff off, so I *deserve*..." or "The neighbors are driving a new car, and I *deserve*..." The really dangerous part is that "I deserve" can quickly become a mindset. Stupid moves in and settles down as a part of your financial routine. Stupid takes up a lot of space and leaves little room for intentionality. And when that happens, you begin to enjoy all the extra little toys you've collected through wasteful spending, and, before you know it, you cross the line from buying those toys with cash to buying them with debt—because you "deserve" it.

As a coach, I want to caution you about this "deserve" thing because it's a dream deterrent. I can remember watching the show *Gilligan's Island* when I was a kid. No matter what plot the professor concocted to escape, Gilligan always ruined the plan. Well, I tell people that when you focus too much on what you "deserve," it can alienate you from what you truly desire. It can put you on an island. I call it Deserve Island! Just like Gilligan's Island, Deserve Island may be easy to find, but it is incredibly hard to leave.

Debt Is Like Quicksand

Let's look at this debt issue on an intellectual and practical level. The average consumer sends 24 percent of their take-home pay to non-mortgage debt.[3] That's a quarter of their income going out the door to debt payments! I want you to take a moment to understand what you could do with an extra 25 percent of your income if it wasn't wasted on payments. Say you earn around $4,000 a month in salary. That would put you at an average salary of around $50,000 a year. If you were one of those average consumers, you'd be paying out $1,000 to student loans, credit card payments, car loans, and other debts. That is $1,000 a month that could be going into retirement. That's $12,000 a year that you could be investing into your dream.

You need to view debt as retirement quicksand. Now, I have never seen anyone fall into quicksand in real life, but I have seen it happen in the movies quite a few times. When those movie characters fall into the quicksand, they don't just vanish into the ground. It's a slow process; at first, it looks like they are on solid ground, and then, all of a sudden, they are sinking. Then they realize that they can't get traction and that they cannot get out. Debt, just like quicksand, slows down your progress, and it often brings your journey toward that dream to a complete halt. Pretty soon you are hoping someone will come along and throw you a rope to drag you out.

There are simply no circumstances where you can possibly rationalize debt. I need you to understand that debt isn't just borrowing money that you don't have from the bank; it also means borrowing from your dream. Every dollar that you send out to debt payments—every dime you willingly commit yourself to for a period of months or even years—is money that you would've, could've, and should've used for investing in your retirement plan. Debt, my friend, always leads to a dream deferred. I hope that's clear!

MISTAKES WE MAKE WITH DEBT

At this point, it's obvious that the biggest roadblock between you and your dream retirement is debt. But some people will claim that there is "smart debt" such as school loans. Let me tell you, though, debt is debt, and it always shows up at your door and demands to be paid each month (with interest), whether you can afford it or not! One of the biggest lies about debt involves the idea that carrying a mortgage is "smart" for tax purposes. We will dispel this ridiculous idea a little bit later in the chapter. Just remember, "smart debt" is an oxymoron. I can talk about that in theory all day long, but what does this mean in practice? Let's look at some of the little cracks where debt tends to sneak in and screw up your retirement plan.

Marketing Lies to Us
Marketing great Seth Godin wrote a book a while back that had one of my favorite book titles of all time: *All Marketers Are Liars.*

And this was coming from a marketer! I'll let Seth's title speak for itself, but I do think I get what he's saying. So many advertisements out there try to pull at your heartstrings and emotions to get you to make a big purchase. Marketers know that if they can get you to feel what they want you to feel, you might rationalize going into debt long enough to make a mistake.

Did you know that we are the most heavily marketed-to country on the planet? Back when I was a kid in the 1970s, we were exposed to around five hundred advertisements each day. Research shows that we are now subjected to over five thousand ads or commercials—every single day.[4] And that number continues to grow. Every commercial or in-app ad on our phone is, of course, trying to move us toward spending money. The goal? To make that big spoonful of stupid go down a little easier.

Car companies are especially good at this kind of thing. I watched a car ad the other day that was working hard to convince me that buying this car was a good parenting investment. The commercial started with a young dad and his little girl, and, by the end, the girl was a teenager driving off in this "safe" car that her dad had bought for her. Man, it made that dad look like the award winner for parent of the year. I mean, he cared enough to protect his little girl with this reliable car! I have to admit, it pulled at my heartstrings a little bit. It was a really good advertisement.

And I'm sure it worked on some dads. I mean, if you're going to be a good dad, you've got to get one of these cars, right? So these dads head over to the lot, pick out a car, and drive home a nice big car loan. But those loan officers don't always clarify the total amount you're going to pay for a car. They tell you the price of the vehicle, and they tell you the amount that they are going to take off. But then they will explain the interest rates at an auctioneer's pace. And it's too late at that point because most people are already emotionally married to the purchase, so they aren't paying attention to the true math. As a result, people tend to buy new cars based on how much the payment is, not on the total cost of the car. We don't ask, "How much?" We ask, "How much per month?" There's a world of difference between those two questions.

You only get to the truth when you look past the ad copy and sales pitch. When we cut away the feelings and emotion around a purchase, we're able to take an honest look at whatever the item is, and then we can decide if it's a smart purchase.

Getting "Fleeced" (Like Good Sheep)

We've talked a bit about sheep already, but do you know what happens to sheep? They get fleeced, right? Now, for those of you who have not seen as many episodes of Animal Planet as I have, I want to explain sheep fleecing. It's where farmers let the sheep's wool grow all big and fluffy, then they give them a haircut similar to mine!

There's a way the American consumer gets fleeced too, without even realizing it—at least until it's too late. I'm talking about the car lease, which is, according to every financial expert I know, the dumbest, most expensive way to operate a vehicle. People who lease cars are paying for a car for a set period of time, but there are plenty of gotcha points in the fine print. And guess what? The salesperson isn't legally required to fully disclose every fee like they would if it were a standard car loan.

One of my early coaching clients was a young man who was living paycheck to paycheck but driving a really nice leased car. We were working on his budget, and he mentioned that he wanted to drive to see his family for the holidays, but he was already over his miles. I dug into it, and, sure enough, he was going to have to pay thirty cents for every mile he was over. By the time I talked to him, he was already going to have to write the dealership a check for $1,500 when he turned the car back in to them, but he still had several months left on this lease. He was not only stuck paying the monthly lease payment, but he was racking up a huge penalty for every mile he drove!

When it comes to your retirement goals, car payments aren't any better than leasing. The average car payment in America is right around $492 a month. But if you choose to drive nice, reliable, used cars that you pay for with cash, your retirement dream could be a reality—with just that one decision.

If you decided to avoid car payments and invest that $492 a month into your retirement instead, you would have almost $2.9 million to fund your dream after thirty years of saving at a 10 percent rate of return. That's almost $3 million—just because you decided to skip car payments. If you had chosen the car instead, you wouldn't have $3 million in your retirement account. Instead, you would have spent $236,160 in car payments over the course of thirty years, and you wouldn't have a thing to show for it.

When I help people look at car payments like this, they start to see those payments for what they really are: a way to grow other people's bank accounts and shrink their own!

Mortgages, Tax Deductions, and Basic Risk

Owning a home is the American dream, but too many people today are confused. Too many people believe that financing a home is the American dream. Having a house is great, but let's be honest: when you have that home paid in full and no longer have to send payments to the bank or mortgage company, now that is true freedom!

This is why it's so confusing to hear people say you should hang on to your mortgage as long as possible for the tax deduction. Holding on to a mortgage simply for your tax deduction is nothing but bad math—I mean *really* bad math. Let me explain. If you are paying 5 percent interest on a $200,000 loan, that adds up to $10,000 in interest payments per year. Because mortgage interest payments are tax-deductible, you get to deduct that $10,000 from your taxable income at tax time, meaning you don't have to pay taxes on that $10,000. You still with me?

So, your taxes on $10,000 (if you were in a 25 percent tax bracket) would be right around $2,500. That's what you'd save on your tax bill as a result of carrying a mortgage all year, and that's why some so-called experts say you should keep your mortgage. But track that with me for just a second: You are going to send $10,000 to the bank in order to avoid sending $2,500 to the government? And people think there's some kind of advantage in doing that kind of thing?

But, still, this myth continues to permeate our culture. I was working with an accountant a few years back. That's right—someone who crunches numbers for a living. He was trying to get serious about his investments and his financial future. We were talking about getting debt free and working the Baby Steps. And you remember, of course, that Dave's Baby Step 2 is attacking your debt, smallest to largest. I remember this guy looking at me a little weird and wanting to debate this concept. I explained that when we talk about basic math, as long as I am borrowing money and paying interest, I am being penalized.

We got around to discussing paying off his mortgage (Baby Step 6), and he started in with the tax deduction argument. Remember, this guy was a CPA. That means he passed a pretty difficult math exam, right? He knew the deal. He was passionately arguing with me about keeping that house payment. I looked across the table at him and said, "Tell me this. If you get sick and can't work, and you can't make that mortgage payment, what is the bank going to do?" He sat silent, so I continued, "They are going to expect you to pay that mortgage, right? Whether you are working or not, that payment requires your attention each and every month."

The truth is, there is more to debt than basic math. The really terrifying downside to debt is risk. In addition to borrowing from your dreams, debt places you at risk. No matter what is happening in your life, no matter what life deals you, that debt will always demand a payment each month.

That may not seem like a big deal when you're working and bringing home a regular paycheck, but what happens if you lose your job? What if you get sick and suddenly find yourself under a mountain of medical bills on top of all your other debts? What if you're married and the primary breadwinner dies or loses their income? What if you suddenly find yourself in an unexpected divorce? Those are real-life risks you face when you play around with debt—even mortgage debt.

When people argue to keep their mortgage payment for tax purposes, I always encourage them to think of better ways to receive tax deductions. If you paid off your mortgage, think about the money you'd be able to generously give to others in need or to your local church. You get the same tax benefit for charitable giving that you get for mortgage interest, but you don't have to be in debt to get it. And, of course, you get to help other people along the way.

Debt always equals risk, and, when your debt is gone, you are free to keep more of your money. You know what this can do for your retirement dreams? It can put them on the fast track! It can turn your bus ride to retirement into an IndyCar race! Think about how supercharged your retirement funding would be if you could contribute the money that you used to pay into the mortgage toward your retirement.

Don't Gamble with Your Mortgage

Of all the crazy things people do to put their homes at risk, the top two would have to be borrowing against your home in order to invest the money somewhere else and taking out a home equity loan for purchases.

We'll deal with the investment thing first. Playing with leveraged investments is a nightmare. This means you are borrowing at a lower interest rate so you can invest at a hopefully higher interest rate. For example, you might refinance your home and get an extra $20,000 at a 4 percent interest rate and then turn around and invest that money hoping for a 10–12 percent return. The key word there is *hoping*. You'd be putting your hard-earned home equity into a volatile investment that could go sideways at any minute. I never, ever want to put my family's home at risk.

The other common mistake I see people make involves HELOC loans—or a home equity line of credit. This is a mortgage loan that is based on the equity in your home. The advertisements may say it's taking advantage of your equity, but I have another way of looking at it. I want you to think of the HELOC as a huge credit card attached to your home, your largest material asset. Even if your goal is to use the equity to pay off other debts, you've got to understand that you aren't *paying off* anything. You're just moving the debt from the credit cards to your house. Despite what the TV commercials say, you simply cannot get out of debt by taking on more debt. And even if I'm going to have the risk associated with debt, I definitely don't want that risk attached to my home!

Keeping Up with the Joneses

Another major pitfall that leads us into debt is probably the most common. It has been around since the beginning of time. It has a lot to do with human nature and the way we compare ourselves to other people. You've probably heard the expression "keeping up with the Joneses." I'll tell you what I call it: fake rich. It really is all about trying to finance an image. Living a lifestyle beyond your means so that you can keep up appearances and fit in with the neighbors is a sure way to wreak financial havoc on your life.

I worked with a young man who was a professional athlete. He was feeling a lot of pressure to keep up with his peers. The other guys on his team had several houses and six or seven car loans, and this young man was following suit. In fact, I think he was trying to one-up the guys around him. But, by trying to keep up appearances, trying to be "the man," he traded the financial opportunity of a lifetime for twenty years' worth of debt! His three homes and dozen cars all pointed back to the fact that he really hadn't done the simple math.

He played professional football, and, in the NFL, the only money that is guaranteed is a player's signing bonus. Nothing else. A pro football player can be cut or traded at any time. The other interesting thing is that most NFL franchises pay checks only nine months out of the year. This little detail came as a surprise to him that first July when he realized he didn't get a paycheck. After nine months of an incredible income, this football star was flat broke. He had spent every penny on useless garbage he didn't really need just to keep up appearances. We had some serious work to do to fix his situation, but he came around. He sold some fancy watches and several cars, and he started to take ownership of his money by changing the things he needed to change so he could invest in his future and his retirement.

This type of comparison mentality is so pervasive in our culture right now, and we're all guilty of it—from cars and homes to cell phones and clothes, we can't help noticing what others have. I have to ask you: are $200 designer jeans really that much different than the $60 pair I'm wearing right now? So many of my former clients went completely broke just trying to keep up appearances, and I see this all the time with the way people spend money on their children. I talk with parents who feel the need to fill their children's toy chest to keep up with the other kids in the neighborhood. Johnny from next door has the new PlayStation, so our son should have it too. Suzy has the new iPhone, so our daughter shouldn't be the only girl in her class without one. Not only does this mentality rob us of ever reaching our retirement dreams, but also it teaches our children the wrong message about how to handle money.

Let me say this one last time: there is absolutely, positively nothing wrong with having some nice things—as long as those nice things don't have you. That means you should not have nice things at the expense of your financial peace and at the cost of your retirement dream.

School Daze

The need to impress other people by what we have isn't just centered on homes, cars, and stuff. Sometimes we make our kids' education the issue. I see this often in families who go into debt *and* put their retirement planning on hold just to send their elementary, middle, and high school kids to private school. I know this can be a touchy subject, but I'm not afraid to talk tough. We have to be honest with ourselves so we can make progress in the areas that matter most. For some people—certainly not all—a high-end private elementary or high school is more about keeping up an image than doing what is best for their kids.

I worked with a wonderful family to help them get their finances in order and begin planning for retirement. The husband was a lawyer and the wife was a doctor. They lived in a part of town where it was socially unacceptable to send your kids to public school. In their social circles, they were expected by their peers to send their children to exclusive private schools. They had no money in savings. They hadn't set aside a dime for retirement. You know where they were investing all of their money? They were spending over $50,000 a year to send their children to school! And we're not talking about college, but a private elementary school. They had this mentality that they were *investing* in their children. When I called them out on their lack of retirement planning, the husband looked up at me and said, rather matter-of-factly, "My children *are* my retirement plan." This couple was fully embracing the Burden Retirement scenario that we talked about earlier in the book.

When Stupid Is Socially Acceptable

We have to realize that while stupid seems socially acceptable, it is still . . . well . . . stupid! It is easy to go back to the car commercials that imply you need a particular type of car to maintain a certain social status or image. Have you seen the Buick commercial where the next-door neighbors drive up in their brand-new Buick? The "non-Buick" family is watching out of their kitchen window, and they determine that the man must've just received a big raise at work in order to have such a great new car! The husband standing in the kitchen gazing out the window says, "Good for him."

His wife, looking longingly at the new Buick, says, "Good for *her*." The commercial, of course, implies that if the husband would only get a promotion and a raise, then maybe they could buy a Buick too! So, in this case, success equals a brand-new car payment every month. That's crazy!

One of the most irritating forms of stupid to me is the idea that all wealthy people carry credit cards. They want you to believe that a credit card can enhance your social status. This is a huge lie. American Express has a new card called the Centurion Card that is marketed exclusively to wealthy customers. It is even made from anodized titanium instead of plastic to give it a more premium appearance. The idea is that other people will see you pull a titanium card out of your wallet and will be impressed.

But here's the thing about the Centurion Card: You pay $7,500 for an initiation fee, then you also pay a $2,500 annual fee. On top of that, you are required to spend and pay back at least $250,000 a year in purchases to maintain your status. There are quite a few perks that come along with the card, but what are they really worth?[5] The truth is, if you are living on a budget, there is no need for a credit card. And no amount of perks can make carrying credit card debt worthwhile! The Centurion Card gets you into some clubs at the airport, gets you some hotel benefits, gives you twenty-four-hour assistance from a real live person, and is the most costly credit card on the planet right now, but I can easily get every one of those same perks anytime I want *without* paying $10,000 a year in fees alone.[6]

I know you may have some fundamentally different views than I do on using credit cards, so let me remind you about my real concern here: there is always a risk involved with incurring debt. And that's not an "every once in a while" risk or a "some of the time" risk. It is a risk that is always present—even for those people who consider themselves "careful" credit users, the ones who "pay it off" each month.

People like to talk about "financial security." You want to know the most financially secure thing I can think of? It's not owing a dime to anyone. When you're debt-free, you can ride out market fluctuations, down markets, and income changes because you don't have anyone beating down your door for their slice of your financial pie. Debt free with a full emergency fund? Yes, please.

PROTECTING YOUR RETIREMENT FROM DEBT

So far, we've focused on the impact debt you pay on during your working years can have on your retirement. We obviously can't move on from this chapter, though, without focusing on a true retirement dream killer: carrying debt into retirement. Let me be crystal clear here. When you retire, you want to owe nothing to anyone. You do not want to have any debt—including a mortgage. Every dollar of your retirement income should go toward funding your dream, *not* paying off debts.

Compare your retirement to a vacation. My wife loves to travel. I'm not as big of a fan, but I do enjoy getting away with my family.

I think my favorite part may be the relaxation that sets in right after I unpack my bags at the hotel on the first day. That's when I can breathe easy because I know I have exactly what I need to make it through the week. I only have what I need, and I intentionally left anything I didn't need at home. That peace of knowing I only have what I *need* and what I *want* is like nothing else.

How does that compare to retirement? Well, vacations usually last about a week, but retirement can last anywhere from twenty to thirty years! So that means there are some things that will need to go with us, and there are some things that we absolutely do not want to bring along. You need to be discerning about what you are going to carry into the last third of your life, and rule number one is that debt cannot follow you into retirement. That's like bringing your nosy, nagging neighbor along with you on vacation—it will just rob you of the joy and peace you should be feeling!

Seriously, Not Even a Mortgage or a Car Loan

Is the home you are living in now the place that you want to live in retirement? If so, then figure out what you need to do to have it paid off before you retire. The earlier that home is paid for, the more money you will be able to put into retirement. Think about how much you send to the mortgage company every month. Now imagine sending that cash straight into your retirement dream. Nothing kicks your retirement savings into high gear like paying off the house and making mortgage-size deposits into your retirement account!

The second thing to consider is whether or not you will want to move. If so, do you want to upsize or downsize? I've worked with several older couples who had a paid-for home, but didn't have a large enough retirement account. Many of those chose to sell the big house that their kids grew up in and downsize into something better suited for empty nesters. In doing so, they were able to pay cash for their new home and put a big chunk of cash into their retirement accounts, all from the sale of their former home. That's a great way to make up some ground in your investments if you have a paid-for home.

If you are doing well in your retirement accounts and want to upgrade, that's great. Just be sure you buy the house right—with a conventional mortgage of no more than fifteen years—and pay it off before the first day of your retirement. If you can't do that, then I'd definitely rethink the move.

And if I don't want you to even have a mortgage, you know what I'm going to say about car loans. We have beaten the car loan issue to death already, so I won't belabor the point. Needless to say, there is *never* a good time to have a car payment—especially as you head into retirement.

As you look at your retirement, think about the car you'll have on day one of retirement and how long it will last. Estimate how many cars you'll need to buy in retirement and when you think they'll hit, and factor that into your estimated retirement account withdrawals. I'm always blown away by the number of people who are surprised by their need for transportation in their retirement years! If you do what we teach, pulling out $10,000 or more for a nice used car shouldn't be a problem, but you won't get there by accident. Make a plan for it.

Cosigning Can Kill Your Retirement Dream

This last thing to consider about debt in retirement is a biggie: never, *ever* cosign a loan for someone else—even your kids. I can't tell you how many times I have seen people make this huge mistake in retirement. You should never, and I mean *never*, cosign for your children's housing, cars, school, or anything else. Cosigning is a huge mistake when you're thirty-five, but it can completely wipe out your retirement plans when you're sixty-five. Just don't do it.

Remember, I began my journey as a debt collector. I know from experience that the second call on a debt collector's list is always the cosigner. When you cosign a loan, you are financially responsible, meaning you are on the hook for that loan! Sounds like common sense, but you wouldn't believe the moms and dads I used to call who acted like they had no idea they were obligated to pay that car loan that was defaulting. In fact, if you are cosigner, you are sometimes the *first* person the creditors will call because they know that you are the one who actually has the money to pay the bills.

I cannot tell you how many people I have counseled about debt over the years who have said, "that is my son's car" or "that is my grandson's loan." What these people never seemed to realize was that they hadn't just buried themselves with financial burdens by cosigning on these loans, but they had actually hindered the financial maturity and growth of their children or grandchildren by enabling them to take on things that they couldn't actually afford to pay for.

In all my years coaching, I have never once heard someone say, "Chris, cosigning that loan for my child was the best financial decision I ever made!" Most of the time, when the issue of cosigning comes up, all I see on their faces and hear in their voices is regret. So I want to be absolutely clear here. If you are thinking about cosigning a loan for someone, picture yourself saying this to the creditor:

> Yes, Mr. Loan Officer, you and I both know my son should not take out this loan. He's been irresponsible with money before, and he will be again. He's had plenty of late payments in the past, and that's sure to continue. His income doesn't even come close to supporting this purchase. So, of course, I know you will one day come to me to pay this bill, which means I'll lose a big chunk of my retirement savings and hand over my retirement dream to you.

You may not phrase it that way, but it doesn't matter. Your signature on the cosign line says all of that and more to the creditor. If that doesn't sound like a conversation you want to have, then don't cosign.

Securing Your Dream by Staying on the Offensive

You must always be on guard about the dangers of debt. Just because you are getting serious about retiring doesn't mean that the credit card applications are going to stop showing up in your mailbox every day. There are always going to be opportunities for stupidity waved in your face, advertised on your television, and flaunted around by your neighbors. You have to play offense! Think of it like football.

When I was in high school, I was able to play both offense and defense on my football team. On offense, the goal is to score touchdowns, right? You're trying to make progress. On defense, you are trying to keep the other team from making any progress. The game is simple enough. But working toward our retirement is just as simple. With credit card debt and debt in general, we have to stay defensive so we don't have that five- or ten-minute lapse in judgment and end up financing something or taking out a car loan. We have to keep stupid from moving onto our side of the field.

But, at the same time, we have to play offense. Here, I mean that we are going to use cash for purchases. If there is something we really want, we aren't going to borrow to get it. I have talked to plenty of millionaires through the years. I have even met a couple of billionaires. But not a single one of them has ever told me that they got there by using credit card points, airline miles, or hotel rewards. None of them gained wealth by using credit. These types of behaviors don't create wealth at all. In fact, they do the opposite.

The people I know who are diligently creating real wealth over the course of many years will tell you that debt is the number-one enemy of progress. So, when I talk about staying aggressive on offense, I mean you need to budget, use your debit card because it is tied to your bank account, and check your statements each month. It goes back to our conversation about the budget and telling every penny, every dime, every dollar where it needs to go. If you don't do that, then you are being robbed of your future. I want you to be offensive-minded and intentional.

Focus is the key here, so let's take a look at these winning strategies to avoid debt and move closer to our retirement dreams. I want you to maintain a fully funded emergency fund of three to six months' worth of expenses like Dave mentioned in the foreword to this book. I want you to stay focused on living debt free. I want you to stay focused about investing for retirement and maintaining those investments throughout your retirement. I want you to stay focused on the fact that your income is your greatest wealth-building tool, and I want you to protect it. You have to be intentional about where the money goes if you want to reach your high-definition dreams.

CHAPTER FIVE

INTENTIONAL INVESTING

A Great Retirement Is No Accident

I have always been a little bit of a history buff. I love watching the History TV channel or reading biographies about the men and women who helped make history. For example, what did it take to build the Great Wall of China? That thing is 5,500 miles long, and the most known and well-preserved section was completed in 1644, long before tractors and bulldozers were invented.

Or think about what it took to plan and execute the Normandy Invasion in World War II. They coordinated 156,000 American, British, and Canadian troops to land on heavily fortified beaches along a fifty-mile stretch of coast to take Normandy back from Germany and turn the war around. What drove those men? What moved them out of the safety of their boats and onto the battlefield?

And don't even get me started about the Space Race and what it must have taken for those first astronauts to sit on top of a rocket and blast off toward the moon. Seriously. They strapped a rocket to their backsides and rode it into outer space! Plus, don't forget all the meticulous planning and organization it must have taken to get them there.

When one of these shows comes on History, I always get sucked in. I can get completely wrapped up in how our nation was shaped, how battles were won, and how the world was changed. And it seems that all of these remarkable accomplishments have some similarities. All of them involved a high level of commitment from those who participated. Each one took a lot of planning. Every single one of these great achievements took some patience. All of them had follow-through. And they all required great execution of a long-term plan.

When I talk about execution, I mean there was a clear goal in mind, whether it was building the Great Wall, taking beaches from the Nazis, or landing on the moon. These operations all required the same key elements. The plan couldn't be rushed. It demanded time to train the people involved, to scout out where they were going, and to make sure everyone had the chance to be fully prepared. These accomplishments weren't accidents, and they weren't quick fixes. To win, the men and women involved put a plan in place and worked toward that plan with focused intensity over a long period of time. That's how they changed the world—and that's how you'll reach your dream retirement.

UNDERSTANDING THE MARKET

As you begin working on a plan for your dream retirement, I want to challenge you to see your plan for retirement as something great—as a gift to you, your children, and others. If you are going to accomplish that dream, the one you visualized in high def, then you need to follow the example of history and do what it takes to change the world—*your world.*

You need to begin your plan with the proper mindset for long-term investing. But before we move on, I want you to revisit your goal. Let's go back and look at your R:IQ number. That number is your target for long-term investing. Once you're out of debt with a fully funded emergency fund of three to six months' expenses, it's time to start aiming all your efforts at hitting that number.

Watch Out Below the Waterline

One of my favorite business books is Jim Collins's *How the Mighty Fall.* It is a treatise on how to keep your company heading in the right direction. One of the many great lessons in the book is about ships. Collins uses a boat as a great metaphor about how to make decisions and avoid mistakes when there is a bit of risk and uncertainty involved.

When I talk to people about investing, the words *risk* and *uncertainty* always come up. People are afraid of what they don't understand. I get that. That's why I like Collins's call to watch out for "waterline damage" when making big decisions. The waterline is the part of the boat that is below the water, the part you can't see unless you dive in and take a close look underwater. That means any damage below the waterline is a huge threat. A hole below the waterline can sink your ship before you ever even know there's a problem.

What does that have to do with your retirement? It's simple: We have to be conscious of the choices we make in our own lives that no one else can really see. We have to be making those right choices "below the waterline" that support our mission. If we don't, our boat will sink, and we'll never reach our dream.

Making poor investing choices—or worse, failing to invest at all—wreaks havoc below the waterline. You may have a big, beautiful home with two luxury cars in the driveway and a trailer hitch for your boat and Sea-Doo. Heck, you may have even paid cash for all those things and have zero debt. Everything above the waterline of your financial life may *look* absolutely wonderful. But if you aren't taking long-term investing seriously, I promise you have some serious damage below the waterline. It's time to dive in and patch those holes.

Demystifying the Market

For a while, one of my sons was afraid of the "boogeyman." It was a battle to get him to sleep in his room each night. If you are a parent, you may have gone through this stage with your kids at some point. It can be as trying as it is entertaining, but you never want your kids to be scared. So, after I sat down and talked to my son, I discovered that an older brother and some friends at school might've passed on some misinformation about the "boogeyman" (probably to entertain themselves). So, all of a sudden, my son was convinced there was something in his closet or under his bed. He wasn't old enough yet to understand that it was just make-believe. It was causing him some serious anxiety!

My job was to talk to my son and debunk the myth. We looked under the bed and checked his closet to get all the facts. And you know what? Once he knew that the "boogeyman" was pretend, he was good.

We often treat investing in the market a little bit like the boogeyman. It can sound a bit scary or mysterious, so we need someone to help us demystify the whole thing. The market isn't some monster hiding under your bed; it is actually a huge tool to help you get to your retirement dream. The problem is that people have a difficult time understanding what the market is and how it works. As a result, they tend to avoid investing in and utilizing the market the same way my son tried to avoid sleeping in his bed at night.

So we need to look at this as adults. Yes, the market can be a little bit complex. Yes, it can be intimidating, especially at first. Yes, it can have some moving parts, but I can help you see it a little bit clearer if you are unfamiliar with it. Once we demystify it, we can begin to use it effectively as part of our plan.

Stock Markets and Supermarkets

The concept of the market, in general terms, is not difficult to comprehend. Markets are simply places where things are bought and sold. For example, you probably buy your groceries at the supermarket. Supermarkets have a lot of things that can be bought and sold. You can go spend a little or a whole lot at the supermarket. You can buy expensive brand names or you can buy generic. You can buy health food or you can buy junk food. The supermarket offers a ton of choices for how you spend your money. Some of those choices, like healthy food, are good for you; other choices, like my favorite nacho chips, are not so good for you. It's not the supermarket that helps or hurts us; it's the decisions we make there.

When it comes to investing, "the market" works the same way. There are actually different types of markets. The stock market is the place where stocks, which are basically small pieces of ownership in a company, are bought and sold. There is also the bond market, the capital market, and a variety of other types of markets, each selling different types of investing products, some good and some bad. So if we went shopping for investments like we shop at a grocery store, I'd help you spot the things you should buy and the things you should avoid.

Just like the products at a grocery store, the prices of investments in the market go up and down all the time. For example, my boys love strawberries, and I usually pick up a few cartons when I go shopping. But I have noticed that the price of strawberries goes up and down throughout the year. They're more expensive during off-season months, but when they are in season, they cost a lot less and are easier to find. There's a fluctuation in the value of strawberries throughout the year, and, as the consumer, I have to factor those fluctuations into my buying decisions.

That sounds familiar, right? We've all seen how different products at the supermarket go up and down in value all the time. That's a great way to think of how the stock market works. Stocks go through similar fluctuations.

Riding the Market Roller Coaster

When I talk about the ups and downs of the market, I start to think about roller coasters. That's a great way to picture the typical movement of the market. I have a love-hate relationship with roller coasters. My wife is an adrenaline junkie. She doesn't just like to *ride* roller coasters; she likes to sit in the very front seat whenever she rides one. Me? I would much prefer to sit toward the back a little so my brain can process the drops and swings and turns that are coming. I want to see it ahead of time so that my body can adjust a bit before that five-hundred-foot drop!

When you get on a roller coaster, you have to be prepared for the hills and drops. You have to be ready for those turns you aren't expecting. And you have to understand what you are getting into before you are locked into your seat. Once that ride gets going, you can't get off. You can't hit a stop button, and you don't want to try to step off as you're dropping down a huge hill. It wouldn't be a pretty sight.

But you know what I have noticed about roller coasters? If you hold on and stay seated, you may have a wild ride, but you end up safely back where you want to be. Parts of the ride may be fun, and other parts may scare you to death. But if you hold on and see the ride through to the end, you usually come out just fine. But if you try to jump off early, well, you are going to get hurt.

Again, the same is true of the market. When you start investing, you have to be emotionally prepared for the values to go up and down. If you aren't prepared for that, you'll make one of the biggest mistakes of all when it comes to long-term investing: jumping out at the wrong time. Let's see why that's such a bad idea.

Jumping Off at the Wrong Time

If you try to keep your eyes glued on each hill, drop, twist, and turn in your investments, you'll stay in a continual panic mode. You'll never be able to relax and leave your investments alone because you'll be too worried about the drop you're in or the drop you think is coming. The problem is, though, that long-term investing only does its magic if you leave your money alone over a long period of time. Trying to "time the market" is a fool's game and has left a lot more people broke than rich.

That's why you have to keep some big-picture perspective about the whole thing. You might be thinking, *How do I keep that perspective?* Well, with investing, the answer is simply time. You can make the market look a certain way if you zoom into one small section of it. Think about it as if you were looking at a small-scale model of a roller coaster you were just riding. If you zoom in really close, you might see only the really high hill or that really steep drop, but that is not the entire track, right? Just like roller coasters, the market will move up and down, and sometimes it just stays flat. If you look at the big picture, the whole model, you can see that, over time, the market is actually a positive thing.

So let's talk about some of the historical ups and downs on the market roller coaster in recent history. If we go back and zoom in on early September 2001, we'd see that the market was going up. That changed dramatically on September 11, when the markets experienced a major drop as a result of the terrorist attacks in New York City, Washington, D.C., and Pennsylvania. People were in such a panic that the markets closed for several days to keep the bottom from completely falling out. When the markets reopened, however, everything crashed as panicked investors pulled their money out of their investments. If you were watching the financial news at the time, you'll remember that every headline and lead story focused on how terrible the situation looked. Investors weren't given much hope, and a lot of people made bad decisions as a result.

Here's what didn't get nearly as much airtime on cable news: just two months after September 11, the markets had returned to September 10 levels. If you zoomed out a little bit, you'd see a pretty steep dip in the market that corrected itself fairly quickly.

Then there was the market crash of 2008. Before the crash, the market looked pretty strong. But during the last quarter of 2008, the market took a serious dive. That's when your 401(k) looked more like a 201(k)! Honestly, it took a while for us to recover from this one, but within a couple of years, the market was back up better than it was before the crash. If you zoomed in only on that last quarter, the market looked terrible; nobody in their right mind would get involved in that mess. And if you zoomed in only on the recovery, it looked amazing! You'd think the market only went one direction: straight up! Neither of those perspectives gives you the entire picture, though. You have to look at the whole thing—the seventy-plus-year history of the stock market (or at least since the merger of S&P in 1941). When you do that, you'll find that 100 percent of the fifteen-year periods in the market's history have made money. The big-picture view of the stock market shows that, if you leave your money alone for a long period of time and invest with the long term in mind, you'll come out ahead.

THE FORMULA FOR SUCCESS

The formula for success is simple: time + compound interest = good results. Time refers to how long you leave your investments alone without panicking and pulling out your money. Compound interest refers to the mathematical secret sauce of long-term investing. Let's talk about time first.

Formula Part One: Time

You might hear about two broad time frames for investing: short-term and long-term. I kind of disagree with that terminology though. Short-term refers to anything less than five years. If you ask me, anything less than five years should be considered *savings*, not *investing*. A five-year-or-less window carries a high degree of risk in the stock market because you never know when one of those roller coaster drops is coming. If you're saving for a house, for example, you don't want the market to bottom out the month before you need the money.

You don't want to put the money you know you'll need in a few years at too great a risk, so you'd choose more conservative options like savings accounts, CDs, or money market accounts. These are terrible for wealth building, but they work okay for short-term savings.

Then there is long-term investing, which is defined as anything more than five years. In your wealth building and retirement planning, you need to be thinking in terms of ten, twenty, and even thirty or more years. When you have that kind of patience, when you think of investing from the long-term, big-picture perspective, then each up and down won't freak you out so much. We'll talk more about the long-term investing options in the next chapter.

Formula Part Two: Compound Interest

The second key in the formula of retirement success involves something remarkable—compound interest. You don't need a PhD in economics to understand how interest works, so let's cover some basics about it.

The most important thing I can tell you about interest is this: **Interest that you pay is a penalty; interest that you earn is a reward.** That means if you're paying interest to a credit card company, you have interest working against you; you're being penalized. However, if you are earning interest on your investments, you have interest working for you; that's the reward of long-term investing. Interest is kind of like an employee who is always on the clock, out there doing the work to get you closer to retirement. If you understand that, then you pass our basic economics course!

When you save money to build wealth, you need to take advantage of the power of compound interest. Albert Einstein called compound interest the eighth wonder of the world. It's like a mathematical explosion. It starts to do things to money that you won't believe. How does it work? Well, let's say you have $1,000, and to make the math easy, let's say you earn 10 percent per year. After the first year, you'd have $1,100. Wait, where did that extra hundred bucks come from? That's your original investment of $1,000 plus 10 percent, which is $100. Got it?

Here's where compound interest starts to kick in. After the first year, you don't have $1,000 sitting in the account; you have $1,100. The next year your $1,100 would become $1,210. Did you see that? Your first year you earned $100, but the second year, you earned $110. That's because you're now earning interest on the interest. The extra hundred bucks you earned in year one is now also growing at 10 percent—that is compound interest. And that's going to keep growing and growing.

If this thing keeps growing like that, you'd earn another $121 in the third year, another $133 in the fourth year, and then another $146 in the fifth year. So five years into this thing, your initial investment of $1,000 has grown to $1,610—and you haven't had to lift a finger!

Now, $1,610 may not look like much, so let's take this thing out forty years. At the end of forty years, say age twenty-five to sixty-five, that initial investment of $1,000 has grown to more than $45,000! You only put in $1,000, but because you started early, you get to enjoy $44,000 of free money! That's the power of compound interest.

Compound interest is a powerful example of interest working for you rather than against you. When this thing really gets going and kicks into high gear, it just goes crazy! Think about it: You put in a little money, then *that* money makes more money, then *that* money makes more money, then *that* money makes more money. It just keeps going, and all it costs you is a little wisdom and a lot of patience.

Compound Interest and Chinese Bamboo Trees

Patience is the key word when we're talking about building wealth. Compound interest will help you reach your dream retirement, but it won't happen overnight. The truth is, even if you're diligently saving toward retirement every month, it will take several years before you really start to see things take off. There's actually a lot going on in those years, but you won't see a dramatic shift. It's kind of like how bamboo trees grow.

Did you know that it takes five years for a Chinese bamboo tree to break the surface after you plant one? Just imagine that. You decide you want some bamboo, you go get the materials, you prepare the ground, you spend a day or two planting them, you water them all the time. And then you wait. And wait. And wait. And then you wait some more. See, you'd have put in all this work, but you never see any evidence that your hard work is paying off. It would look like nothing's happening.

The truth is there's a lot going on under the surface; you just can't see it. But then, one day five years later, a bamboo shoot pops out of the ground. Then another. And then another. And you want to know something about Chinese bamboo trees after they break ground? You can actually *see* them growing! They grow so fast, experts say you can actually sit there and watch them grow! Amazing, right? Well, that's what happens with compound interest. It works behind the scenes and you may not be able to see anything for years, but then all of a sudden it will show unbelievable growth.

I'll give you another example of the power of compound interest just to make the point even clearer. Let's say you got a $50,000 inheritance in your mid-twenties. A lot of people would blow that money in a week with a new car and some other stuff they didn't really need, but not you. You learned about the power of compound interest, and you wanted to put it to work for you. So, instead of blowing the money, you invested it and got an average 8 percent rate of return.

After one year of 8 percent growth, that investment would be $54,000. Not bad. You earned $4,000 in a year without having to do anything! But let's keep this thing going. After ten years, you'd have $107,946. After thirty years, your $50,000 investment would be worth $503,132. And if you left that money alone for forty years, you'd have $1,086,226! That is 95 percent growth! It's more than $1 million of that free money we talked about!

So, if you had invested that money at age twenty-five, you'd be a millionaire at sixty-five—and you wouldn't have had to do anything, right? Well, not really. You see, your patience would've earned you all of that money. Now remember, during all of those years your investment might've been on the front seat of that roller coaster ride. Your investment over those years would've made money and lost money. It would've even stayed level for a while, but all that time it just kept working for you. You didn't worry about it at year sixteen when it went way down or year twenty when it went way up. You had a long-term view, so you just left it alone. When you do that, compound interest takes over and builds wealth.

MANAGING RISK FOR A BETTER RETURN

We've talked about the concept of risk already, but now I want to get specific. There are certain types of risk that scare people away from investing. But here's the thing: I don't make decisions based on fear. Sure, you want to acknowledge the risks and make wise decisions, but when risk turns to fear, and that fear keeps you from making *any* decision, you get stuck. And when you're stuck, you don't do anything. You sit and hide. When you are paralyzed with your money, you totally miss out on the power of compound interest. Every year you put off the decision to invest, you are losing tens or even hundreds of thousands of dollars. If you want to be scared of something, be scared of that. Be afraid of retiring broke because you let risk keep you from investing.

Like I told you earlier about my son and his fear of the boogeyman, if you learn to understand something, it takes away the mystery and can keep you from getting stuck in your fear. If you can just understand some basics related to risk and return, it can definitely help you feel more comfortable and confident when it comes to long-term investing.

Investing Risk #1: You Could Lose Money

I won't lie to you. When you invest in the market, you have the potential to lose your money. Of course, there are things you can do to minimize that risk, but it's always there. It's always a possibility.

Remember, the market is a roller coaster. When you have money invested, that roller coaster means sometimes you'll be making money, and sometimes you'll be losing money. That's just how it works; you can't avoid it. The idea, though, is that over a long period of time, you come out way ahead. That's why it's so important to keep a long-term perspective.

The ups and downs in the market are generally referred to as "market volatility." Sometimes when people read their quarterly statements and see that they've lost money, they panic and actually pull their money out of their investments. They jump off the roller-coaster in the middle of the ride! To make matters worse, they're selling their investments when they are at the worst prices. That's the wrong way to go. You want to *buy* when the price is low and *sell* when the price is high. When I see a big dip in the market, I act like the investments are on sale! That's when I try to pull some extra money together and make some new investments.

We talked earlier about patience, and that is exactly how you need to deal with this part of the risk. Like I said before, 100 percent of the fifteen-year periods in the stock market's history have made money. Think about that. This includes some pretty rough times in the market's history—such as World War II, the Great Depression, the Oklahoma City bombing, 9/11, and, yes, even the 2008 financial disaster. So the truth is that you can minimize the risk of losing your money by investing it for the long term. You have to make at least a fifteen-year commitment if you are going to do this. Investing for the long term will allow you to ride out the ups and downs that are a natural progression of the market.

Investing Risk #2: Getting Beaten Up by Inflation

We are all familiar with the effects of inflation whether we realize it or not. Every year, things cost a little more, don't they? Every year, it feels like your money buys a little less—because it does. That is because of inflation. For example, let's say that inflation averages 3 percent per year. That means things cost 3 percent more today than they did a year ago. But that also means your money is worth 3 percent less this year than it was last year, because you can't buy as much with it.

So, if you were to put $100 in a cookie jar today, you might only be able to buy $97 worth of stuff next year, then maybe $94 the next year, and only about $40 worth of stuff in twenty years. So, after twenty years when you open your cookie jar, your $100 bill looks more like two twenties. So much for the security of stashing your money in a cookie jar!

Here's a way to really feel the impact of inflation. Let's look at the difference between just a couple of 1970s prices and the prices of those things now. First, in 1970 you could buy a gallon of gasoline for 38 cents![1] That's crazy! You could have filled your whole tank in 1970 for the cost of a couple of gallons today.

And how about buying a house? In 1970, you could purchase a new house for about $25,000. Today, the average new home for a young family will cost you about $268,000. That is a huge increase! That means your $25,000 house value from 1970 wouldn't even be a 10 percent down payment today!

So, if you had set aside $25,000 in a cookie jar forty years ago to buy your retirement home and you were ready to retire today, you would only have enough to buy a retirement bedroom—attached to your kid's home.

See, people who are scared of investing may just stick with saving cash throughout their life. That's the old image of someone stuffing the mattress with hundred-dollar bills or, like we said above, hiding everything in a cookie jar. But the problem is, the cookie jar carries risk too. Sure, you could lose your money in an investment, but you'll also lose money even if it is sitting in a cookie jar because of inflation. The point I'm trying to make here is that you aren't staying free from risk by staying out of investments; in fact, you're guaranteeing that you'll lose money over the long haul if you stick with cash in a cookie jar.

So, how do you avoid the risk of inflation? This one is pretty simple: You need to earn more than the rate of inflation. Your investments need to run faster than inflation to avoid being tackled from behind.

Investing Risk #3: Putting All Your Eggs in One Basket

This risk is the scariest of them all. You know the image: If you put all your eggs in one basket and your basket breaks, what happens? You lose all your eggs. And all you have left is a mess. Nobody wants that.

The biggest danger here is putting too much of your money into any one type of investment, no matter what that investment might be. If that one particular investment takes a loss, especially a *serious* loss, you risk losing significantly more money. The dot-com bubble of the late nineties is a perfect example of this type of financial risk. When the bubble popped around 2000, some companies went bankrupt and many investors lost a lot of money because they were so heavily invested in dot-com interests. Some people even lost everything.

Another example is Enron. *Fortune* magazine called Enron "America's Most Innovative Company" for six years in a row in the late nineties. Enron was an energy company that saw their net worth mushroom to over $100 billion in just a few years as they branched out into dot-com business. However, at the same time, they also branched out into corporate fraud, and it all ended in a huge financial scandal at the end of 2001.

Enron filed bankruptcy, and the financial collapse of the company impacted thousands of people. Many employees and investors lost everything because most of them had put all their financial eggs in the Enron basket. There were even news reports of people jumping out of the windows because they realized they had lost everything.

I was a financial coach at the time, and I counseled a guy who had worked for Enron. He was in his mid-fifties and he, like so many others, had invested all he had in Enron stock because of how fast the company was growing. He lost over a half million dollars. And, because the company folded, he also lost his job. He was devastated. No job, no money, no savings, and no retirement—it was all gone.

You might be shaking your head thinking that you would never make that mistake, but hold on for just a second. It was their company, so they felt a sense of pride and ownership. They felt like they were being loyal to a company that had served them so well.

Plus, Enron looked like a once-in-a-lifetime investment back then. They were on fire! But the employees didn't understand the level of risk involved.

So how do you avoid the risk of losing all of your money? Diversification. Now, *diversification* is one of those ten-dollar words financial people throw around, but it's not complicated. It simply means to spread your investments around. Spreading your money across several different types of investments levels out the roller coaster ride a bit and lowers your risk overall. I'll talk more about some strategies for spreading your investments out a little later.

Try Dollar Cost Averaging to Minimize Risk

We shouldn't talk about minimizing risk without also covering another strategy called dollar cost averaging (DCA). This is a behavior methodology of consistent, ongoing investment purchasing. Dollar cost averaging pretty much removes the temptation of trying to time the market or trying to guess what part of the roller coaster you are on. People who try to time the market play a dangerous game of jumping in and out of their investments because of market fluctuations. In my experience, timing the market is based more on luck than science, and it can cause a lot of headaches for the average investor. That's why I recommend a consistent investing schedule like DCA.

In layman's terms, dollar cost averaging means that you are committing to buy a dollar amount of a particular investment over time. Let's say you have $4,000 to invest, and you want to put it all in a new miracle hair-growth treatment called Follicle Frenzy. Hey, a guy can dream, right? Anyway, you have some choices with your $4,000. You could invest it all in one lump or you could spread that investment out over several months. Which works better?

If you decide to put it all in at one time, what happens if you just happen to pick a day when Follicle Frenzy hit a record high of

$100 per share? That means your $4,000 would have bought forty shares ($100/share × 40 shares = $4,000). Done deal.

Or you could have tried the dollar cost averaging approach. If I were dropping $4,000 into Follicle Frenzy, here's what I would do. I would decide up front that I'm going to put in $1,000 a month for four months instead of investing all of it at once. Then, once we get into it, let's say we discover that Follicle Frenzy's stock price is all over the place month to month. It's pretty volatile, which means the per-share price is going to be more expensive sometimes and a lot cheaper at other times. Here's what that might look like each month:

- Month 1: $80 per share = 12 shares
- Month 2: $100 per share = 10 shares
- Month 3: $75 per share = 13 shares
- Month 4: $50 per share = 20 shares
  Total shares purchased over four months = 55 shares

At the end of four months, because I had committed to buying $1,000 per month, I was able to minimize the risk of paying too much at the stock's high point ($100 in month two). Instead, I spread my investments out over time and was therefore able to take advantage of the lower prices the other three months. Just look at the difference between month two and month four. Something weird happened in month four, and the price dropped all the way down to $50. Because I was investing $1,000 a month regardless of the price, I was able to buy twice as much in month four as I did in month two. See how that works? It's just like the supermarket. If you have $10 to spend on soup, you can buy more soup when the price is lower and less when the price is higher. The market works the same way!

And here's the real benefit. If I had invested my entire $4,000 at one time when the price was $100 per share, I would have only been able to buy forty shares. However, by spreading my investments out over four months, I was able to take advantage of the dips in the market. As a result, I was able to end up with a total of fifty-five shares! The average price of those shares over the four months was about $72 ($4,000/55 shares = $72), which is a lot better than the $100 per share it would have cost all at once and at the wrong time! So, for the same $4,000 investment, I was able to purchase fifteen more shares of Follicle Frenzy!

If this sounds complicated, know that if you are using automatic payroll deductions, such as in a 401(k) or Roth 401(k), to invest in a retirement plan, you are *already* doing this. That's one reason I love company-sponsored retirement plans; they simply cut a certain percentage out of your paycheck every month and help you invest steadily over a long period of time. Even if you don't have that option at work, you can still do this on your own. Just work with an advisor to find a great mutual fund to invest in, set a certain dollar amount to invest each month, put that on an automated contribution plan, and boom! You're taking advantage of dollar cost averaging by spreading your investing purchases out on a regular, consistent schedule.

INVESTING YOUR WAY TO YOUR
RETIREMENT DREAM

Here is the greatest news about investing: I have watched it work firsthand. I have opened portfolios of countless people and seen how faithful and patient investing has paved the way to their retirement dreams. We said early on that funding your retirement dream is completely up to you. That lotto ticket probably isn't going to work out. Publishers Clearing House isn't going to show up at your doorstep. And the government certainly isn't going to fund the dream you'll spend decades planning. Bottom line: the Retirement Fairy isn't coming!

Investing is a fundamental piece of reaching your dreams. The money you save while you're working is the income you'll have in retirement. And remember, your retirement income is completely in your hands. That's what the R:IQ is all about! I've been in the money game a long time, and I believe in the market. If you follow the basic principles we've been discussing through this book so far, investing will work for you.

The last thought I want to leave you with—and we will discuss this at length in a later chapter—is the truth that you don't want to do this stuff on your own. I told you the story earlier about hurting my knee playing football and finally going to the specialist. Well, the truth is that you need an expert to help you—a true investing professional. Not someone who is always trying to sell you stuff. I want you to find someone who is patient and will explain the market to you. I want you to make sure you avoid the people who are out there peddling get-rich-quick formulas for your investments. Stay patient, be conservative, keep shopping in the produce section of that market, and you will end up with a healthy retirement! You also have to keep in mind that you are setting out to accomplish something great. And great accomplishments take time, planning, attention, and patience.

Now that we've covered some basics about investing, I think it's time to dig into the meat and potatoes of your investing options. Not all investments are created equal! Even if you're ready to invest, you still need to know which investments are great and which ones are terrible. That's what we'll hit in the next chapter.

CHAPTER SIX

THE INVESTING MENU

Understanding Your Options

My grandmother wasn't just an amazing person; she was also an unbelievable cook. I've already told you about her phenomenal chili and my terrible attempt to make it when I went away to graduate school. Even after she gave me the step-by-step instructions for her recipes, it was almost impossible for me to have the dishes come out as good as her versions. So when I drove home to Kentucky for Christmas break that first year of graduate school, I had two specific goals in mind. First, I wanted to spend some time with my family—specifically my grandma. Second, I was on a mission to learn exactly how she made some of my favorite food.

We spent time in her kitchen during that break and had some of the best conversations we'd ever had. And she also let me cook with her. As I paid close attention, I realized that there were things that just came naturally to her, things she had learned from trial and error over the years that were difficult to explain to someone over the phone. That's why I always had so much trouble re-creating her dishes! It wasn't enough to simply follow the instructions on paper; I had to learn from the master.

You see, I learned the "secret" was the little dashes of *this* and the drops of *that* she added to these dishes—all natural instinct for her. As we cooked, I quickly realized it was far more than just the ingredients that made her cooking so great. It was also her timing. It was the mixing, juggling, and blending of all those different ingredients that made those dishes taste spectacular. She understood how everything needed to be put together: just when to add the spices, just when to turn the heat down, just the right amount of time to let things simmer. It was like she was ballroom dancing or directing a symphony! Over that break, I learned that it was the *nuances* that made my grandma's cooking so phenomenal—and I wanted to learn the whole process.

I tell you that story because it might help you understand what this chapter is about. To be successful with investing, you can't just know the ingredients. No, you have to understand the nuances and the timing and how everything should blend together to get you on your way to the retirement of your dreams.

The "ingredients" in your recipe for retirement are the different types of investments available to you in the market. We'll cover the main options you should know about and especially those you should take advantage of, and I'll try to help you understand the special nuances of each along the way. But, before we jump into this discussion, I need to give you a disclaimer—one that I have mentioned several times before. You need to consult a professional about your retirement plan and options. I'm not talking about a friend or the guy in the cubicle next to you at work either. This is your dream, and you can't afford to take advice from someone who doesn't know any more than you do about this stuff. Work with a pro who knows the ins and outs of all of these options and who can arm you with the knowledge you need to make your own investing decisions.

LET'S TALK ABOUT ASSETS

Before we dive into specific investments like IRAs or mutual funds, we need to get a big-picture view of these things. When it comes to individual investments, the bigger picture refers to asset classes. Got your nerd goggles on? Good, because we've got to understand some financial concepts that are important for your long-term success, but that may be a little boring for your short-term entertainment.

Investments are broken down into broad categories based on the type of investment they contain and the investment's risk and return profile. Pretty much every investment you could think of falls into one of four asset classes or categories: cash, bonds, stock, and real estate. Let's lay some investing groundwork by walking through a basic explanation of each type of asset.

Cash Assets
Cash assets are your basic banking options, such as your checking, savings, and money market accounts. These are all relatively safe places to park money for short-term saving because they carry an extremely low degree of risk. They are also the best places to keep your emergency fund, which Dave explains in the foreword of the book.

Another form of cash asset would be the CD (Certificate of Deposit). People like to think CDs are good for long-term investing, but I disagree. A CD is basically a bank account with a certificate that says you put your money in the bank and will leave it there for a certain amount of time. If you've ever gotten a receipt for a deposit into a normal savings account, you pretty much got the CD experience—but you didn't have to tie up your money for one or five years to do it.

Cash assets may be safe, but they aren't entirely risk-free. They carry a low rate of return, meaning you won't make much on your money. That leaves you open to the risk of being run over by inflation. We've already seen how stuffing your money in a cookie jar is a bad long-term plan. Most cash assets are just a half step up from the cookie jar.

Bond Assets

A bond is basically a loan agreement between a borrower and an investor. The bond issuer agrees to pay the investor back with interest over a specified period of time. A bond is basically a certificate that a corporate or government entity uses when they need to raise money (for a building project, for example) without outright borrowing the money from a bank. So, in order to raise that capital, they issue bonds to investors.

The issuer of the bond promises you, the buyer, that they will pay out a set interest rate after a fixed amount of time, called the maturity date, which could be anywhere from one to more than thirty years, depending on the specific bond. For example, if you purchase a bond for $100, you would know up front that the bond would earn a set rate of return, maybe 6 percent. And you also would know the date that bond will mature. When a bond matures, it simply means you can cash it out and the issuer will pay you.

Let's take a quick look at the different types of bonds that are out there. The first type is the government bond, or what people refer to as the "treasury bond." This is generally considered the safest bond you can purchase because the US Treasury backs it. Interest that you earn on this type of bond is exempt from state and local taxes, but not from federal taxes. While there is little risk involved with these bonds, government bonds also carry some of the lowest yields.

The second type of bond is a municipal bond. Municipal bonds are issued by state and local governments and are popular as tax shelters. These bonds typically mature in thirty to forty years, and the interest you earn is exempt from federal taxes and sometimes even from state and local taxes.

Then there are corporate bonds, which are issued by companies. The interests on these bonds are taxable. They are higher risk, but they are also higher yield. The risks involved with these types of bonds are related to the creditworthiness of the company that is selling them. Corporations also issue the final type of bond I want to briefly touch on: the high-yield bond. This one is commonly referred to by investing experts as a "junk bond." These bonds are more like a roll of the dice because they are issued by companies without a strong credit history and tend to be high risk, but they also promise a high return.

People can get confused about bonds pretty easily, but it's really not that complicated. I'll give you an example to show how all of this would play out in the real world. Let's say Carl's Colossal Cookies has decided to open a second location but doesn't want to go to the bank for a loan. So Carl decides to offer ten bonds to raise the $100,000 he needs to open the second location and get it running. Rick agrees to buy one of the bonds for $10,000. The $10,000 is called the "face value" of the bond and just indicates how much Rick loaned Carl.

In exchange for the loan, Carl agrees to pay Rick an annual interest rate of 8 percent on the loan, which is also referred to in fancy bond talk as "the coupon," but it simply means the interest rate. So Rick will receive $800 in interest every year for the agreed-upon life of the bond. In this case, Rick agreed to loan Carl the $10,000 for a total of ten years. So, each year for ten years Rick would earn $800 as interest on the loan.

If Rick needed to cash out the bond before the ten years was complete, he would not get all of his money back. But, at the end of the ten years, the bond would reach "maturity," which just means it would be time for Carl to repay the original $10,000 loan amount to Rick.

That's it. A bond is just a loan between a borrower—someone who needs money—and an investor—someone who has the money to loan. But before we move on, I need to cover some important questions that people often ask me about bonds: *Is there risk involved with bonds?* Well, yes, there is definitely risk. *Should you use them as part of your investing plan?* No, I don't recommend bonds as part of your investment plan. People mistakenly believe bonds are "safe" investments that have slightly lower rates of return than equities. But single bonds can sometimes be extremely volatile and go down significantly in value. Bond mutual funds can at least be tracked for historical returns, but they do not offer the returns in equity that mutual funds do. This part of the conversation starts to get a lot more complicated, so this is something you'll want to discuss with your financial advisor.

Stock Assets

We discussed stocks a bit in the last chapter, but it's time to go a little deeper. Stock represents owning little bitty pieces of a company. It's kind of like a bunch of bricks in a building, and you own one or more of the bricks. It's different from a bond because you aren't *loaning* the money. You're using your money to literally *buy* a piece of the company. Since you own that piece, you are entitled to a share of any profits the company makes. And, as a shareholder, you get to participate in some of the decision-making for the company.

Stock prices are driven by the performance of that company. If the company's earnings go up, so will the price of their stock. So stockholders earn money by selling their stock *after* it has grown because of the company's success. The other way to earn from stock is called a dividend. This is a quarterly payment that some companies will pay their stockholders, which is a way for the company to reward their stockholders for maintaining ownership in their company.

Again, let's see what all this means in a real-world example. Let's say Bob, an avid mountain biker, wants to start his own bicycle sales and repair business called Time to Ride. He discovers he can get the business up and running for $100,000. The problem is that Bob only has $20,000 to invest in his business. So Bob issues stock in Time to Ride and breaks the ownership down into ten shares valued at $10,000 each. Bob has $20,000, so he keeps two shares for himself and finds eight other people to invest $10,000 each.

So, there are ten total shares of stock valued at $10,000 each, and the company is worth $100,000. That means each share of stock represents 10 percent of the ownership of Time to Ride. So each of the investors *owns* 10 percent of all the bikes, tools, parts, building, and even the earnings the company makes.

After a couple of years, Bob has done pretty well, and Time to Ride is now valued at $200,000. So, each share of stock, which is worth 10 percent of the company, is now worth $20,000. That would be $200,000 divided by the ten shares of stock. That means each of Bob's investors has doubled their initial investment. Not bad.

Of course, at any point along the way, a stockholder could sell their share of stock and transfer the ownership of that piece of the company to someone else. That's how people make money buying and selling stocks. The idea is that you buy low and sell high, meaning that you buy it cheap and sell it when it's worth a lot more than you paid for it.

So, how are stocks related to the market? You've probably heard the term "stock market," right? The stock market is a large group of financial markets from all over the world. It's a marketplace for buying and selling stocks. You may have heard of the Dow Jones or the S&P 500. These are a couple of the various reports, kind of like report cards, on the performance of all markets. They help us know if the market is going up, going down, or staying flat.

That's what stocks are and how they work, but let me caution you here: I do not recommend investing in individual stocks! Single stocks are far too risky. It is much better to diversify in mutual funds than to put a pile of money into one particular company. Remember my friend who had invested his entire retirement in one company? You know that little business from Texas called Enron that was all over the news when it folded? That is a perfect example of why I recommend diversifying. But if you have your financial house in order and you really want to own a stock just to play around with, limit those single stocks to no more than 10 percent of your investment portfolio—and be emotionally prepared to lose that money!

Sometimes people take issue with me on my stance on single stocks. To explain my position, let me tell you about a trip I took to Vegas. I was sitting on the airplane one early morning in Nashville, getting ready to take off for a speaking event. Now, if you have ever been on one of those early flights at oh-dark-thirty in the morning, you know most of the time everyone is sleepy and quiet. But not this flight! See, this one was heading for Vegas! It was buzzing with energy. People were talking excitedly about their plans. They were high-fiving, hugging, and participating in all kinds of crazy behavior for that early in the morning. You know why? They were all going to get rich! They were going out to the desert, they were going to double their money, and they were going to come back filthy rich! I will never forget the energy of that crowd when we touched down in Vegas that morning. That little signal went *ding* telling us we could get out of our seats, and the seat belts were so loud it was like applause. It looked like people were being unleashed from their seats! They were ready to *run* to the casinos.

Now, the funniest moment was a day later when I was getting

on a plane to go home *from* Vegas. I'll be honest. That plane was full of the saddest, sickest group of folks I had ever flown with in my life. Nobody was smiling. No one was talking. Heck, a couple of people looked so pale that I was worried they might keel over right there in their seats. Not a single person got on that flight chatting or smiling or bouncing around like the next millionaire. I'm pretty sure most of those people who had gone to Vegas to win had lost money. That's how casinos stay in business! You've heard the expression, "Whatever happens in Vegas stays in Vegas," right? Well, I'll tell you what *else* stays in Vegas: your money!

Here's the point: single-stock investing is like playing the tables in a casino. Everyone is looking for the next Apple or the other Big Thing that is going to hit big, but the truth is you can't guess the success of companies or the growth of an individual stock. Unless you have a crystal ball and a magic wand, I'd stay away from single stocks.

Real Estate Assets

The fourth major asset class is real estate. These assets basically represent land or anything that is permanently fixed to it (houses, apartments, condos, office buildings, retail space, and so on). There are three broad categories in real estate: residential, commercial, and industrial.

Real estate investments are probably the most hands-on, time-consuming investments you could make. I tell people as a general rule to avoid real estate unless they have a real passion for it. We've all seen the talking heads on late-night television explaining how you need to add real estate to your portfolio, but the problem is that real estate is a huge responsibility—one that many investors simply aren't ready for. But, if you're interested in this as part of your overall investing plan, let's at least look at some particulars you need to know.

First of all, you should only consider real estate once you have the cash on hand to buy the properties. That's right: cash. You should *never* take out loans for a real estate investment. Why? We covered that in our debt chapter: a loan is a risk. If you take out a mortgage, you have introduced risk into your financial situation, and like I told you before, no matter what is going on with your job, your health, or your financial situation, that mortgage loan payment is going to knock on your door every month. Our goal as we move toward our retirement dream is to mitigate risk, right?

The second thing to think about when you are considering real estate is location. I had a client call me to talk about his portfolio. He was living in Indiana, but he had purchased several investment properties in California during a time when he had lived in Los Angeles. After he was transferred back to Indianapolis, he was no longer able to check up on those properties and deal with his renters. He was spending a ton of money on plane tickets to fly out there and resolve issues he was having. It was a big source of stress for him, and he was in a mess. I'll tell you what I told my client: You don't want to be a long-distance landlord. If you are, you will probably have to hire someone to handle that property for you, which will create another expense.

And, speaking of expenses, you need to remember that you are ultimately responsible for the upkeep and maintenance of the property. So, if the air conditioner goes out and you have some sweaty, irritable tenants, it's your job to fix it immediately. That's why I advise people to not only pay cash for real estate investments, but to also have a cash emergency fund set up specifically for those investments. That way, you always have the cash on hand to replace that air conditioner or water heater when—not if—it breaks. And, of course, you can't forget to factor in the costs of property taxes, interest, and insurance.

The thing I am concerned about often when it comes to real estate investments is that they can tie you down financially. You want to invest in things that get you closer to your R:IQ number and dream retirement. I've done a lot of different kinds of investing over the years, and I've never had to replace the roof on my 401(k) or fix the air conditioner in my Roth IRA! The point is, real estate often becomes more of an expense than an investment to buyers who don't know what they're doing. If you've got a big passion for real estate, a high tolerance for risk, and a big pile of cash to throw at it, real estate may be fine for you. Just don't go into it blind to all the risks and expenses involved.

SO WHAT'S A MUTUAL FUND ANYWAY?

Mutual funds are a major part of the market and personally my favorite type of long-term investment. You've probably heard a lot of people talk about mutual funds. But what is a mutual fund? And how do they work?

Mutual Funds Demystified

In the simplest explanation, mutual funds are formed when investors pool their money together to invest in something. For example, let's say I'm going to open a mutual fund and I need some help; I need some investors. So I find some people to invest in this fund, and each person invests $100. Picture a group of people each putting $100 in a bowl, leaving me with a big bowl full of cash. Now, what just happened here? These people just *mutually funded* this bowl of cash. It's a *mutual fund*. This isn't that hard, is it?

What I buy with this money, as the manager of the fund, tells you what kind of fund it is. If I were buying bonds with this fund, we would call this a Bond Mutual Fund. If I take the money out of the bowl and buy stock in international companies, or foreign companies, we would call this an International Stock Mutual Fund. You with me?

Common Types of Mutual Funds

Of course, you can buy mutual funds directly, but chances are your company's 401(k) is full of them. So I want you to be able to identify the four most common types of mutual funds represented in 401(k)s. Remember, different types of mutual funds have different objectives that impact the risk and potential growth of the funds. The four main types of mutual funds are Growth and Income, Growth, Aggressive Growth, and International. There are plenty of other types of funds, but, again, these are the most common.

Growth and Income funds are more predictable and the calmest type of funds. Next, you will find Growth funds, which are fairly stable funds in growing companies; the risk and reward of these funds is somewhere between Growth and Income funds and the Aggressive Growth funds. Now, Aggressive Growth funds tend to be fairly aggressive and all over the place; we call them the "wildchild" funds. And then there are International funds that represent companies from around the world and places outside of your home country.

When I understood all of this, I spread out my investing evenly across these four types of funds. That gave me exactly the kind of diversification I was looking for. Not only are the investments automatically spread out among many individual companies within the mutual fund, but I'm spreading out my investing across four different *types* of funds. That's my sweet spot, but you need to figure it out for yourself and decide what is best for you in your situation.

Understanding Market Caps

In your 401(k), you might see some other terms you don't understand, including the word *cap*. Cap refers to capitalization, which means money. It really just describes how much money a company is worth. For example, one company might be described as being a ten-million-dollar company compared to another company described as a ten-billion-dollar company. A company's value is determined by multiplying their outstanding shares of stock by the price per share. Say what? Look at it this way: If a company has a million shares of stock, and each share is valued at $50, then that company's market cap is $50 million. That's one million shares times $50 each, right?

Small Cap funds are "small money" companies (companies valued below $2 billion). Medium Cap funds represent "medium money" companies (companies valued between $2 billion and $10 billion). And then Large Cap funds include "large money" companies (companies valued above $10 billion). This is where most of the name-brand companies that you and I know are.

Now, if I, the mutual fund manager, were putting together a Large Cap Mutual Fund, I would buy stock in some large companies. These could be companies like Apple, FedEx, Home Depot, Microsoft, or Walmart. This mutual fund might include ninety to two hundred different stocks from large companies. That would make this a Large Cap fund. And most of these large companies are growing, so that would also make this a Growth Stock Mutual Fund.

With any fund, as the value of the overall mutual fund goes up, so do your returns. But within the fund, some of the company stocks may go up in value and some may go down, but the overall value of the fund should go up over time. Your return comes as the value of the fund increases over time.

KEEPING YOUR MONEY SAFE FROM TAXES: TAX-FAVORED PLANS

If you want to make the most of your money, you need to understand how to shield your investment from taxes as much as possible. I want you to be able to take advantage of every legal means of avoiding taxes. And please notice that I said "legal means" because we are following the letter of the law and staying true to our integrity. I want you to pay every dime you legally owe in taxes; I just don't want you to pay one dime beyond that! Using the right kinds of investments and managing taxes will be a big key to reaching your R:IQ number, so pay attention.

Basic Investing: The Tax Terms

Let's begin this conversation by understanding the tax terms. *Tax-favored* refers to any investments that are given special tax treatment under the law. One type of tax-favored option includes tax-deferred plans. This refers to investments like a 401(k) or 403(b) whose contributions come out of your paycheck *before* you pay income tax on the money. Since your contributions to these plans are pre-tax—meaning the money is invested before you pay income tax—this kind of investing lowers your current taxable income and gives you the chance to invest more money now (by avoiding those taxes), which in theory should allow you to enjoy even more growth on your investments. However, you will pay income tax on your withdrawals at retirement. That's where the tax-*deferred* part comes in. It just means you're deferring—or putting off—paying those taxes until you take the money out at retirement.

Then there are tax-free plans like the Roth IRA and Roth 401(k), which literally grow tax-free. You fund these plans with after-tax dollars—meaning you pay income tax on the money before you contribute to the investment. The upside is that you pay zero taxes on your withdrawals at retirement. This is huge! It's basically free money. We'll talk more about the Roth options a little later.

Employer-Sponsored Investment Plans

Now that we have done a quick overview of the basic tax investment terms, we have to talk about the investment plans that are sponsored by employers. These are called Qualified and Non-Qualified Plans. The first, a Qualified Investment Plan, is a retirement plan that is established by an employer for all employees. The appeal for the company using this type of plan is that it helps them attract and retain really good employees. This type of plan typically provides tax breaks for the employees so that the taxes on retirement contributions are deferred. It also minimizes present income tax liability by reducing the employees' taxable income.

There are two basic types of Qualified Plans. The first is the defined benefit, which is essentially a pension plan with a guaranteed payout. The risk in this type of plan is on the employer to save and invest the contributions. The second type of Qualified Plan is called a defined contribution. This would simply be something like a 401(k). This type of plan has its own guidelines to specify how your contributions can be made, how old you have to be before you can receive distributions without a tax penalty, and how much your employer can contribute to the plan in the form of matching. In this type of plan, the risk is on the employee to save and invest in the plan.

The second type of employer-sponsored plan is called a Non-Qualified Plan. This refers to any tax-deferred, employer-sponsored plan that does not meet requirements set by the Employee Retirement Income Security Act (ERISA). Non-Qualified Plans are often designed to meet specialized retirement needs of key executives and other select employees. Within this particular classification, there are four different varieties: deferred compensation plans, executive bonus plans, group carve-out plans, and split-dollar insurance plans. The contributions made to these plans are usually non-deductible to the employer and are usually still taxable to the employee who is benefiting from them. Taxes in these plans for employees are generally tax-deferred.

I know some of these terms, plans, and guidelines are super nerdy. You don't have to be an expert, though. I'll say it again: my goal is to empower you to have an informed conversation with your financial advisor. I promise, I won't be testing you on all these terms later!

What Exactly Is a 401(k)?

Now let's go back to the 401(k) for just a moment. A 401(k) is a retirement plan that companies can offer you to help you save for retirement. We normally refer to the 401(k) as an investment, but it's technically not an investment itself. Instead, it is the *tax treatment of an investment.* The term "401(k)" simply refers to the section of the tax law that allows companies to provide a tax-deferred retirement plan for their employees. The 401(k) itself could contain any type of investment, but it's usually full of mutual funds as the primary investing vehicle. If you work in public education or for a nonprofit, your employer may offer a 403(b) instead of a 401(k). These two basically work the same way, so nearly everything I say about the 401(k) also applies to the 403(b).

How common are 401(k) plans in America? The US Department of Labor reports that there are over five hundred thousand companies in the United States that offer 401(k) plans. Fifty-one percent of those companies also offer a Roth 401(k) option for retirement, which allows for tax-free growth on your 401(k). There are reportedly over eighty-eight million participants nationwide. That means more than 80 percent of all full-time workers who are eligible for 401(k)s actually participate.[1] Forty-six percent of company plans have an auto-enrollment feature with a default 3 percent contribution rate. Of employees who participate in a 401(k) plan, their contribution rates average between 5 and 7 percent.[2]

Those numbers actually paint a pretty good picture. It's easy to look at that and assume that 80 percent of all employees are actively working toward their retirement dream. Keep in mind, though, the stats we've already looked at regarding retirement savings, because the numbers aren't pretty. Only half of eligible 401(k) participants have $10,000 saved; 36 percent have less than $1,000 saved; and only 22 percent have over $100,000 saved. If you've got $100,000 in your 401(k) at age thirty-five, you're doing great. But if that's what you have at fifty-five, you've got some work to do.

Roth 401(k): Your Company's Tax-Free Option

We said before that about half of all companies that offer a 401(k) include the Roth 401(k) option. Let me say this up front: If your company offers the Roth 401(k), take it! It's a great deal. Here's why: you get the benefit of tax-free growth on your contributions, which could literally save you hundreds of thousands of dollars or more at retirement!

With the Roth option, however, your contributions are made with after-tax dollars, meaning you'll pay income tax on that money before it makes its way into your 401(k). So, it's a little bit more expensive on the front end, but the payoff in retirement is off the charts!

One quick note about the Roth options: Only your contributions grow tax-free. If your company offers a match, which we'll discuss below, your contributions will grow tax-free and your company match will grow separately in a tax-deferred account. So you'll essentially have two accounts growing side by side, and you'll pay taxes only on the retirement income from the match side of the account.

Don't Put Your Retirement on Autopilot

I mentioned that many companies have an auto-enrollment feature that automatically puts employees into the 401(k) at a 3 percent contribution rate. I'm glad that companies are being proactive about helping their employees save for retirement, but there are a few problems with auto-enrollment. First, you never want to put your retirement dreams on autopilot. You've got to stay plugged in and in control the whole time instead of letting some automated system manage your retirement. Second, saving only 3 percent isn't enough! Remember

Baby Step 4 from Dave's foreword of this book? We recommend saving 15 percent of your income for retirement until you pay off your home. At that point, you should save even more. You're not going to fund your dream retirement with a measly 3 percent contribution rate. Third, the automatic selections you might get could be totally wrong for you, but you'd probably never know. Overall, I recommend that you do not "auto" your retirement at all.

Years ago, I met with a gentleman in his early fifties, and we were taking a look at his portfolio. He had started investing in his early thirties when he was single. For the past twenty years, his investing had been based on his risk level as a single thirty-year-old. He had basically used the "Crock-Pot" approach to his retirement: he had thrown everything in there twenty years ago and just left it to simmer. The problem was, his life had changed drastically over two decades. He was now married and had several children, yet his investments were far riskier than he needed them to be at his stage of life. His portfolio had far too much risk in the mix.

Fortunately, he hadn't run into trouble yet, but he realized he needed to change it. He needed to do consistent checkups. He realized he couldn't just roll with the status quo. You see, as your life changes, so should your portfolio. You have to keep your finger on the pulse of what is going on. Think about my grandma's cooking. We were able to talk and enjoy our visits, but we stayed in the kitchen because she always wanted to keep an eye on what was happening around that stove. Your investments should be handled the same way. Live your life, but keep an eye on what's going on in your retirement accounts. That's one reason I suggest scheduling quarterly—or at least annual—meetings with your investment professional.

Free Money: The Company Match

One of my favorite terms (and it should be one of yours as well) is *company matching*. We could also call it *free money*. I get excited about free money! Company matching is when your company offers to match a percentage of your retirement contribution. So, for example, your company may offer a 3 percent match. That means they'll match you dollar-for-dollar up to your first 3 percent in contributions. If you earn $50,000 a year and take advantage of a 3 percent match, your company is basically giving you an *extra* $1,500 a year to invest toward retirement—for free!

Obviously, you should always take advantage of a company match, but you need to make sure you're ready before you start. What does "ready" look like? It means you're completely out of debt except for your house (yes, that includes credit cards, car loans, and student loans) and you have a fully funded emergency fund of three to six months' worth of expenses. If you aren't debt-free with a full emergency fund, those need to be your top priorities before you start saving for retirement. Get focused, and get those things done! Once you're ready, using your 401(k) up to the company match should be the first thing you do with any investing dollars.

IRA: The Do-It-Yourself 401(k) Plan

If you don't have access to a 401(k) or 403(b) at work, or if you want to do investing beyond the 401(k), which we'll discuss in a minute, you need to take a look at the IRA. Contrary to popular belief, the IRA doesn't stand for "Individual Retirement Account." It's not an account at all. Instead, it stands for "Individual Retirement Arrangement." *Arrangement* is the key word here. It means that IRAs get a special tax treatment under the law, similar to a 401(k).

An IRA is a tax-deferred treatment on different kinds of investments. So, you could have mutual funds, annuities, or even real estate inside your IRA. Again, the IRA is just the tax treatment; you could have most any kind of investment wrapped in an IRA. And since it is tax-deferred, you will pay tax on the distributions you take at retirement.

Of course, you'll remember that "Roth" and "tax-free" are some of my favorite words, and that applies to IRAs too! The Roth IRA allows you to contribute after-tax dollars to get completely tax-free growth on your investment. That means you won't pay any taxes on all that wonderful growth when you start drawing out your retirement income. This is huge, and it can save you a ton of money. Say you work really hard and you end up with $4 million at retirement. If that money is in a traditional IRA, you'd owe taxes as you withdraw your money. Taxes on $4 million could be a full $1 million! Ouch! But if that $4 million was in a Roth IRA instead, you'd owe *zero* in taxes. All of that money is yours! So, if you qualify, the Roth IRA is definitely the way to go.

Anyone with an earned income or a non-income producing spouse can open an IRA or Roth IRA. However, there are contribution limits each year, meaning you can only contribute a specific amount into the account annually. Plus, there are income limits for Roth IRAs (but not regular IRAs), which means you can't take advantage of a Roth IRA if your annual income exceeds the maximum income set forth in the law. And, of course, there's an age limit when you have to stop contributing and when you have to start withdrawing the minimum distribution. All those limits and ages change all the time, so I'm not even going to bother putting them in this book. They'd be out-of-date by the time you read this! Just talk about it with your financial pro to get the up-to-date information.

Now, if you've left a job where you had a 401(k), I always recommend doing what's called a *rollover* into a new IRA. A rollover just means that you move your entire 401(k) account into a new IRA. When you do that, you get a lot more flexibility and have access to more funds to tailor your account to fit your needs. But here's my big warning: do not bring that money home! You want to do a *direct transfer*, which means the money moves from the 401(k) directly into the new IRA. If it comes to you first, you're going to be subject to all kinds of fees and penalties. Don't do it!

You can also roll over a 401(k) into a new Roth IRA, but you'll have taxes due up front if you do that because a Roth uses after-tax dollars. This can be a great idea, but only do it if you have the cash on hand to pay the taxes without having to pull that money out of the investment itself. Figuring this out, of course, is another reason you need a professional to give you advice in these types of situations.

Investing 15 Percent of Your Income

We've talked about 401(k)s, 403(b)s, IRAs, Roth options, real estate, single stocks, and a ton of other things. At this point, your head may be swimming. But don't worry. It gets easier with practice. For now, I just want to make sure you have a solid plan for getting started with your retirement savings.

Again, you're ready to start only when you're out of debt (except the house) and have a fully funded emergency fund of three to six months' worth of expenses. If you're there, you're ready to start investing 15 percent of your income. Here's how I suggest doing that: If your company offers a match on a 401(k) or similar plan, take it. Invest up to the match. If they offer a Roth 401(k), you can just invest your whole 15 percent there. That's pretty simple, right? You get the match and you can get tax-free growth on your whole 15 percent without having to do anything else. Done!

If they don't have a Roth option, then invest only up to the match. Then, put the rest in a new Roth IRA. So, for example, if they match up to 3 percent, put your first 3 percent in the company plan, and then put the remaining 12 percent into a Roth IRA. If you're a high-income earner and max out the contribution limits of the IRA before you hit the 15 percent mark, go back to the 401(k) to finish it off. And, of course, if your company doesn't have a 401(k), just start with the Roth IRA.

NEARING THE FINISH LINE: USING
SOCIAL SECURITY WISELY

When my kids were young, they loved for us to read to them at bed-time. As they grew older, I began to understand that "story time" was more of a ploy to avoid going to bed! But, one thing I noticed was that most children's stories have a happily-ever-after moment to send kids to sleep with good thoughts. And they should! If we could choose, we'd all have a nice, neat, storybook ending, right? For people nearing age sixty-five, the goal of Social Security was to help promote that happy ending. I can imagine the Social Security bedtime story reading something like this:

> Once upon a time, in a land far, far away, there was a kind-hearted old man named Uncle Sam. In this special place, when people reached the age of sixty-five, all of their finan-cial needs were taken care of by old Uncle Sam, and everyone lived happily ever after.

The reality is that counting on Social Security to meet all of your needs is a fairy tale. It's not going to happen. Unfortunately, I have known too many real people (and I can still see their faces) who believed this story. And now their retirement dream is far, far away.

Social Security and Withdrawal Considerations

I said before that Social Security—however much, if anything, you get in retirement—should be the icing on a delicious cake that you baked with your own hard work. But, as much as I don't want you to count on it as your only source of income, the truth is that Social Security can be an awesome blessing—if you use it the right way.

The age at which you begin drawing Social Security benefits really matters. For anyone born in 1960 or later, full retirement age is currently considered sixty-seven years old. "Full retirement age" is an important distinction. This refers to the age when you will receive 100 percent of your full, calculated benefit. That's why I always encourage people to hold off on Social Security benefits until *at least* age sixty-seven.

You can, however, start drawing Social Security benefits sooner than that if you want or need to. The earliest age to begin receiving benefits is age sixty-two. That may sound better than waiting five more years until age sixty-seven, but here's the thing: the earlier you start, the less money you bring home. If you start receiving benefits at age sixty-two, you would only receive 70 percent of your full, calculated benefits. That means you'd be intentionally giving up 30 percent of your Social Security income for the rest of your life! That's a bad plan.

If you waited two more years, until sixty-four years of age, you would receive 80 percent of your full benefit. If you took it at sixty-five, it would be 85 percent and at sixty-six years of age, it would be 93 percent. Then of course at age sixty-seven you would arrive at the full 100 percent. What I want you to hear is this: If you start receiving Social Security benefits *anytime* before age sixty-seven, you are losing money and you'll never get it back. If you start at age sixty-four and take 80 percent of your benefit, you will *always get* only 80 percent. It won't pop up to 100 percent when you hit the age sixty-seven mark. This is a decision that will affect your retirement income for the rest of your life, so be careful here.

Now here is the thing that a lot of folks don't know: *If you wait until age seventy to begin taking those benefits, it would increase your payout to a maximum of 124 percent!* Did you catch that? Getting 124 percent of your benefit sounds suspiciously like some of that free money we've talked about—and you know how I feel about free money! Unless you will absolutely depend on those Social Security benefits to fund your retirement, I recommend holding off until age seventy. If you've been saving and investing for yourself like we've been talking about, and if you truly view Social Security as "extra" money, then this shouldn't be a problem. However, there's no reason to wait any longer than age seventy. The benefits don't get any better by waiting longer than that, so once you hit seventy, dive in!

Of course, these rules and regulations can change at any time. The information you read here may be out-of-date already, so be sure to discuss them with your financial advisor as you work on your retirement plans.

Keeping Social Security and Medicare Benefits Straight

The other thing that gets a little confusing for people at this stage of retirement is dealing with Medicare. The application age for Medicare is sixty-five. If you don't plan to take Social Security benefits that early, make sure that you sign up for Medicare alone at age sixty-five.

Because Medicare, like Social Security, is a government program, there are a lot of confusing variables and people often get mixed up dealing with these two concerns. I can't tell you how many people I've talked to who *thought* they had signed up for Medicare but actually hadn't! Check with your financial pro and make sure you're signing up for what you need, when you need it.

PUTTING ALL THE PIECES TOGETHER

Now, I know we have covered a lot of nuts and bolts in this chapter. It reminds me of the Spider-Man bike I tried to put together for one of my boys' birthdays. You've probably been there a time or two. You see, in my house, everyone knows that Daddy is not the "put things together person." My wife is the high-detail person. She loves that stuff. She gets out the directions and spreads them out on the floor. She gets all the pieces and organizes them by their numbers in the proper piles right there where she can see it all. Then she reads through those directions in English and Spanish and even in French if she has to! But I am telling you, she puts stuff together better than the picture on the box!

When Dad puts toys together in our house, there are all kinds of parts left over and lying around. In fact, I have so many leftover parts from when I have put toys and bikes together that I could open a spare parts store for parents when I retire! I like to fly through it and get the thing done. I am not as meticulous as my wife.

Retirement, however, requires you to be a little meticulous in how you put things together. You want to lay those parts out and know exactly where every piece goes. You want your retirement to look as good as or better than it does in the picture you keep in your mind. The more careful and patient you are with it, the closer your retirement will look to that high-definition vision you saw in your R:IQ.

Now that we have the pieces identified, we need to talk about some things that will derail your retirement plans faster than pretty much anything else: your behaviors. Buckle up, because the next chapter is all about you!

CHAPTER SEVEN

YOUR BEHAVIOR

The Best Friend and Worst Enemy
of Your Retirement

One of the things I value most about traveling the country to speak is that I am often inspired by how many hard-working people I get to meet along the way. I'm talking about people who get up and go after it day after day, not just when they feel like it, but on the good days and the bad days. I am always inspired to know that our country is full of innovative and earnest workers.

But I have also become aware, through my years of financial counseling and getting to know the folks who attend these speaking events, of a reality that keeps me up at night. It is a sad truth that is going to have an impact on several generations of Americans and one I want to change: the majority of these hard-working folks are allowing themselves to just live *for* the day instead of living *in* the day. You might be wondering what I mean by that. Living *for* the day doesn't mean you don't work hard; it just means that you have no real long-term plan beyond the eight hours in front of you. You are just worried about the day or the work ahead, and you pretty much ignore the future (kind of like the ostrich with his head in the sand).

But living *in* the day means you are working today with an eye on your goals for tomorrow. It shows that you're focused not just on what's going on today but also on where you're headed in the future. It's like reading a map. A map is only useful if you know two things: where you are and where you want to go.

Don't misunderstand me. I don't think we have a work ethic problem; I think we just have a focus problem. I truly believe that the world is filled with hard-charging, hard-working folks. Many of them just don't have a plan for their money or retirement. That's sad because it means at the end of all of their hard work over many years, they'll likely retire broke and stressed. But, if we could approach our finances with the same focus, passion, and intensity that many of us apply to our careers or personal goals, I think many of our stories would be different.

The statistics show a nightmarish reality. Forty-five percent of working-age households have no retirement savings at all. That is almost half! Among people ages fifty-five to sixty-four, the average household retirement savings is only $12,000. You and I both know that isn't going to get you to a comfortable retirement. How about this one: for 22 percent of retired married couples and 47 percent of retired singles, Social Security makes up nearly 90 percent of their monthly income![1] We have talked about this before, but it isn't going to be good long term to live off that "icing." I have a feeling that there will be quite a few people feeling sick about their Social Security in the coming years. And if you think the 401(k) will save the day, get this: 34 percent of employees do not contribute enough to receive the full company match![2] That means many people are just leaving free money on the table!

Now, I know that the statistics can paint a pretty sad picture, but I also know from firsthand experience how true they are. I can put names and faces to these numbers, which is why I'm driven to get you to see retirement differently! So, now that we have focused on the market and what investing actually is, it's time for us to get to the root of the problem—our behaviors.

You see, 401(k)s and Roth IRAs are awesome tools, but they only work if you actually contribute to the plans. The days of working for one company for thirty-five years and retiring on a full pension are over. Your retirement is 100 percent up to you. That means we've got to deal with the behaviors that keep so many people from taking advantage of all the wonderful investment options we've been talking about. If we can identify the bad behaviors and focus on the good, it will get us one step closer to an inspired retirement!

STAYING VIGILANT OVER THE LONG HAUL

Sure, plenty of people aren't investing for the future, but a lot of people actually are. That's a great start, but it can also be a dangerous place to be if you're not careful. Even if you're up and running on your investment strategy, and even if you're starting to build some wealth, you have to be on guard against investing beyond your knowledge. If you're not careful, a little bit of success will make you forget the discipline and patience that got you there. Or, as I like to tell people, having some success can make you arrogant enough to be ignorant. That means you constantly have to check yourself to make sure you are staying on the plan. You have to stay vigilant.

Now, you are probably thinking, *I am vigilant! I would never do anything to get off of the plan!* I promise, this can sneak up on you without you knowing. I once worked with a really bright, hard-working gentleman who was fortunate enough to inherit a home.

So, all of a sudden, this young guy and his wife had no mortgage. His grandparents had given the house to him. What a gift—and an opportunity to carry on a legacy!

He moved his family into the house and, for the first four months, he and his wife were able to jump-start their retirement plan by investing the money that had been going into a mortgage payment. Then he started talking with a buddy who was into day trading. Simply put, day trading is a method of buying and selling single stocks for very short terms—usually less than a day. So you might buy a stock in the morning and sell it that afternoon. These are always really volatile stocks, and you have no way of knowing if they're going to skyrocket straight up or come crashing straight down on any given day. Based on what we've said about long-term investing throughout this book, you won't be surprised to hear that I think that day trading comes with a stupid degree of risk! It is gambling disguised as investing.

Remember what I said about the danger of having a little success? This guy with the paid-for house was between jobs, and his friend talked him into doing a little trading on his own. He had just enough success at first that he went off the deep end. He took his friend's advice and decided to get serious about day trading. Can you guess what he did? This guy took out a $125,000 home equity line of credit on his home and used that money on high-risk day trading—without telling his wife! Now, this was a pretty smart guy who, for the most part, made solid financial decisions. But no one is immune to stupid!

You know what happened next? He lost all of that money day trading—every single penny of the $125,000. G-O-N-E. He was left with only a new monthly mortgage payment and a very confused, scared, and angry wife—all because of a couple hours of stupid. Like I said, if you are going to be successful, you have to stay vigilant against stupid.

Investing Requires Focus!

I learned the importance of focus back in my days playing college football. As a successful team that was competing for championships at Georgetown College, we all had to learn how to drown out the outside voices and focus on what our teammates and coaches were saying. I learned that the outside voices were always misleading and distracting. Success meant that you couldn't get swept up in what was being said by the media or anyone beyond your inner circle of that locker room. I learned to live *in* the day instead of living *for* the day, to stay intent on what was right in front of me (each individual play) while keeping the ultimate goal (a national championship) in mind.

It was a great lesson and one that I quickly discovered could be applied to investing for retirement. I want you to think of your family as your team and your handpicked financial advisors as your coaches. And I want you to think of your retirement as that national championship game. As you work toward that goal, you're going to see and hear a lot of distractions—just like I heard on the football field. But success means that you're going to tune out everyone except for your team and your coaches. Those are the people who are in the game with you, and they're the ones helping you reach your dream.

There Are No Excuses

Playing football also taught me the importance of taking ownership of my actions and never making excuses. It was another lesson that has impacted the way I handle my finances and can help you in your efforts toward a dream retirement. One of my favorite coaches once told me, "Successful players don't make excuses; they make plays." Coach Horning was an incredibly intense leader who was always reading books about motivation and quoting guys like John Maxwell or Zig Ziglar. He was really into positive thinking.

Of course, Coach Horning's messages were not new to me because they were the kind of things that I heard all the time at home. Mama Hogan has always been special to me—not just because she is my dear, sweet mother, but also because of her devoted love and support for me all my life. When I was a freshman in high school, she took up cross-stitching and made me a few things that I still keep to this day. One of the cross-stitched items reads, "If it is to be, it's up to me." My mother helped me understand that if I really wanted something, I had to put in the focus, effort, and hard work to achieve it! I'm grateful for my mother's wisdom, as it served as a foundation for me in my formative years. And so I was locked into those same messages when I arrived at college to play for Coach Horning.

I'll never forget coming off the field in the middle of an intense football game when Coach came up to me and asked me why I had missed a tackle. I looked at him and said, "Coach, the guy has been holding me all game and the referee isn't calling a penalty on him!" The truth is that I was giving him an excuse. Coach squared up to me nose to nose, looked me right in the eye, and said, "Hogan, an excuse is the skin of a lie wrapped in a reason!" Now that isn't the typical kind of thing you hear from most guys in an intense situation like that, but that was how Coach would teach us.

As I walked over and sat down on the bench, I couldn't stop thinking about what he said. Coach was like Yoda, always trying to use a "Jedi mind trick" on us. He was always challenging us and giving us something to think about between plays. I was probably eighteen years old at the time, and I just wanted to play football, not earn a philosophy degree!

Before I ran back onto the field, Coach hit me with the same line again: "Hogan, remember, an excuse is the skin of a lie wrapped in a reason!" But that time, I finally got what he was trying to say. It didn't matter if someone was holding me, and it certainly didn't matter what the referee called or didn't call. It was my responsibility to simply make the play. His words reminded me of the truths that Mama Hogan taught me all my life. If I wanted to win—in life, in football, in my finances—I had to put in the effort and cut the excuses. My success was—and still is—entirely up to me. I never made any more excuses from that point forward.

So how does this relate to planning for retirement? When you start looking at this retirement situation, you are going to feel like you are being "held" sometimes. Excuses are the easy way out. Excuses are easy to pick up and use because you can find them lying around almost everywhere in our culture. The truth is that you will have to retire someday, and, when that day comes, you won't care about all the reasons why you thought you couldn't prepare for that day. There are no excuses. When you come to the end of your work life unprepared, there will be no one else to blame but yourself. So don't give yourself an out. Making excuses is destructive behavior, so make sure the buck stops with you.

WHY PEOPLE RETIRE BROKE

Dave Ramsey likes to say that personal finance is only 20 percent head knowledge and 80 percent behavior. That's definitely true of retirement too. I could go on and on about investing strategies, mutual funds, IRAs, Roth 401(k)s, and a thousand other things, but you could still retire flat broke. People generally don't enter retirement with no savings because their plan didn't work; they retire broke because they didn't have a plan in the first place!

I've watched far too many of my clients walk themselves off a financial cliff because they thought they just needed facts. The truth is, though, that facts only get you 20 percent of the way there. If you want to win at the retirement game, you've got to take control of the behaviors that might keep you from investing. So, with that in mind, let's take a look at some of the top reasons why people hit retirement with no money.

Reason 1: They Don't Invest

Once you get past all the excuses people make, the number-one reason people have no money when they arrive at retirement is because they refuse to invest. Sometimes it's because they have a low-risk tolerance and are just scared. Sometimes it's because they're confused and don't know what to do. Sometimes it's because they spend too much time watching cable news and get freaked out about interest rates and the ups and downs of the market.

You see, the finance nerds of the world like to argue about the rate of return on money, and they are completely correct: higher interest rates yield higher returns. No kidding! But here is the bottom line that you need to hear: 8 percent, 10 percent, 12 percent, and 15 percent of zero money invested is still zero! Market returns mean absolutely nothing to you if you're not investing.

You have to take an *active* approach to your own financial future. It is your retirement, no one else's. You need to know yourself and your risk tolerances, but you also need to know where to go and find help. Investing is a lot like going to a salad bar or a local sandwich shop. You kind of understand what you like on your salad or sub. Your choices reflect your tastes and your preferences. You may try some new stuff from time to time and discover that you like it. But you have to balance what you think tastes great with what is healthy so that you maintain your long-term physical wellness. You want to be in this thing for the long haul. Investing requires the same mindset.

Reason 2: They Jump Off

Remember how I told you that I'm not too fond of roller coasters? It's not a fear, per se; let's call it a healthy awareness! I told you earlier that

I think I have learned to tolerate them over the years for my wife's sake, but you know how I learned to actually tolerate riding them? Well, it is a pretty simple answer, and there is nothing fancy about it. I didn't get hypnotized, I didn't find a roller coaster drug, I didn't take up amusement park meditation, and I didn't discover some special prayer to help me get through it. No, I've actually learned to tolerate roller coasters by following this less-than-profound strategy: *I rode some roller coasters.*

I would never have gotten better at tolerating coasters if I had never gotten on one. That's how I view investing. *Nothing* can make you more comfortable with roller coasters better than actually taking a ride!

Think about it: you can watch a roller coaster go around or examine a scale model of a roller coaster, but riding that thing is a completely different experience. There is this roller coaster at Kings Island in Cincinnati called The Beast. The Beast isn't much to look at. It's this big, old, wooden thing that was built decades ago. It doesn't look that scary from the ground, but man, riding it is a whole different experience. It shakes and rattles and goes ridiculously fast, and you feel a little out of control because it isn't a smooth ride like the newer ones. It took me a couple times riding on that thing before I could tolerate it. The Beast is a little like the stock market.

Let me give you an example. In 2008, when we had the big market dive, many people went back to the mentality of "See, there it goes again. The market is just not something we can trust." They went through that first drop on the coaster and panicked. Remember, though, we looked at the stats showing how the market actually recovered from this big dip. At the end of the day, all this attitude does is give people an excuse to not be intentional with their investing. They just jumped off the coaster! Sometimes, I believe people *want* an opportunity to make those kinds of excuses. It's like this self-fulfilling prophecy. And there is a huge group of folks out there who want to blame the market for their lack of results in preparing for retirement!

But what I need to reiterate to you is that, when you ride that investment roller coaster *long term*, you have to go in eyes wide open and aware there will be ups and downs. The key is to keep your seat belt on, keep your bottom in the seat, and hang on for the long haul. After all, the best part of a roller coaster is usually the very end.

So, even when the market goes down and everyone else is freaking out, I don't want you to be stressed. Why? Because you're plugged into a plan that works. You're following a budget. You're out of debt and you're investing. And remember what we talked about in the last chapter: When the market goes down and you consistently invest, you are actually buying things on sale. When the price goes back up, you are actually experiencing what they call "gains."

But again, I have watched thousands of people get terrified when they see the ups and downs of the market and let the fear just overwhelm them. Fear is what keeps people from embracing their future. Fear is a lose-lose proposition. Instead of refusing to invest or refusing to stay in the game, I want you to refuse to lose. If you don't consistently invest over a long period of time, or if you jump in and out all the time, you probably won't make it to your high-definition retirement dream.

Reason 3: They Make Stupid Decisions

I already told you how one stupid decision caused a former client to lose $125,000—and almost his marriage—practically overnight. Let me tell you about another dumb move I know about. This is a story I know really, really well. Too well, in fact. In this case, I was the one who was stupid.

I was newly married, and my wife and I were both working. We were making good money, and I decided that I was going to dabble in some stocks. So, we put about $2,500 into some AOL shares. The next thing you know, we looked up and it had more than doubled. We were obviously excited about this, so we added some money to it, and I bought some more because I thought we were riding a wave that just wasn't going to run out. Before we knew it, we had $10,000 tied up in stock with that one company. Talk about undiversified! But we thought we were winning, so we kept piling on the stupid!

The next thing we knew, our $10,000 grew to $15,000, and then to $20,000, and all the way up to $25,000. Remember, we were newly married and a lot younger, so $25,000 was a huge piece of our financial puzzle. But instead of getting wisdom and guidance from an investment professional, I just stayed the course. I firmly believed that if my stock could grow to $25,000 so quickly, then surely it would continue on to $50,000, $75,000, or even $100,000 over time! What could go wrong?

I'll tell you what could go wrong: I could get even stupider. So that's what I did. Before long, there was a "little bit" of a correction in the market, and the stock got a little shaky. You'd think that would have been my cue to get out. Wrong! Instead of getting out, I decided to double down. You know what that ended up doing? It doubled my losses!

My stock quickly went from $25,000 to $1,500 before I finally woke up and made some adjustments. This was the penalty I paid for not getting the proper guidance and not being aware of my risks. So you see, my friend, I have done my time with stupid. I have earned the right to warn you away from the danger. All these years later, I still think back to that dangerous game I played with AOL. When I'm feeling particularly irritated about it, I'll get my calculator out and figure out how much that $25,000 could have grown by the time I retire. That realization makes me sicker than being on a roller coaster.

The lesson here is that you are always one stupid decision away

from wrecking your retirement dream. You will never be so successful or so wealthy that you can dive headfirst into stupidity. One bad
risk on a single stock, one afternoon of day trading, one impulsive
hour in the showroom of a luxury car dealership—all it takes is one
moment of letting your guard down to undo years of hard work.
Always measure the long-term impact of these kinds of decisions,
and keep your guard up against stupid!

Slow and Steady Wins the Race

Not too long ago, Dave Ramsey and I were in California teaching
our Smart Money event. When it was over, this young guy waited
patiently in line to talk to me about his situation. He told me that
he had recently pulled everything out of his 401(k). Strike one! The
reason he did it was that he had listened to all of his friends who
were panicking about the stability of the market, and he took *their*
clueless advice over the wise advice of his financial advisor. Strike
two! Now, this man was nowhere near retirement age, so cashing
out his 401(k) meant that he lost a fortune in fees and taxes. He
kissed about 40 percent of that money good-bye before it ever made
it to his bank account. Strike three! You're out!

By the time I met him, this guy, probably in his early forties,
had $250,000 just sitting around in a savings account earning noth-
ing. He had unplugged some great investments, paid a huge penalty
for early withdrawal, and completely lost the earning power of all
that money he had flushed down the toilet. I remember standing
there, looking at him a little dumbfounded because he seemed to
be a highly intelligent man. The problem was, he was getting really
bad advice.

I see this happen all the time. His broke friends—all of whom
were up to their eyeballs in debt—decided to tell this man, who
had done a fabulous job saving, how to invest his money. And he
listened! I had to ask him, "If your friends don't handle their own

finances well, why would you take investing advice from them?" He just stood there quietly. He knew he had made a huge mistake.

Investing over the long haul is hard. You have to be strong enough to weather the financial storms that pop up. It may take a while to see any real gains (remember the bamboo tree?). There is no such thing as getting rich quick. There is no magic formula for building wealth overnight. You know what the secret ingredient is for wealth building? Patience. Fear, anxiety, and impulsiveness are the enemies of patience, and they'll all lead you into retirement broke. Don't let them! Keep your eyes on the goal and keep moving toward your dream—slow and steady.

YOU NEED PROFESSIONAL HELP! REALLY!

We have addressed a few of the most common behaviors I see getting in the way of people's retirement dreams, but now I want to address one of the biggest: the mistaken belief that you can navigate the retirement waters alone. I believe the most important investment behavior you can engage in is to go out and find a professional investment advisor. A good financial advisor will get you past what you *think* you want to do and help you choose the right options for your situation. That phrase "help you choose" is extremely important. You never want to pay someone to make your decisions for you; that's *your* responsibility. An investment advisor's primary job is to teach you how things work and empower you to make your own decisions.

An investment professional is essential to your financial well-being. They should be able to help you peek behind the curtain and understand what is really going on with your investments. They will make sure your money is working as hard as you are. As we discussed in the last chapter, a solid advisor will help guide you based on your particular situation, meaning specific to your level of risk, your financial situation, and the retirement that you want to have. It is a win-win situation. So why exactly do so many people avoid getting help with investing?

What Keeps People from Sitting Down with an Advisor?

Getting some professional guidance sounds like perfectly normal behavior, right? Then why do so many people avoid getting help from an investment advisor? It is like those people you meet who never go to the dentist. I mean, the dentist isn't always the highlight of your week, but if you go consistently, it is good for your health and usually not a terribly painful experience, right?

I believe that folks avoid finding a good investment advisor for a variety of reasons. So let's take a quick look at them so you have the knowledge to fight off those feelings.

Excuse 1: Guilt and Shame

A lot of the folks I talk to don't get help because of guilt and shame. They simply don't want to face their own reality, let alone show their mess to anyone else. We've already talked about how destructive guilt can be and how debilitating shame can be. These two emotions can keep us in ostrich mode forever, preventing us from ever getting the help we desperately need to move forward.

Some people feel guilty because they didn't get serious about investing until later in life. Others feel shame because they made some really poor choices related to loans and withdrawals. The common thing about both groups is that they don't want to invite anyone into their financial house because they are afraid of being judged. I get that. You think it was easy for me to tell you how much money I lost in my stupid AOL experience? We've all done stupid things with money! It's a truly universal experience, and if you want to get on track to retirement, you've got to get over any shame you feel about your past mistakes. The past is in the past. The goal here, wherever you're starting from, is to move forward. Besides, you'll be dealing with a financial professional. I promise, whatever mistakes you've made, it won't be anything an investment professional hasn't seen hundreds of times before.

Excuse 2: Pride

I've talked to plenty of people over the years who have avoided getting help from a pro because of sheer pride. They carry this idea that they can do it all on their own, and the thought of getting some help makes them feel inadequate. Please! Do we feel this way in any other part of our lives? We go to doctors and lawyers for their professional expertise. Why on earth would we not need the help of a financial expert?

I have a friend who is a great auto mechanic. He loves to share some of the ridiculous things guys say when they drop their cars off for repairs. "Yeah, well, obviously I could fix it if I just had the time." "Sure, I can tell what's wrong with it just by listening to it, but I won't spoil the fun for you." There's this societal pressure that makes some men feel completely inadequate if they can't diagnose the rattling noise in their car!

You have to let it go, be open about what you don't know and what you need to learn, and bring in the experts to teach you what you don't know. Whether it's with travel directions or your retirement plan, the only place pride will lead you is over a cliff!

Excuse 3: Feeling Like It's Too Late to Learn

I meet a lot of older folks, too, who feel like they should already know all of this, but they don't understand it and feel like it is too late to learn. You have probably heard that old saying "you can't teach an old dog new tricks," right? Well, that is a huge lie. You are never too old to learn something new! And you are never too old to start investing toward your future.

Excuse 4: Ignorance and Cynicism

I also find that people can feel intimidated talking with advisors about their financial situation. The actual process of finding help can be intimidating to folks because they are ignorant about the process. People generally don't understand where to go to find the help they need. There is this common attitude that says, "I don't understand this stuff and I never will." People say this to me as if that somehow excuses them from ever having to retire. Claiming ignorance is a total cop-out. Saying that you don't understand will not dismiss you from reaching a point in your life when you can no longer work.

Then there is the cynical approach, which honestly is just another form of ignorance that people dress up to sound smart. The problem with cynicism, of course, is that it ignores the proven fact that long-term investing builds wealth over time.

A TOUR GUIDE FOR INVESTING

Have you ever been to the Bahamas? I have, and it is beautiful. I can show you some amazing pictures and tell you a little about the Bahamas that most folks never learn about when they travel there. But first, let me share a story about my trip that might help open your eyes as to why it is so important to find a professional that can help you get to your retirement dreams. We have talked several times about how you need to think about retirement as one long vacation, right? I have asked you to imagine all of the things that you want to do with your life, and I've explained that we get to experience bits and pieces of that when we actually spend time on real vacations right now—those moments when we put our feet in the sand and have no meetings, no coworkers to deal with, no project deadlines hanging over our heads.

My wife and I were vacationing on this little island and were doing all of the usual touristy stuff, but we wanted to make the most of our time so we decided to hire a local tour guide. He was someone who came highly recommended when we began to ask around. He lived there on the island and knew all of the cool places that the usual tourists didn't know about.

This guide took us off the beaten path, away from the usual tourist spots, and showed us some of the most beautiful places on the island. It made our vacation! I mean, we learned about some local restaurants that we would've never found on our own, and he showed us some scenery and beautiful beaches that only the residents of the island knew about.

What did it do for us? Well, it took our vacation to a completely different level. Our pictures were far more beautiful, our dining experiences were way more interesting, and we were able to relax on some of the most scenic beaches that you could ever imagine—all because we took the time to investigate and paid a small fee to get a little advice from someone who knew the lay of the land. Our experience was totally different than most of the people who had traveled there for vacation.

Tour guides help you experience things that you never could've found on your own. And this is exactly what an investing professional can do for you on your way to retirement. Think of that investment advisor as a native of the market. It's their job to know the best restaurants and beaches and to help you maximize your time there. You see, for anyone who has that high-definition retirement dream, your investment professional can help show you ways to get there that you would never just find on your own. They reside in that space and know the ins and outs of the investing landscape.

How Do Investment Advisors Get Paid?

Once you decide to get the help you need with your investments, you should go in understanding exactly how an investment professional gets paid. There are several relatively straightforward ways that you will compensate a professional advisor.

The first way is fee-based, which means that the investment professional will charge you a flat fee annually. This will usually be a small percentage of the value of your investment accounts. You'll sometimes see this called a "wrap account," meaning all the administrative and professional fees attached to the investment are *wrapped* up together, fixed, and charged on a regular quarterly or annual schedule. They will let you know this up front during your initial conversation or meeting. To be clear, you will not be writing a check to the professional; the fee is typically deducted from your investment account.

The second way is commission-based, in which you will pay a commission to your professional. This is usually based on the amount of money you contribute to your investment accounts. So the more you contribute, the more you *both* earn. That's called a win-win situation!

Finally, there is the avenue of proprietary funds, which means your advisor sponsors or manages certain investment funds. The advisor generally offers funds that are managed by his employer. The fund usually carries the name of the institution. For example, when I worked at the bank, the bank would offer their investment to customers. These investments were sponsored by the bank. Be sure to ask your investment professional so you can understand clearly what the fund is, who is managing it, and how it's performed historically. I have heard some horror stories of people being "sold" underperforming proprietary funds simply because they didn't know to ask.

It's important to understand how your investing professional gets paid. Whether they work for a fee or for a commission impacts the short-term and long-term expenses associated with your investment. However, the most important thing is to find an advisor you can trust and who has the heart of a teacher. No compensation model will protect you from a crook or someone who doesn't want to spend time helping you understand what you're investing in. So make their compensation part of the overall discussion when considering a certain professional, but never base your decision strictly on their compensation.

Questions for an Investment Professional

No matter how they are compensated, you always want to ask your potential advisor a few solid questions before you do business with them. This person could become part of your financial team—a key coach who helps you achieve your retirement dream. That means you need to view your initial meeting with them as a job interview. Remember, this person is going to work for you. You're in charge, and you make the decisions—starting with whether or not you're going to hire this person.

Before we get to the questions, and I know I have said this before, it is worth pointing out again that you have to determine up front if your potential advisor has the heart of a teacher. It is vital that you are working with someone who is comfortable helping you understand the entirety of what you are doing with your finances. In my opinion, you shouldn't tolerate working with anyone who isn't patient and good at clearly explaining everything in terms that you can understand. Remember, you never want to do anything with your money that you don't totally understand. The advisor's job is to prepare you to make your own decisions, not to make them for you. If they can't teach you how this stuff works, they're not the one for you.

Most of the questions listed below are pretty self-explanatory, but, before we get there, I want to start with the big one. This is the question that you should ask before spending a dime on an investment your advisor recommends. You ready? Here it is: "Do you personally invest in this fund yourself?" You see, I want to invest in the funds that the advisor is so confident of that they invest their own money. Basically, this question lets you know if they're willing to put their money where their mouth is!

Now on to the questions to ask your investment advisor. Hang on to these questions because they will be helpful in locating an investment advisor whom you will be comfortable working alongside:

- *Can you tell me about your experience as an investment professional?*
- *How long have you done this type of work?*
- *What type of clients are you looking for?*
- *What is your general investment philosophy?*
- *What is your approach to investing?*
- *What do you think is best for your clients?*
- *What is your outlook on customer service?*
- *How will I have access to you for questions?*
- *How often will I be able to communicate with you?*
- *How are you compensated?*
- *Do you have any favorite funds?*

This is a great set of questions for that initial meeting. You'll be able to tell a lot about the advisor by the manner in which they answer them. You should never work with someone who seems impatient or makes you feel uncomfortable about asking questions. Fortunately, there are plenty of good advisors out there who are also skilled teachers and will serve as excellent tour guides as you begin to invest for your own future.

INVESTING BEHAVIORS: FINAL THOUGHTS

Before we wrap up this crucial chapter on investing behaviors, I want to make sure I hit a few final points that can make or break your retirement planning. These last few things will give you a more solid foundation when you are ready to walk through the door into retirement.

The Three Ds of Investing

We have discussed how important it is to have a plan. Once you begin to put that plan in place and execute your journey toward retirement, I want you to hang on to a few ideas that will help keep you on track. I call them the Three Ds of investing.

Dreaming

The first D is dreaming. You have to continue to remind yourself of your goals and dreams. Understand that the the what, or the substance, of your retirement is literally that high-definition visual of your dream. Dreaming requires staying focused on what you want your retirement to be able to do for you.

Determining

The second D is determining. What will you need to do to achieve your dream? This is where the R:IQ tool will help guide you. You see, knowing the road you are on and where you're heading means you will end up with a better retirement. Choosing to nurture that retirement dream also means meeting with a professional and talking about what you need to do. You also move closer to your dream by being aware of the changes and tweaks that should be made along the way and by choosing to contribute and invest money over a long period of time. These are all decisions that you make every day, and each one impacts your retirement. You need to determine what will move you closer to retirement, and then act on it!

Discipline

The third D is discipline. Discipline means you get in the habit of doing the right things over and over again. It is persistence over time. This means that you are working your plan based on your R:IQ number. You are protecting your retirement, and you are safeguarding your dream. You're not withdrawing too much, and you're not taking unnecessary risks. Staying on the path (sticking to your retirement investment plan) gives you peace of mind when you are armed with knowledge. You have to be disciplined enough to know that this is a twenty-, thirty-, or forty-year game plan!

Discipline can often be boring because it usually isn't flashy or sexy. But it is essential to your success. In fact, I might go so far as to say that your investing habits *should* be fairly boring! That probably means you are on the right track.

Danger Language

Speaking of discipline and investing as a boring process, I want to reiterate that you should always be quick to "throw a flag" when you don't understand something. I want you to watch out for these terms when you deal with investing:

- *Timing the market,*
- *Hedging your bet,*

- *Day trading,*
- And, yes, be wary when you hear the phrase *investment opportunity*!

We're trying to live our dreams, and some of these phrases may sound pretty exciting. So here's my little tip: If something in your investments sounds fresh and exciting, beware! These are the types of phrases that should make you question whether you are protecting your retirement dream. Make sure you're taking the right step in the right direction. Beware of those who will prey on arrogance, ignorance, and fear.

When you hear phrases you don't understand, do me a favor. Ask someone who knows. Remember, you need to behave the same with your investing future as you would with your physical health. Whenever you have a serious health issue, you go to a doctor. You ask the questions, run the tests, get second opinions, and listen to the diagnosis, right?

Don't get sucked into believing that you can self-diagnose your physical *or* financial health with a little help from Google. Find an advisor to call when you have questions or when some "opportunity" sounds too good to be true.

Prescription for Investing

If you have followed the Baby Steps Dave explained at the beginning of the book, then you have already laid the solid groundwork for proper investing. Now you just have to stay focused. The truth is that investing with cash actually forces you to make wiser decisions—just like you are more cautious when you use real money as opposed to debt.

Let me leave you with this one final point of emphasis: If you are approaching your investments with the proper mindset, you should always be able to say, "I don't care what the quarterly account statement says today because I am working on a long-term plan." Remember, good investing takes patience, and we already know that the long-term plan means there is no debt, that your investments are equal to the level of risk that you can handle, that you have the patience to maintain that long-term mindset, and that you are armed with the knowledge you need to make your own decisions with the help of a trustworthy financial coach.

Finally, no matter where you are in your retirement planning, I want you to remember that you are never too young or too old to begin investing. All the time you have is all the time you have! Of course, the urgency and opportunities change as you get older, and that's what we're going to cover in the next chapter.

CHAPTER EIGHT

USE THE TIME YOU'VE GOT

Retirement by the Decade

I am 'such-and-such years old,' so what should I be doing for my own retirement planning?" It is one of the first questions I usually get from people when they approach me at a speaking event.

Here's the deal: When it comes to saving and investing for retirement, nobody, no matter their age, feels like they got started early enough or with enough money. No matter their age, salary, or financial circumstances, everyone I talk to looks back and thinks of all the things they could have or should have done better. But, there is no time to waste on "I wish I had." The feelings, emotions, and energy spent wishing the past were different are a complete waste of time! Like the old saying goes, hindsight is always 20/20. Forget the "wish I had" moments. I want you to put all of that wasted emotion behind you and remember that it is never too early and it is never too late for you to begin investing for retirement.

All the time you've got is all the time you've got! So let's see how to make the most of it.

YOU ARE THE "PLAYER-COACH"

I am going to spend most of this chapter breaking down your retirement planning by age and telling you what you need to focus on in your twenties, thirties, forties, fifties, and beyond. But, before we get there, I need you to understand your role in the retirement conversation no matter how old or how young you are: you are the "player-coach" of your retirement.

Let's talk for a minute about the different roles that coaches and players are responsible for. As a coach, it is your job to guide people as best you can and put them in the right position to win. So the coach's work is cerebral and tactical; it is all about planning and positioning for success, right? But then as a player, you don't have to worry about designing a game plan so much. It takes a little tactical engagement, but you are mainly concerned about your assignments out there on the field—the work right in front of you.

The thing you need to see is that, as you work toward your retirement dream, you must balance being both player and coach. Not only do you need to go out there and execute "on the field," but you also need to spend time on the game plan, from plotting the big schemes to attending to the little details that put you in a position to win.

From Baby Steps to Baseball

Before we jump into the age-specific advice, I want to remind you of a few of the big commandments for retirement planning that will apply to you no matter how old you are. Whether you are twenty-five or fifty-two, you need to stay on track with the Baby Steps that Dave described in the foreword to this book. That means you need to have an emergency fund of three to six months' worth of expenses in place before you even think about investing. It also means that you are out of debt except the house and are committed to staying out of debt for the rest of your life. Once you're debt-free with a full emergency fund, it's time to dive into retirement by contributing 15 percent of your income toward tax-favored plans, which we covered in Chapter Six. Then, once you pay off the house, you can throw even more money into retirement and start building some serious wealth.

When we talk about the timelines of retirement planning, I want you to think about a baseball game. There are some fascinating similarities between baseball and retirement planning. Both are slow and steady games. Another interesting similarity is that the intensity of baseball often depends on the situation in which you find yourself in a particular inning of the game. If you are behind by a couple of runs in the fifth inning, you are going to need a little more focus and intensity, because time is starting to run out. Mistakes aren't quite as serious in the first or second inning, because you know you have a long game ahead of you. However, as you get to the fifth or sixth inning, the mistakes are more problematic simply because you don't have as much time to make up for them. Can you see how that same dynamic applies to your retirement plan?

RETIREMENT PLANNING BY THE DECADE

In this chapter, I want to provide you with some important mile markers or inning-by-inning advice so that you can make the proper adjustments to your retirement plan based on where you are in your life. Remember, different phases of the game will always call for a slightly different strategy and execution. So let's take a look at how to approach our high-definition dream—decade by decade.

Retirement Planning in Your Twenties
(First and Second Innings)

Retirement planning in your twenties means taking advantage of the opportunity to get an incredible jump start. It is a great time to learn how to control your lifestyle and to really allow the miracle of compound interest to work for you. Your twenties are where you really begin dreaming about what you want your future to look like—from your career to your family to your retirement dream. You could say this is where you really become an adult, which, honestly, is hard to do if you never get out of your parents' basement! This is the decade when you're supposed to grow up and give your adult life a great start.

Starting the Game

In a baseball game, your twenties would be the first and second innings of the game, right? This is really where the game is getting started. You are settling in and getting a feel for what the contest will be like—the weather, stadium, opposing pitchers, and batters. The thing to remember is that, even though you are still feeling out the conditions of the game, you should still be competing to win from the very first pitch.

Here's what I mean: Yes, you'll spend your twenties getting a feel for what you want to do professionally, who you want to marry, and what your life as an adult is going to look like. You'll probably even make some dumb mistakes you'll laugh at when you're older. But none of that excuses you from investing in your long-term future. You see, your twenties are actually the best time to lay the foundation and the groundwork for a successful retirement. How do you do that? Assuming you are debt-free, I strongly recommend setting up an investment account and allowing the wonder of compound interest to get to work on your behalf. Why not put a couple of runs on the board in the first inning?

You also need to remember to leave your investment money alone and let it grow. In your twenties, I would definitely meet with a professional investment advisor who can help direct you to the right investment choices related to your age. You no doubt have a lot to learn at this point, so let the pro teach you what you need to do to get a great start.

Put Compound Interest to Work

Let me take a moment and remind you what compound interest can do if you start investing in your twenties. If you begin making investments at twenty-five and let the compound interest work for you for forty years, you will be a millionaire—period. And it won't even be that hard. Heck, investing just $100 a month from age twenty-five to sixty-five at a 10 percent rate of return comes to more than half a million at retirement, and anybody with a job and no debt should be able to swing $100 a month![1]

Now if you are reading this in your twenties, you may be thinking, *Age sixty-five? That is so far away!* I get that. But ask someone in their sixties how quickly time seemed to pass between their twenties and sixties, and they'll tell you it happened almost overnight. The compound interest clock is ticking, so do not buy into the lie that you will have "plenty of time later" to invest. The truth is, you *do* have plenty of time to invest—and that time should start now! Even a small regular investment in this decade of life can yield incredible growth. And when it does begin to grow, I want you to remember, no matter your situation, unless you're one day facing a bankruptcy or foreclosure, never cash out your investments. Leave them alone and let compound interest do its magic.

I remember a time in my twenties when I suddenly realized that I'd really built up some money in a 401(k). I had been serious about saving even at that young age, but I wasn't immune to stupid. My wife and I were moving, and we decided that we *desperately needed* some new furniture to fill up the house and, while we were at it, a new car to park in our new driveway. The truth is, we were young and stupid, and were trying to keep up with the Joneses. I know that's never happened to you, right? Right.

We obviously didn't have enough cash on hand, so I went to the one place where I knew I had some money: my 401(k). I withdrew $20,000 out of the account, which only ended up being $10,000 after penalties and taxes. That's right: I threw away almost $10,000 of my money!

Now, just take a moment and consider the opportunity cost of that situation. If I had simply left the money alone, that $10,000 I lost would have grown to almost another half million dollars by retirement. I didn't just throw $10,000 out the window, I threw a half million out. To make matters worse, I can't even remember what that stupid furniture looked like. The lesson, of course, is to leave those investments alone in your twenties. Don't even think about touching them.

Start Dreaming Early

I also think it is important to begin to dream about retirement in your twenties. I know it may sound crazy, and I know it won't totally take shape, but I want to challenge you to begin thinking of what your retirement might look like. You see, people who can visualize their dreams and goals have a much better chance of getting there than people who don't. Even in your twenties, you can use the R:IQ tool to formulate a plan. And the great thing about beginning to invest in your retirement dreams during your twenties is that it will help you avoid those "Oh, crap!" moments later in life. And so what should you do if you haven't begun investing for retirement yet? I have two simple words for you: start now!

Retirement Planning in Your Thirties (Third and Fourth Innings)

Your thirties are the time to begin seriously looking toward what you want your retirement years to look like. Taking control of your spending is more important than ever. If you don't, your spending will take control of you! This is when you really form lasting relationships and start having a family of your own (if you haven't already started). I like to say that your thirties are your planning years. It is when you should get really serious about developing a plan to achieve your dreams for retirement.

Settling into the Game

If your thirties were part of that grand baseball game at the American Retirement Ballpark, we would be in the third and fourth innings. Our game is really developing at this point; there are probably some runs on the board for both teams. You are working as player and coach to adjust your game plan and execution to put yourself in the best position to be successful.

The nerves and insecurities of the unknown that come with the first two innings are gone, and you can no longer take anything for granted. Mistakes made here can put you behind in the later innings of the game. In real-life terms, those mistakes usually look like unreasonable lifestyle choices—especially in your thirties. I always tell people that you shouldn't let your thirty-five-year-old lifestyle cramp your sixty-five-year-old retirement plans!

Your thirties are when you really need to get down to business. You need to have a plan for your life, you need to talk about that plan with your spouse and family, and you need to get to work executing that plan. This is the time when your long-term dream should come into clear focus.

Increasing Your Contributions

This is usually a key career decade for most working adults so, as your income grows, your retirement contributions should grow as well. You definitely want to be intentional about increasing those contributions bit by bit throughout your thirties. It's game on!

We already saw that just $100 a month from twenty-five to sixty-five would come to more than a half million dollars at retirement. But if you bumped up that investment to $200 a month at age thirty-five and let that run for the next thirty years, you wouldn't have a half million; you'd have more than $800,000! And again, $200 a month in your thirties shouldn't be too great a sacrifice if you're staying away from debt and budgeting your money the way we've discussed.

If you didn't invest in your twenties and you're just starting out, don't be discouraged. If, for whatever reason, you didn't start investing until age thirty-five and then invested $200 a month, you would end up with almost $450,000 by age sixty-five. If you got a little more aggressive and bumped your monthly investment up to $370, you could make up some ground and still hit that $800,000 figure by age sixty-five.

Think about that for a moment, because $370 is far less than the average American car payment per month. So many people in their thirties tell me they can't afford to invest, but then I find out they're spending $500 or $800 a month on stupid car payments! Don't tell me you can't "afford" to invest if you have a car payment. What you're really saying is that you've *chosen* to put your money into a new car instead of putting it into your retirement dream. Personally, I'd rather save up and pay cash for cheaper, used cars now so I can be a mega-millionaire later. But maybe that's just me.

Retirement vs. College Savings

If you have kids, your thirties are also the time when you should start investing for your children's college education—if you have the extra money to do so. Keep in mind, though, that your retirement should always take priority over your child's education fund. Yes, I know that is a countercultural thing to say these days, but it's the wisest move. Besides, wisdom is usually countercultural anyway.

Before you let some kind of weird, misplaced parental guilt settle in, let me explain it simply. There is a 100 percent chance that you are going to retire someday unless you die first. But, despite what you believe, there is only a 65 percent chance that your kids will actually go to college.[2] You have to pay attention to the percentages because they don't lie. Did you know that 49 percent of parents would be willing to tap into their own retirement savings so they could help their children with tuition?[3] Look, I love my boys, but that's just a bad plan!

It is not your *responsibility* to pay for your kids' college. Your kids can (and probably should) pay for at least part of their own education, and they can do that with a little bit of planning and a job. In fact, there are a lot of studies out there that show this approach is actually more beneficial to your kids and will help them take their college education a little more seriously. The bottom line is that I don't want you to steal from your own retirement to help your children attend college.

Staying Away from Stupid

I also want you to stay allergic to stupid in your thirties. Remember, stupid doesn't discriminate by age; it can hit you equally as hard in any decade. Don't buy into the lies of the media that I've warned you about. Don't get caught up in the ads and commercials telling you why "you need this" or how you are "incomplete without that." Just live your life and focus on the important stuff like your relationships and dreams.

So how does stupid sneak into your thirty-something life? Life is extremely hectic in your thirties—your children are young, your career is taking off, you're always busy, and you're always tired. Busy, distracted, and tired can lower your guard when stupid is looking for a way into your life. So make sure you have a plan and stick to it!

Avoid competing with others over what you drive, where you live, or what you wear. You need to stop comparing yourself to your parents' lifestyle. You may not be at the place where you have the money it takes to live like they are living. Keep in mind that it took them a long time to get to where they are now! Remember what I said about keeping up with the Joneses earlier. Behind all that nice stuff, the Joneses are really broke and stressed out. Their life may look pretty good from the outside today, but let me tell you, you don't want to be in their shoes when retirement arrives.

Building Your Legacy

You already know (or you're about to learn) that having kids intensifies everything in your thirties. Life is not just about you anymore. And having kids dramatically increases the pace of your everyday life. You are in the position of really settling into your role as the *provider* for your family. Your decision-making changes in so many ways. I mean, just think about what you have to drive! This is when you are making that transition from the cool little sedan to the big ol' minivan. You take on this greater sense of responsibility because now there are people who depend on you.

This is the time of life when you need to make sure your insurance plans are complete and in shape to cover your entire family.

(We will talk more about how to handle that in the next chapter.) In addition to your responsibilities, it is also a time when you begin to realize the connections and joys of parenthood. When I became a parent, it changed my perspective of my own parents and grandparents and helped me consider what a family legacy really means.

This is the decade when your parents begin to discuss what they might leave to you. And, through that process, you begin to consider what you will be able to leave your own children someday. And I am not just talking about finances here. I am talking about your words, your actions, and your life decisions. I believe one of the most significant questions you can ask yourself is, *What can I do that will have a generational impact on my family?* These are the important considerations you face when you see your parents playing with your children and you start to understand firsthand how important it is that your family is connected across generations.

What If You Haven't Started Yet?

I hear the same question all the time from people in their thirties: "What should I do if I haven't started investing for retirement yet?" My answer is simple: "Get started now!" The great thing about your thirties is that you still have time to let compound interest do some incredible work for you. The R:IQ tool will show you that you will have to invest more each month than you would have if you had started out in your twenties, but let me tell you, this is still a pretty manageable number for most folks, and you are still capable of reaching that high-definition dream!

Retirement Planning in Your Forties
(Fifth and Sixth Innings)

Let's just deal with it: When you get into your forties, you really begin to feel the pressure. Retirement is no longer some myth out there on some faraway and distant island. This is the time of life when people start dealing with kids heading to college, aging parents, estate planning, disability, career ups and downs, and a million other things—but it is also the time to double down and really get intentional about retirement.

The Pressure's On

I suppose that your forties could be considered your pressure-building years. Retirement is not only real, but it is actually looming out there in the visible distance. In our baseball analogy, this is where we hit the fifth and sixth innings—right in the middle of our game. And this is the point in the contest where, as the player-coach, you feel the pressure to keep the lead if you are ahead. And if you are behind in the game, there is definitely an urgency to intensify your efforts in order to get back into the game.

In our forties, the decisions we make will carry straight into our retirement years. Long-term decisions, like the ones that require fifteen- to thirty-year commitments, can and will impact our retirement. For instance, a new thirty-year mortgage at this point will run far into retirement, and that's something you absolutely don't want to happen. This may also be the decade of big career changes. We need to consider how taking promotions, making job changes, relocating across the country, and sometimes even job losses will impact our long-term retirement goals.

There's no easy way to put this: This is the decade when you start to run out of time to fix your mistakes. This is when small mistakes are no longer small. Hear me when I tell you, though, that that doesn't mean your mistakes are insurmountable. I'm just saying they are a little more formidable to overcome than they were when you were twenty or thirty years old. I always tell people that if we put retirement considerations on a medical injury scale, we would move from stable (in our twenties) to serious (in our thirties) to critical (in our forties). That's just another way of saying that your forties are really time to get after it.

This is also the time of life when people forget their dreams because of regret. I talk to so many people in their forties who have lost their motivation and have gotten off track. Why? Because this is when all of the financial and emotional pressures of life seem to converge: with your kids, college planning and saving, lifestyle expenses, caring for aging parents, and so on. And if you have made some mistakes financially, this can be a crushing time because each area of life seems to have certain unavoidable demands attached to it. But it is not hopeless. In fact, it is never too late to get started. If this is how your life feels right now, take all of that pressure and use it as the strongest motivation you have ever had to turn your financial life around. Quit looking out that rearview mirror and get moving in the right direction.

Keep Increasing Your Contributions

As your pay increases in your forties, you should definitely focus on bumping up your retirement investing. If you've been investing all along at this point, let me show you some of the numbers again: We started out saying that investing $100 per month starting at age twenty-five could grow to more than a half million dollars by the age of sixty-five. Then, if you bumped that up to $200 per month at age thirty-five, your final figure could grow to more than $800,000.

If, starting at age forty-five, you could bump that up another $100 and invested a total of $300 a month for the next twenty years, you'd likely top $880,000 by age sixty-five! That's not bad! However, you're starting to see the diminishing impact of compound interest at this point too. Adding an extra $100 a month doesn't have as much of a bang on your retirement total as it did in your thirties, does it? That's why starting early is so important!

Starting Late in the Game

If you are in your forties and just now getting started, let's continue looking forward for a minute instead of worrying about what you haven't done yet. If you waited until the age of forty-five to start investing for retirement and you invested $300 a month for twenty years, you would probably end up with a little over $250,000 by age sixty-five. That's *something*, but we need to do a little better than that. Hey, we still have twenty years to go, right?

We've been playing around with $100, $200, and $300 in our examples, but that's mainly because the math is easy. If you're doing this stuff for real, you're investing 15 percent of your income into retirement. Just for fun, let's say you have a household income of $56,000, which means your 15 percent monthly contribution would be $700. Let's run the numbers on that and see where you'd land in retirement.

If you invested $700 per month for twenty years with a 10 percent rate of return, you would land at around $533,930. And if you were able to work and keep contributing until age seventy, you would end up with $916,311.

If you have a higher income or got *really* aggressive and invested $1,000 a month at a 10 percent rate of return from age forty-five to sixty-five, it would hit $762,757. And again, if you kept working and saving until you were seventy years old, it would grow to $1,309,015. Boom! You're a millionaire, baby!

Okay, that's a whole lot of math. I can geek out on math all day long, but I've tried to avoid it too much up to now. Here's the point of running all these numbers for you at this stage. A lot of people in their forties have nothing in their retirement accounts.

Remember the story of James and Judy from Chapter One? They had lived a lush lifestyle, but they got to age sixty-five with nothing in retirement. What would have happened if they had changed their ways at forty-five instead of sixty-five? They still could have become millionaires! If you're sitting there in your forties, I want you to hear that there is still a lot of hope to be found in the R:IQ tool, an investment calculator, and a good talk with a financial advisor. The math can still work for you, but it all depends on what we talked about in the last chapter: your behavior. If you change your behaviors today, you can still have an awesome retirement dream!

Guarding Your Behaviors

Speaking of behaviors, one of the most common pitfalls I have noticed for people in their forties relates to attitude. I believe these are the years where you are most tempted to fall into what I call the "I deserve" trap. You see, in your forties, you start to look back and feel like you need to be rewarded for all your hard work. You can lose sight of the plan and fall into stupid by buying a new car . . . or boat . . . or house. You might've behaved like this a little bit in your twenties, but that new toy you "deserved" back then might have just been a new cell phone or a new computer. But by the time you hit your forties, the price tag on those toys has gone up quite a bit.

You can easily convince yourself that you "deserve" the new sailboat or the new house on the lake just because you are approaching midlife. The counseling-psychology types call this kind of "I deserve" decision-making a "midlife crisis," but I just call it stupid. You aren't just borrowing from the bank when you make these poor decisions; you are borrowing from your dream. You are living *for* the day instead of living *in* the day. The next time you are having one of those "I deserve" moments, remember that you are only one choice away from knocking your great retirement down to a not-so-great retirement.

And so, what should you do in your forties if you haven't yet started investing toward retirement? You have to begin now. You need to meet with your financial advisor and talk about how best to maximize your earning potential for retirement based on your own circumstances and your income. If you are not yet out of debt, then you need to work to pay off those creditors and start using the money from those monthly payments to fund your retirement. It is never too late to right the ship!

Retirement Planning in Your Fifties
(Seventh and Eighth Innings)

We've been talking a lot about baseball but, again, I played football. I remember playing in a really big high school football game against one of our rival schools. It was halftime, and we were losing to Montgomery High School 7–0. I can recall every detail about that game: the faces of the guys, the color of the paint in our locker room, the other team's uniforms, many of the plays, and even the weather that night on the field. Our coach was chewing us out in the locker room, trying to get everyone fired up. Now, I played both offense and defense in high school, and I had been playing hard in that first half. But Coach looked at me and said, "Hogan, you are running the football like a two-hundred-twenty-pound oaf!" He was trying to find a way to rally the team, but what he really did was make me mad. So I got up from my chair and walked up to him in front of the entire team. I looked him in the eye, pointed my finger at him, and, loud enough for the whole locker room to hear me, said, "I want you to give me the football! And I want you to keep giving me the football! And we are going to go out there and win this game!"

On the first play of that second half, I looked at the offensive linemen in the huddle and told them, "We are just better than this, fellas!" You know what happened in that exchange? Coach knew what he was doing: he lit a fire under all of us. As a result, we went back out on the field and pushed the other team around for the next two quarters of the game. And Coach kept calling plays to give me the ball. We won the game 21–7.

In his brilliance, our coach gave us exactly what we needed: a kick in the pants to get us emotionally involved in the game we were playing. Did I get mad at the coach? Heck yeah, I did! But he challenged me to play harder. He motivated me to do something. Sometimes we just need a proverbial slap in the face to get our wheels turning and really get us motivated.

Get Mad, but Get It Done

If you're in your fifties and you haven't yet done much to plan for retirement, I'm sorry, but you need a little of my old coach's motivation. At this point, shame and regret are done; there's no time for that. The past is in the past; you can't change it. Now's not the time for regret. Now is the time to get completely, passionately ticked off at your situation! No, you're not yelling at *yourself*; you're yelling at your empty retirement accounts. That's just not going to cut it! You're only ten to twenty years from retirement. It's time to get off the bench and put yourself in the game of your retirement planning.

As your coach, the reason I am using this kind of tone is because I can't afford *not* to. If you are sitting there in your fifties, I need you to hear me loud and clear: if you keep doing stupid things with your money, you will end up broke in retirement. I have already told you what that looks like, and I'm telling you again that it is not okay!

That "Oh!" Moment

When we talk about your fifties, we are looking at the perspective years. This is when the reality of a looming retirement begins to sink in for most people. You can't afford to stay in ostrich mode in your fifties, because the countdown clock has started; you can hear and see it ticking away, and it is a little scary. This is usually when folks have one of those "Oh!" moments that we talked about back in Chapter Two.

Remember, there are three "Oh!" responses. One is, "Oh, yeah! We are on track!" That means everything looks good and you are sticking to the plan. If you began investing early, your fifties are typically the decade when your investments reach their first million-dollar mark. And if they reach the million-dollar mark early in your fifties, well, that means you can potentially reach the two-million-dollar mark or more before you hit your sixties! The thing you need to understand with investing and compound interest is that it takes a while to get to the first million, but once you are there, the second million comes along a lot quicker. How incredible is that to think about?

Another "Oh!" response is, "Oh, boy! We still have some work to do!" You've probably done *some* investing, but your projected figures are not where you want them to be. The encouraging part is that you can still do some things to adjust your investments in a positive way. This is a perfect time to sit down with an expert and take a long, hard look at what you can do to improve your retirement options.

Finally, there is one last "Oh!" response, and this is where far too many people in their fifties fall. This group looks up and says, "Oh, crap! We're in serious trouble!" This group has little to nothing saved for retirement. It is the group of folks who really begins to panic. Even at this stage, though, it is not too late! Even the folks who hit their fifties and find themselves in "Oh, crap!" mode can still begin to invest and make some choices that can have a surprisingly positive impact on their retirements.

The Seventh-Inning Stretch

If we were playing on that great retirement baseball field, we would probably find ourselves in the seventh and eighth innings at this point. The outcome of the game is starting to become a little clearer. You are thinking in lucid terms about what the next play should be. If you are way ahead in the game, then maybe you should make some changes. You might get a little more conservative in your play-calling because you want to protect that lead. Or you might adjust your game plan a little bit to put some more pressure on and close out the win. If you are behind in the game, you are probably faced with making some big changes.

Of course, a lot of people get discouraged at this point and some even concede defeat. But listen: it is never too late to rally! It is never too late to make some changes and at least be competitive at the end of the game. Maybe you roll through a couple of relief pitchers, maybe you go to your bench to shake up the batting order, maybe you give a fiery speech in that dugout—but if you are behind, I want to see you dig your cleats in and try to make it a game!

Keep Up the Momentum

If you began investing back in your twenties, you are probably in pretty good shape at this point. But don't let up; you have to keep stoking that fire. If you started at age twenty-five with $100 per month, then bumped that up to $200 per month in your thirties, and then again in your forties to $300 per month, you would be on track to see your investments grow to around $880,000!

Now, in your fifties, if you added another $100 to your monthly contributions, you'd be investing $400 per month for the remaining ten to fifteen years. At that rate, your investments could grow to just over $900,000 at ten years and almost $1.5 million at fifteen years.

Like I said before, if this is all you're doing, you aren't doing enough. Don't get so caught up in the $100/month example that you lose sight of the big picture. The goal should be to invest 15 percent of your income *until you pay off the mortgage.* Once you are 100 percent debt-free including the house, which often happens in the fifties decade, I want you to throw as much money as you can into retirement. Go wild! Don't just walk across the retirement finish line; run like you want to break the tape!

Starting from Nothing at Fifty

If you haven't done much investing, there are still some things you can do to make headway. Let's say you have only done a little bit of work and you have $50,000 sitting in a retirement account. You still have anywhere from ten to twenty years to add to your investment and allow it to grow. If you start investing $500 a month and earned a 10 percent rate of return, just beginning right now in your fifties, you could see your investments grow to $234,874 in ten years' time, $418,560 in fifteen years' time, and $714,390 in just twenty years!

Granted, that doesn't get you to the $1 million mark, but it certainly puts you in a better position than you're in now sitting there with just $50,000 in the bank. And let's say you really buckled down and started putting $700 a month toward retirement. That could look like this: $276,948 in ten years, $502,440 in fifteen years, and $865,595 in twenty years! Remember, the more you add to your investments, the more you will potentially earn over time. And you know what I am going to say here: it is never too late!

Keep Your Guard Up

Like I've said before, it is so important that you sit down with an investment professional to get advice. They can help you speed up the process a little, but keep in mind that you should never take shortcuts or cut corners anywhere. I know it can be tempting in your fifties when you feel like you are behind. Make sure you are diversified and allowing compound interest to work for you. Remember, we want to run away from those phrases that we talked about in the last chapter and be wary of people who use terms such as *timing the market, day trading, hedging your bet*, and *investment opportunity*!

Be Realistic About Your Dream

I need to be clear here, even though you may not like what I'm going to say: if you are just now beginning to save and invest, you are going to have to *adjust your expectations* for retirement. First of all, you aren't going to retire early. As long as you're physically able to work, you're going to have to a while longer. Just get your mind around that now, and make sure that your retirement age isn't something you are unwilling to adjust. Also remember that delaying your retirement, especially your Social Security benefits, until age seventy can have a significant financial impact on your retirement lifestyle.

If you are just starting out in your fifties, you are also going to have to set some boundaries with your kids and possibly your parents. You are going to have no choice but to say no to some things. You are by no means canceling your trip toward retirement; you are just making some adjustments to the direction and destination.

If you haven't changed your priorities yet, your priorities will change you. The principles that you need to follow don't change but, as I said earlier, your urgency needs to drastically change. You need to understand that each little delay can make things worse.

Even a six-month delay could cost you a fortune. Working on your retirement should become your new hobby—right now, this very minute. The key is that you shouldn't give up. Remember that your retirement is not an age; it's a financial number. Stop thinking about how old you are and start thinking about how much money you are going to need for your dream to become a reality. Now, are your choices going to be mind-blowingly awesome? Maybe not, but the thing to get excited about is that you do still have choices.

Find Money You Already Have

If you're behind where you want to be, it's time to get creative and begin to look for money that you already have. For example, do you have a house you could sell? Could you downsize or rent and invest the equity from the sale of your home?

I talked with a lady in her fifties at an event recently, and she asked what she could do to accelerate paying off her school debts. She had gone back to graduate school in her forties and was still carrying that around in her fifties. She was doing a great job paying off that debt, but her retirement was looming. As we were talking, she explained that she had $250,000 in equity in her current house. This was the home where her kids had grown up, so she hadn't even considered letting it go. But I explained that if she sold the house and downsized, she could pay off the school loans and still have $150,000 to invest. I'm not lying to you when I say that she looked at me like I had just invented fire. She never would have thought of that, but getting a pro's outside perspective changed her entire retirement!

Your fifties are when you need to take a look around and figure out what can be sold. At this stage, if you are getting an inheritance from your parents (just remember not to count on one), you can plug that into the retirement equation. Will you be one of the last people on earth to get some kind of pension income in retirement? How much will Social Security add to your income? This is the time when you set everything out on the table and take inventory of what you have, what you need, and what you can do without to help you get to a livable retirement situation. Even if you're starting from scratch, there are still options for you to pull this thing off!

Retirement Planning in Your Sixties and Beyond (Ninth Inning)

Your sixties can go in two directions: They can be considered your pride years or your paddle years, depending on the choices you have made throughout your life. Either you will be able to embrace the want-tos, have some pride about what you have accomplished, and be able to enjoy the legacy you have built for your family, or it will mean that you have to keep your head down and continue paddling on through the have-tos of life. But this is the decade in which, no matter what you have done, you are now face-to-face with the realities of retirement.

Approaching the End of the Game

In our baseball analogy, your sixties would be the ninth inning. Time is definitely running out. If you are far ahead in the game, then you can relax a bit and begin to enjoy the victory. Have you ever watched a sports team near the end of a really big game when they have a huge lead and the victory is certain? They begin to relax and smile and celebrate and hug in the dugout or on the sideline. The strain of competition is fading, and they start to really enjoy the moment. I would love to see you there.

If you have been working at this retirement dream for a while and began investing in your twenties as I recommend, you are likely looking at $1 million or more in your retirement accounts. That's great! Just keep in mind that you can enjoy your success without getting lazy. Talk with your investment professional to adjust your investments so that your wealth is protected and continues to grow.

If you have no retirement savings, retirement now simply means you do the best that you can. I understand that, at this point, you must be anxious about your future. Maybe you're beating yourself up for not taking action sooner. Don't. None of that matters now. All the time you've got is all the time you've got, remember? Keep looking ahead to where you're going, and let where you've been fade off into the background.

It's Still Not Too Late

What action should you take if you're in your sixties with no savings? I would give you the same advice as if you were in your fifties: you need to make some major adjustments to your expectations. Your retirement reality probably won't match your retirement dream, but there are still things you can and should keep doing to move forward into an enjoyable retirement—and avoid the Burden and Nightmare retirement options we discussed earlier.

Even in your sixties, with some careful planning and disciplined budgeting, you can still build up some type of retirement fund. So here is what you need to focus on: You have to keep working as long as you are healthy. You should max out your 401(k) contributions and get company matching funds if you can. You should take advantage of "catch-up savings" provisions, which allow you to contribute more in your fifties and sixties if you haven't been saving enough before then. And, if you and your spouse max out all of your retirement savings options from age sixty to seventy, you could actually still end up with a sizable retirement account, in some cases up to $250,000.

But, remember, you still have to take care of the basics. The Baby Steps still matter, even if you have gray hair or no hair. Paying off your debt as soon as you possibly can is an absolute must. You should definitely consider selling your house and downsizing to something much smaller that you can pay cash for (or rent) and use the rest of the equity for investments. You should definitely delay taking Social Security until age seventy to get the most money possible (see Chapter Six). Also, it is important that you sign up for Medicare benefits at age sixty-five to help with your medical costs.

A Legacy to Be Proud Of

This is the point when you should also be focusing diligently on your legacy, knowing that a very small amount of your legacy is actually related to money. Your greatest gift during this season will be your time. Sit down and tell your family your stories. Let them record you on video. Giving your time should be a priority whether you have prepared all of your life for retirement or are living out a difficult retirement situation. Your greatest gift to your family will be your presence.

My last bit of wisdom for someone in their sixties and beyond would be this: Whatever you do, no matter what decisions you make, please don't leave your children a legacy of debt and trouble. If you've made a mess, then do your best to clean it up. Don't compound your children's grief at your eventual passing by leaving them a financial web to untangle.

A WORD ON COACHING

Throughout this chapter, we've focused on specific things to do in each decade of your adult life. However, I have to tell you that I would sit down and coach a seventy-year-old in the same way that I would coach a forty-year-old. The wisdom of having a plan and sticking to it, of staying away from stupid, and of leaving behind the pretenses of being "fake rich" go way deeper for me than just financial teaching. We are talking about inspiration!

So, no matter your age, I want to leave you with a few questions: *What are your priorities? Who is important to you? What do you want to leave the ones you love? What do you want your legacy to be?* These questions capture the essence of what retiring inspired is all about.

CHAPTER NINE

WHO DO YOU TRUST?

Assembling Your Dream Team

I t was one of the first nice days of the new year. You know, one of those days when the winter finally breaks into some sunshine and warm temperatures. My wife was out shopping while I was home with the boys. I was sitting at the desk working when they came in all excited about the pretty day outside. They had been cooped up in the house most of the winter, and they wanted to get their bikes out of the garage and go ride for the first time in months.

Of course, they needed me to come down to the garage and help them get their "equipment." Now, by "equipment," they meant the kneepads, elbow pads, and helmets their mom had bought them—you know, all the stuff that is necessary for a kid to ride a bike these days. You see, I tend to have an old-school mindset, so my first thought was, *They already know how to ride their bikes.* And my second thought was, *I certainly didn't need body armor to ride a bike when I was a kid!*

I told the boys, "Look, guys. You're Hogan men. Just get out there and ride without all the gear this time. You'll be fine!" In all fairness, they were just going to be on the driveway in front of our house, so what could go wrong? They protested a little bit and asked what would happen if Mom found out. I cut them off mid-sentence and said, "Oh, you'll be fine. Get out there and have fun!" You probably know this isn't going to end well, right?

So they headed out the door to hop on their bikes for the first ride of the new year. Then, about three and a half seconds later, my boys came busting through the garage door screaming and crying like trauma victims. My youngest son had a skinned-up elbow, my middle son had a skinned-up knee, and the oldest had a huge knot on his head! Each kid was blaming the others for what happened. "He got in my way!" "We ran into each other, and I had to ditch my bike!" I could barely see straight through that dense fog of trauma and drama.

I got them all situated on the couches in the living room and ran to grab some bandages for the skinned knee and elbow and an ice pack for the bump on the head. It looked like I was running a MASH unit right there in my living room. While I was wrapping up the scraped knees and elbows, I suddenly had a terrifying thought: *The kids weren't wearing their knee and elbow pads.* That thought caused me to look over at my oldest, whose entire noggin was now being taken over by Mount Saint Head Wound. *Oh no,* I thought. *My wife's firstborn child wasn't wearing his helmet. And she's going to get home at any minute.* This wasn't going to be good.

That realization hadn't finished flashing through my head before the garage door opened and my beautiful bride came walking in with a couple of shopping bags. I met her at the door as fast as I could because I was trying to direct her toward the kitchen and away from the carnage in the living room. It didn't work. The boys heard their mom's voice, and they immediately began crying like overly dramatic extras in *Saving Private Ryan*.

My wife walked into the living room and saw the huge bump on her son's head. While she was waiting for an explanation, Head Wound looked up at me with this wide-eyed expression, trying to ask with his eyes, "What do I tell her?" He knew that Dad was about to get it from Mom. His brothers weren't as concerned. Just as I was about to explain, Skinned Knee and Busted Elbow started yelling from the other sofa, "Daddy said we didn't need to wear helmets! He said he is the man of the house and he knows better!" Betrayed!

The boys weren't the only ones who did some time on the sofa that day! But the truth is, I was only in trouble because I had everything available at the house to keep my kids safe, but I didn't take advantage of any of it. I didn't do the things I needed to do to protect my children. I let my guard down just for a second, and life came in and messed things up.

As we're talking about retirement, this story is a good reminder that one little accident can cause a world of trouble. In order to protect your retirement dream, you've got to take advantage of all the "equipment" designed to keep you safe. That equipment includes key insurances, tax and estate planning, and real estate decisions. And trust me, nobody is an expert at all of this. That's why this chapter is going to talk about building your "dream team" of experts, advisors, and professionals to walk with you through this retirement planning maze.

LEARNING TO PLAY BOTH SIDES

I have told you a little bit about my time playing on the football field. The thing that is unique about the game of football is that you have players who train and practice specifically to play on offense, and then you have players who focus specifically on mastering defense. Football coaches spend time working on schemes and game plans to address each skill set. You need the same mindset when it comes to your retirement. You have to work on both offense and defense if you are going to be successful.

A common mistake in retirement planning is that people sometimes focus primarily on the offensive: building wealth. Most people don't go around expecting bad things to happen, but we all know better. We have worked on your plan for retirement, but we aren't quite finished yet. You have stated your dream, you have visualized it in high definition, you have laid out the plan and the path toward that dream, and now you are working to make that dream a reality. But the next step is just as important: I want you to make sure you don't leave that dream unprotected! You've got to learn to play defense too.

What do I mean by that? Well, we are going to explore what it looks like to put on your helmet, kneepads, and elbow pads as you set off on this journey. And if there's one thing I've learned from years of financial coaching and encouraging folks to pursue their dreams, it's this: You cannot do this by yourself. If you are going to make a dream happen, you have to put together a dream team to help get you there!

Playing Offense

We've spent quite a bit of time discussing the "offensive game plan" of your retirement thus far. These are the four major strategies that you use specifically to *build* your wealth. Let's recap really quickly:

First, make sure that you have an *emergency fund* of three to six months' worth of expenses in place. And, as you near retirement, one school of thought is to actually boost up your emergency fund. If your age is an issue, or if you are for some reason uninsurable, you will definitely need to dramatically increase the size of your fund. In fact, if you are uninsurable, I would recommend that you set aside as much as one to two years' worth of expenses in an emergency fund.

Second, you absolutely must practice the discipline of *budgeting* in order to get to your dream! I don't care how much money you have (or don't have). You will never outgrow the need to budget. The day you stop budgeting is the day you start moving backward in your retirement.

Third, you should get out and *stay out of debt*. Treat debt like it is the plague! One of the keys to winning in retirement is staying allergic to debt before and during retirement.

Fourth (and we spent several chapters on this), you must *invest*. You need to make sure you get help from a professional investment advisor so that you can grow your wealth and stay on track. Keeping money in a cookie jar, stuffed in your mattress, or even in a basic savings account won't take you into retirement.

Playing Defense

We have spent most of our time in the book talking about offense, so I want to spend the rest of this chapter talking about defense. Remember, your retirement is totally up to you. It's your job not just to build wealth, but also to keep it safe! There are many ways to protect your dream, and a lot of that defense depends on assembling a team of pros to help you build *and protect* your dream retirement.

Let's go over some parts of the defensive strategy you'll need if you are going to make it to where you want to go. When I talk about defensive strategies for retirement, not all of them mean protecting your retirement *after* you arrive there; a lot of this information will help you defend your dream as you are working toward it.

First, *budgeting* is not only an offensive strategy; it is also defensive.

You have to continue your budget even *after* you arrive at retirement! Budgeting is a life skill and isn't something that you should ever get out of the habit of doing, even after you have arrived at that high-definition dream.

Second, you need to *stay vigilant about your wealth*. If you are not being vigilant in your defense, you can fall into some mistakes that can actually bankrupt you. So don't get lazy.

Third, like my boys and their bicycles, you need to *put on your safety gear*. There are some specific strategies that you can "put on" to safeguard your wealth, and we are going to spend some time talking about those in this chapter.

Putting on your safety gear means that you need:

- The proper *insurances* in place
- Wise *estate planning* practices
- Help handling your *taxes* properly
- Counsel in *managing your retirement accounts* the right way
- Insight on how to address *housing issues*
- Confidence in *picking a dream team* of professionals that can provide you with the direction you need to bring it all together

Remember, you can't do all of this by yourself! So let's jump into what is important for your defensive game plan.

INSURANCE: THE UNSUNG HERO OF YOUR RETIREMENT

Insurance is a critical piece of your financial plan. You cannot neglect this area of planning because, if you do, someone or something could easily steal or destroy your dream. Believe me, no one really likes to pay insurance premiums. You may feel like you are just throwing your money away when you pay those premiums. You probably think of all the other things you could do with that money. But I also believe that you really don't want to face the possibility of something bad happening to you!

Believe it or not, I've talked with plenty of coaching clients who honestly believed that *not* talking about insurance would somehow protect them from getting sick or hurt. It's like they believed that just thinking about the possibility of an early death would cause a piano to fall from the sky and take them out!

That is just ostrich-mode thinking, just living life with your head in the sand. Here's a reality check: Bad stuff is going to happen to you. You're going to get sick. You may have a car accident. A guest visiting your home may fall and get hurt. You might get sued. I am not being pessimistic either. This is just life. Ignoring the possibility doesn't keep it from happening; it just keeps you from being prepared if—or *when*—life steps up and punches you in the face. Insurance is what protects your investments in the event of life happening.

Insurance has one and only one job: to transfer risk away from you and onto the insurance company. See how that little word *risk* keeps popping up throughout this retirement discussion? That's because mismanaging risk in all its forms can wreck your finances. If you are not covered properly, an accident or a lawsuit could plunge you into serious debt or even bankruptcy. And the simple truth is that if someone else (the insurance company) assumes that risk for you, then you get to keep your wealth and retirement savings.

Insurance: The Good and the Garbage

There is a wide array of different types of insurance available today. Some are good—*extremely good*. In fact, some are absolutely essential to your long-term success and protection. We'll cover those in detail. But the truth is, there's also a lot of garbage on the market today. These are terrible, fairly useless insurance products that you don't need and that are a waste of money. Let's start there.

Under no circumstances do I want you to waste your time with these types of insurance policies:

- Credit Life or Credit Disability
- Cancer or Hospital Indemnity
- Accidental Death
- Prepaid Burial
- Mortgage Life Insurance

All of those are designed to play on your emotions. *What if I get cancer?* Good health insurance covers cancer. *What if I die before we pay off the house?* Your spouse can use your term life insurance money to pay off the house. *What if I die unexpectedly in an accident?* Again, term life insurance will leave your survivors with money whether you die in an accident or from an illness. Dying in a plane crash would be tragic, but it wouldn't make you double dead! You've got to get past emotions and use some wisdom in your insurance decisions.

And, as a general rule, you should stay away from all the different types of insurance policies that offer what I call "fancy options." Your insurance should be like your investments—fairly straightforward and easy to understand (assuming your insurance agent has the heart of a teacher).

So if those are bad, how do you know which ones are good? Here are the seven types of coverage I recommend everyone to have:

- Homeowners or Renters
- Automobile

- Health
- Term Life
- Disability
- Long-Term Care
- Identity Theft Protection

But even with the information I'll share below, you still need to get some quality help. That's why you need an insurance specialist on your dream team—someone you trust who can sit down with you and explain these insurances to you in a way that you understand. I also recommend you use an independent insurance agent or broker who can shop multiple companies to come up with the best policy for you.

Homeowners, Renters, and Auto Insurance

Most people don't forget to carry adequate homeowners insurance. In fact, it's required as part of most mortgages. What they do forget, though, is to perform routine checks to make sure their coverage keeps up with their home's increasing value. Always make sure you have enough coverage to replace your home and its contents in the case of disaster.

Now, one type of insurance that a lot of people don't think of is renters insurance. If you are renting, whether it's a house or an apartment, you must have renters insurance, sometimes called contents insurance. Why? Because your landlord's policy will not cover your stuff if something happens to the property. That's not a cheapskate thing either. The homeowner or building owner doesn't have the legal obligation to protect your belongings. That's *your* job. So if you're renting a house and it burns down, renters insurance is the only thing that replaces all your stuff.

And, of course, you need some auto insurance if you own a car. Most states require this anyway, but the minimum coverage they require is usually way too low. However, if you have a fully funded emergency fund, you can save money on your premiums by going with a higher deductible. Also, you can usually get a good discount if you keep your home and auto insurance with the same insurance company. And don't be afraid to shop around for the best deal on quality coverage. These are all things you want to talk to your insurance professional about because getting in an accident with insufficient coverage can wreck your retirement dream.

You should also make sure that you have a sufficient amount of liability coverage on each of these policies. Liability coverage will protect you from lawsuits and loss resulting from injuries that you're legally responsible for (car accident, someone falling in your home, etc.).

Umbrella policies are also a great idea once you begin to build some wealth. An umbrella policy simply provides an extra layer of protection in the event of a lawsuit. You can think of it as a bonus pack on top of your liability coverage that steps in in extreme cases, like if you're sued for $1 million! That much umbrella liability is not that expensive, and it's the best way to protect your assets once you build some wealth.

And don't forget to review all of your policies, coverages, and rates annually to make sure you have enough coverage. And keep in mind that the minimum coverage required by the state is usually not enough.

Health Insurance

If you haven't been paying attention to the news for the past few years, let me give you the basic state of affairs in the world of health insurance: it is ridiculously complicated, it is terribly expensive, and it is an absolute necessity! I need you to go out right now and get it if you don't have it. Medical bills are consistently one of the leading causes of bankruptcy. You should first consult with your human resources department if you work for a company, or talk to a health insurance professional if you provide your own insurance, in order to evaluate all of your available options.

You only have to turn on the news for one evening to know that health care laws change all the time, and that's not going to slow down in the foreseeable future. It would do you no good for me to get too detailed or specific on this topic because the laws may be different by the time you finish reading this sentence. That is exactly why you need a player on your dream team who specializes in health care insurance, so you can make sure you have the correct coverage you need for you and your family.

Since we are talking about retirement, you may be wondering about Medicare. Great question! Medicare is a government program for seniors that provides some insurance to help cover medical and health-related services. Medicare is basically a form of social welfare (or social protection). Talk to a professional advisor who can help you with the information related to Medicare. Like anything that is run by government agencies, Medicare involves a lot of choices that might seem complicated, and it also involves a lot of deadlines that might not be completely clear to you. You need to make sure you have a solid understanding of the program so that you can make the best decision available to you when the time comes.

Most people will sign up for Medicare at age sixty-five. If you are still working after the age of sixty-five and haven't signed up, you need to make sure that you sign up within eight months of when you stop working. Remember though—and I say this because I have coached many people who were confused about this—Medicare is not the same as Social Security, and it is not free. In fact, it still involves premiums for coverage and requires co-pays for most of its services. You should also remember that Medicare does not provide any type of coverage for your dependents.

Life Insurance: A Warning

I want to tell you about my friend Steve Maness. He's one of the most remarkable people I will ever know. When I first met Steve, he and his wife, Sandy, were doing a lot of volunteer work, a passion he and I had in common. I was immediately drawn to Steve, his huge heart and passion for life, and his deep-seated drive to inspire and help others. His commitment to serving others was made more impressive by the fact that, at the time I met him, he was battling an aggressive form of terminal brain cancer.

We became fast friends, and I was able to walk him and his beautiful wife through the process of preparing for death. I learned so many lessons from Steve and Sandy about how to handle tragedy with grace, love, and dignity, but I also learned from these remarkable people that life happens no matter who you are. Tragedy can strike no matter your age, religion, race, socioeconomic status, or charitable spirit. Though they were wonderful people, tragedy had come to the Maness family.

I began my relationship with Steve as kind of a coach, giving him advice on how to set things in order, and he gracefully invited me in as a friend and allowed me to walk through this difficult time with him. I could write an entire book on the courage, faith, and inspiration I witnessed in Steve's life. But I think the thing that stands out most is how much he loved his family. You see, long before Steve was diagnosed, he had already put term life insurance in place—just in case. He knew, even as a young man, that Sandy depended on his income, and he loved her enough to make sure she would be taken care of if anything ever happened to him.

Something did happen to Steve. He got sick. He died. And three days after his passing, with tears still streaming down Sandy's face, she gave birth to their first—and only—child.

Over the next few months, I worked to honor Steve and Sandy

by doing the best I could to help her cope with all the financial questions and challenges that she faced after his death. The good thing was that they had the time to prepare together. They made plans; he made sure she knew where the vital information was and whom to talk to. I was able to connect them with the insurance and investment professionals who could help Sandy get through that tough time of transition after his death. But all of that would have been so much harder if Steve hadn't already taken care of his life insurance. He refused to leave her broke *and* in mourning.

When you think about life insurance, I want you to think about my friend Steve. It is an absolute necessity, and leaving it out of your plan can be devastating not just to your family's retirement, but to their ability to survive after your passing. If you're prone to ostrich behavior, it's time to get your head out of the sand and love your family enough to get this done—today!

Life Insurance: What Kind and How Much?

Life insurance has one and only one job: to replace your income after your death. If you have people who are dependent on your income, then life insurance shouldn't even be a question. Get it.

I recommend only term life insurance; whole life or cash value plans are bad ideas. They may look good at first because they have a savings plan built in, but I always want you to keep your insurance and your investing separate. You'll make the best use of your money by paying for term life (more coverage for less money) and investing in the retirement plans we've already discussed.

Since life insurance is used to replace your income, I recommend getting twelve times your annual income in coverage. So, if you earn $50,000 a year, you'd get $600,000 in term life coverage. If you earn $100,000 a year, you should have $1.2 million in coverage. That way, if your survivors invested the insurance benefit and that investment earned 10 to 12 percent, the annual rate of return could actually replace your lost income without eating too much of the principal. And make sure that you have coverage for your spouse even if they are a stay-at-home mom or dad. If you have a spouse at home taking care of the kids and something happens to them, you'll need additional income to pay for child care.

Now, you might be reading this and thinking, *Chris, I am twenty-three and have no one else dependent on my income. Do I need life insurance?* The answer is no. Life insurance is for your family, for the people who are dependent on your ability to earn an income. If you do not have a family or dependents, then don't worry about it yet. But, you will need to make sure that you have a fully funded emergency fund to take care of your final expenses.

Or, if you're older or already a millionaire, or if you're worried about a term life policy expiring in twenty or thirty years, remember this: The need for life insurance is not permanent. If you and your spouse are in your sixties and have millions in your retirement accounts, you are what's called self-insured. If something happened to one of you, the other could probably make do with the millions you already have. Again, though, this is all stuff to cover in detail with your insurance professional.

Disability Insurance

I find that disability is the most commonly overlooked of all the insurances that you need. That doesn't make sense! Not only is disability insurance extremely important, but it's also one of the best deals in insurance.

Statistics are clear that you actually have a greater chance of being disabled than of dying during your working lifetime. What will your family do if the primary breadwinner gets hurt in their thirties and suddenly can't work anymore? Where will you get thirty-plus years' worth of income? That's where disability coverage comes in.

A disability will result in a loss of income. So you want to protect yourself and provide for your family by having disability insurance, which will provide a monthly income stream based on a percentage of your gross income for a period of time.

There are two types of disability insurance: short-term and long-term. As you can imagine, short-term disability insurance generally covers you for three to six months, although some policies have benefits that can last up to two years.[1] I'm personally not a big fan of short-term disability. If you have a fully funded emergency fund of three to six months of expenses, you should be able to handle any short-term problems.

Long-term disability insurance provides you with a longer term of coverage if you are too injured or sick to work, and I definitely recommend long-term disability coverage. These policies come with different features you'll want to explore, but keep in mind there is usually a six-month waiting period before benefits are paid. That's another reason you want a nice, big emergency fund!

If your company offers disability as part of their group plan, buy it. You won't find it any cheaper on the open market. If they don't, put this on the priority list for your next conversation with your insurance pro.

Long-Term Care Insurance
People are definitely living a lot longer these days than they used to, but a lot of those years can require a high level of personal care. That makes long-term care (LTC) insurance a necessity. It covers nursing homes, assisted living facilities, and in-home care. According to research quoted by Time.com, you can expect to spend around $212 per day for nursing home care.[2] That's $77,000 a year, and prices are only going up! Spending your last several years in a nursing home can completely destroy your retirement account. That's why LTC coverage is so important.

When you investigate this with your insurance professional, make sure to review what exactly the policy will cover, what it will not cover, and the limits of the policy before you decide to purchase it. Make sure that you shop around and allow your pro to help you find the best option for your particular situation.

Identity Theft Protection

Did you know that every two seconds in America, someone becomes the victim of identity theft?[3] It is a staggering statistic, and I am afraid that those numbers will only get worse over time. That's why it is more important than ever to make ID theft protection part of your insurance plan.

It is becoming increasingly difficult—probably impossible—to prevent ID theft entirely, so you need to be ready. You need protection that not only monitors your credit report (you could do that for free yourself), but also provides a counselor to clean up the mess involved with identity fraud. If you get hit, you could lose hundreds of hours of your life trying to straighten things out. That's a risk you can live without.

You need coverage that provides restoration services and a counselor who can work with you to help clean up the mess left behind when your identity is stolen.

ESTATE PLANNING: DOING THE DETAILS WHILE YOU STILL CAN

Like I said earlier, it is sometimes difficult for us to consider the bad things that can happen in life, but we still have to be prepared. While insurance is a huge part of protecting your wealth, it is not the only thing that you must do. Your wealth is your responsibility—before and after your death. Your grieving family members won't automatically know what you wanted them to do with your estate; they need you to tell them. The process of putting your wishes on paper and systems in place for handling your money after you're gone is called estate planning.

You Need a Will

A will basically establishes a plan for the distribution of your assets. Everyone over the age of eighteen *must* have a will. It's easy and inexpensive to put one in place, so there's really no excuse for not having a will. If you don't have one, get one right now. I'm serious!

Having a clear will in place can prevent problems among your heirs. It's your written declaration; it's your way of saying exactly who gets what and what goes where. It also makes sure the government doesn't step in and make those decisions for you. A good will leaves little room for arguments and petty disagreements among surviving spouses, children, grandkids, and everyone else who may pop up wanting a piece of your stuff. Protecting your wealth—and your family—from this mess is one of the last gifts you'll leave the people you love.

Make sure that you identify an executor of your estate, someone you trust, to oversee the terms of the will. And within the will, I also highly recommend that you establish a legal guardian for living dependents. Make sure to update your beneficiaries on plans such as life insurance, IRAs, and your 401(k)s. And, along with the will, I also recommend that you leave instructions for your own funeral, but never prepay burial expenses.

Laws and regulations concerning wills are specific to the state where you live, so if you move to another state, you'll need to tweak your will. In most states, you must have two witnesses sign the will with you and also have it notarized. And if you have your own business, you also want to make sure that you have instituted a plan for succession.

A Living Will

A living will is also known as a health care directive. Now, I understand that this is one of those worst-case scenario plans, but it is also essential to your estate plan. The living will is a document that sets out the medical care plan you desire in the event that you are seriously injured or are otherwise unable to communicate. This document provides direction for medical care if something happens that leaves you with life-threatening injuries. It also provides what is known as a "DNR," or "do not resuscitate," directive that clearly states your wishes regarding what measures should be taken to save or prolong your life.

Without a living will in place, these incredibly painful decisions will be in the hands of your family—who will already be suffering from the shock and fear of something happening to you. Again, if you love your family, don't put them in that situation. Make your own decisions on paper before the situation ever comes up.

The living will is usually coupled with a health care power of attorney, so you'll need to specify who you want to be in charge when or if you can't speak for yourself. You definitely need to work with an estate planning professional to set this up properly.

Power of Attorney

A durable power of attorney (POA) allows someone whom you identify and trust to direct your assets and investments. You need to identify who the person (or people) will be for your power of attorney. The person you select will have the ability to transact business on your behalf, open and close accounts, transfer funds, and so on. Legally speaking, this person will be able to act with your authority, so be careful whom you choose!

This is a critically important item to have in place as you get older. Back in my banking days, I got to know a young couple who were regular customers, and I chatted with them when they visited the bank to do business. One day, my friend came into the branch to let me know his mother had an accident and was in the hospital in serious condition. He wanted to know what needed to be done to make sure he could access his mother's account to keep her bills paid.

This is where we ran into a roadblock that my buddy wasn't expecting. No one, not even a child, can access someone else's bank accounts without prior permission from the account holder. You'd have to be a joint signer on the actual bank account or there would need to be a durable power of attorney already in effect. Neither of these things had been done! So, we had to begin a long, uphill battle in order to get him access to his mother's account. It was a lesson that I will never forget, and I always share it when I'm speaking on financial planning. So, please, if you have elderly parents, even if it's awkward, have a conversation about a durable power of attorney. It will save everyone plenty of heartache and valuable time and money in the long run.

Establishing a Trust

You can actually limit estate taxes by setting up trust accounts in the names of your beneficiaries. With a trust in place, your wealth would move into a trust at the time of your death, rather than moving directly to your heirs. At that time, a trustee (designated third party) of your choosing would oversee assets on behalf of your beneficiaries.

Trusts usually avoid probate and offer you several benefits. The chief benefit is that a trust allows *you* to control your wealth and dictate where you want it to go. It also lets you control your legacy by protecting your estate from an heir's creditors and from beneficiaries who aren't great at managing money and who would squander whatever you leave them. And, of course, it's a great way to ensure that any inheritance to younger children is managed well until they are capable of managing it themselves. Also, by keeping your money out of probate, a trust helps maintain some degree of privacy while also offering key tax protections.

A revocable trust, also known as a living trust, allows you to retain control of the assets while you are still alive. In a living trust situation, you can change your mind and revoke that trust if you need to for some reason. While a revocable trust avoids probate, it is usually still subject to estate taxes.

There is also an option called an irrevocable trust. This one is more complicated and definitely something you don't want to rush into without some serious thinking and good counsel. The thing about an irrevocable trust is that it transfers assets out of your estate and into a trust while you're still alive—and it cannot be altered once it is executed. In an irrevocable trust, the assets are removed from the estate and are no longer subject to estate taxes, which is why it might make sense for some people. However, this also creates some big hassles that you may not want to deal with. Be sure you know what you're getting into before you even think about this one.

Again, this is a place where you should definitely enlist the help of a professional, because there are a wide variety of different trusts, and you want to choose wisely.

TAX PLANNING: KEEPING THE GOVERNMENT OUT OF YOUR MONEY

There are two guarantees in life: death and taxes—and unfortunately, you must plan to deal with both of them. We already spent some time covering *tax-favored investments* in our chapter on investing, but we need to dig a little deeper into the tax minefield to make sure you get to keep more of your money.

Estate Tax

An *estate tax* is a tax on the value of a person's assets within their estate. It is mostly imposed on the assets that are left to someone's heirs after their death. However—and this is important—estate taxes are not imposed on the transfer of assets to a spouse. So don't worry about your future widow or widower getting hit with a huge estate tax bill. The bigger concern is to make sure your wealth is passed down to the next generation safely once you and your spouse are gone.

Estate taxes can be high, so careful planning in this area is an absolute necessity. Keep in mind that federal estate taxes allow for a certain amount to be passed on to heirs tax-free but, like everything with federal regulations and taxes, the rules change all the time. That means you *always* need to make sure you have the right professional guidance to help you.

Gift Tax

If you have a dream of writing your adult child a check one day to help them buy their first home, pay attention. Believe it or not, giving someone (including a child) a big cash gift can open them up to a huge tax bill. Welcome to the gift tax!

A *gift tax* is a tax on the transfer of assets (including money) to another individual, even a family member. A gift asset is considered anything that you give for which you do not expect something in return. However, there is some wiggle room before the taxes kick in. The federal gift tax exclusion amount tells you how much you can give without creating a tax burden. That exclusion amount changes often. As of 2015, you can give a gift up to $15,000 in a single calendar year to an individual without taxes being due.

There are some perfectly legal and moral ways to get around the gift tax. First, you can gift the cost of medical, dental, and tuition expenses without any tax penalty if you pay the provider directly.

Second, there is an exclusion that could allow you to pay five years' worth of exclusion amounts into a 529 college savings fund all at one time. In order to do this type of thing, a special gift tax return would need to be filed but, again, there would be no tax on that gift. Third, remember that the exclusion amount is *per individual.* Say, for example, that your adult son is married and you want to give the couple a $25,000 cash gift. If you write one $25,000 check, they'd be subject to the gift tax. However, if you wrote one $12,500 check to your son and another to your daughter-in-law, there would be no gift tax. In that case, you legally gave two separate $12,500 gifts, which would be covered by the gift tax exclusion.

There are many rules and regulations related to gifting assets to children, grandchildren, and others, and those rules change often. Having that tax professional on your dream team can help make sure your loving gifts go where you want, which is probably *not* to the government!

Charitable Giving

A *charitable gift* is a gift that is made to a nonprofit organization, charity, or private foundation. A note about charitable giving: I believe that if you are handling your financial life properly, you should always be actively giving. Charitable giving is a heart thing, and I believe that it is essential to bless others with the success you have in your own life.

A charitable gift is usually in the form of cash, but it can also be in the form of property, vehicles, appreciated securities, clothing, or other assets or services. This can be as simple as donating clothing and household items to Goodwill or the Salvation Army, and it can be as complicated as donating millions of dollars to build a new hospital!

As with everything else, the government has all kinds of special rules that apply, especially to the donations of certain types of property such as cars, inventory, and investments. However, charitable donations are tax-deductible as long as you give your gift properly. That's not always as simple as it should be, so this is one more thing to discuss with a tax pro.

Retirement Accounts

We have talked over and over again about the best way to protect your retirement accounts: leave them alone until you are ready to retire! Stay on that roller coaster. Now, that said, there are some things you can do to help protect your 401(k) from taxes until you start taking withdrawals at retirement.

First, do not cash out or bring home a company 401(k) when you leave the company. You should instead do a direct transfer to an IRA. Direct transfers from one tax-deferred retirement plan to another are not considered "distributions" and are not taxable as income or subject to penalties. You, of course, need to work with your investment professional to make sure this is done properly.

Second, never borrow against your 401(k). The 401(k) loan is pretty common today, but that doesn't make it smart. This short-sighted mistake can create a huge mess for you. I've seen it happen way too often with my clients. Here's the deal: if you borrow against your 401(k) and then leave the company before it's repaid, you're stuck with a crisis. And don't tell me you won't leave the company. You could find a dream job and move. You could get fired. You could die. Any of those things would trigger a big tax problem and put your money at risk.

So, if you leave your job with an outstanding 401(k) loan, you have ninety days to pay back the full amount. If you don't, the penalties and taxes become due, which could cost you up to 40 percent of the value of your loan. That means a $10,000 loan, if not repaid, could end up causing you to throw $4,000 out the window! This is a big mistake!

Your 401(k) is there for your retirement, not your home renovations. Unless you need the cash immediately to avoid either a foreclosure or a bankruptcy, leave that money alone and let it grow.

REAL ESTATE: THE INVESTMENT YOU CAN LIVE IN

The next order of business is to consider the best plan for your home. People don't always understand that their home isn't simply their biggest purchase; it's often their greatest investment. But unlike a 401(k), it's an investment you get to live in!

Mortgage Basics

The first ground rule when it comes to mortgages is to hate debt. I'm serious. Mama Hogan always said, "Chris, we don't hate." Well, that's true—except when it comes to debt. I hate debt, and you can tell my mom I said so.

However, I won't yell at you for getting a mortgage as long as it's a reasonable mortgage that follows a few simple guidelines. No matter what, I want you to make sure that you take on a monthly payment that is no more than 25 percent of your take-home pay on a fifteen-year fixed-rate loan with at least 10 percent down. When the dust settles after closing, you should also make sure that you still have a fully funded emergency fund. That's not furniture money! And seriously, none of this thirty-year mortgage nonsense. That's a waste of tens of thousands of dollars in interest over the life of the loan, and it keeps you in debt twice as long by enabling you to buy a house you can't afford.

Why only a fifteen-year mortgage? Well, let's pause and just look at the numbers by comparing a fifteen-year to a thirty-year mortgage. If we have a $225,000 mortgage on a 6 percent loan, the fifteen-year loan payment would be $1,899 per month. The thirty-year mortgage payment would be $1,349 a month. So you'd save $550 a month on your mortgage payment with a thirty-year. That's why people do them. However, after just ten years, the fifteen-year loan has a balance of $98,210, while the thirty-year loan has a balance of $188,292! During those ten years, you would have paid almost $162,000 on the thirty-year mortgage but would have only knocked $36,708 off the loan! That's more than $125,000 that you completely flushed down the toilet over ten years. That's insane!

The second ground rule when it comes to mortgages is to make sure it's paid off before you retire. A paid-for house when you retire is a total game changer. You have basically freed up more money for investing when you have a paid-off mortgage. And you need way less money per month for living expenses if you have no mortgage payment. This, of course, means that you don't need as much from your retirement investments, so you can leave more money in the retirement accounts to keep them growing. Besides, when my time on this earth is done, I'd rather toss my kids the house keys instead of my mortgage papers.

To Upgrade or to Downsize?
The other question I often hear concerning housing in retirement is whether or not you should upgrade or downsize your home. This is actually a really smart question to ask as your income and lifestyle change. Does your retirement house need to be as big as the one that once housed your whole family? What is the cost to you in order to maintain that extra space?

I have a friend whose father-in-law downsized to a small house after retirement so that he and his wife would be free to travel without worrying about mortgage payments or keeping up space they didn't need. For fifty-one weeks a year, this is the perfect situation. But for one week during Christmas, all of his kids and grandkids come to stay at that house, and they really have to cram together to stay there. This exact situation is what keeps too many retirees in big homes they don't really need. But according to my friend, the grandkids love the experience. They sleep in sleeping bags in the living room with their cousins, watch cartoons and Christmas movies, bake cookies, and have a fantastic time for those few days. The truth is that sometimes we worry more about space and accommodations than we do focusing on togetherness, right?

Now, I also know it can be tough emotionally to sell the house where you raised your kids. Those walls usually have a million memories, and the thought of leaving them may break your heart (or your adult children's hearts). This is something you really need to consider. However, I'd never let my grown children dictate my living situation. If you're ready to downsize but plan on keeping a big house simply because it's what your grown-and-gone kids want you to do, it may be time to put a sign in the yard!

Passing On Your Home

Another interesting concern I deal with from time to time is people wanting to deed their house to their heirs while they are still alive. This is almost always a terrible idea. When you deed property to your children while you are alive, you are basically giving them a gift. If you deed your home to you children, their tax basis is then determined by what *you* paid for that home. Then, if they sell the house, they have to pay taxes on the new value difference.

Huh? Okay, look at it like this. Say you paid $50,000 for your home thirty years ago. Thinking it's a good idea, you decide to deed your house to your kids while you're still living. Then, when you die, they sell the house for $250,000. Those are perfectly reasonable numbers when you consider the thirty years of appreciation on the house. What happens is this: your kids have to pay taxes on thirty years' worth of appreciation, which comes to $200,000! If you had just left it to them in your will and they turned around and sold it, the taxes would have been based on the home's value on the day they took possession. This one decision can save your children tens of thousands of dollars in unnecessary taxes.

If you intend to pass on your home, the best idea is to create a will that leaves the property to your children in a simple trust to help them avoid probate and some of the taxes. This is generally complicated, and I recommend that you consult a professional estate planner to help you with this to make sure you are doing it correctly.

The Reverse Mortgage Trap

Some of the worst scenarios I hear about when I am talking to folks who are nearing retirement are related to the new fad of reverse mortgages. A reverse mortgage is simply another debt, and it is one of the most expensive ways to get money. A reverse mortgage is a home loan that provides payment based on the equity that you have in your home. In a regular mortgage, you make regular payments to the lender. In a reverse mortgage, you receive money from a lender, and you don't have to pay it back as long as you still live in the house. You are not required to make a payment on the loan at all. Then, the loan is paid back from your estate at your death. Sounds nice and easy, right? Wrong.

There are too many disastrous consequences and hidden penalties in the fine print of these agreements to count, but I'll quickly hit a few. First of all, this choice decreases anything that you were planning to leave to your heirs. Second, you also must continue to pay property taxes, homeowners insurance, and upkeep on the home. And third, if for some reason you cannot pay the property taxes, then you can actually end up in default on the loan and the lender gets to take your house. How would you like to end up suddenly homeless in retirement? No thanks!

You know that retirees are the targets for this garbage arrangement by who is hired to do the television commercials. You don't see the current celebrities on those ads, do you? Nope, but you will see Pat Boone, Robert Wagner, Alex Trebek, and Henry Winkler peddling for the reverse mortgage industry. Can you guess why that is? It's because those are the trustworthy celebrities that today's retirees remember from their favorite shows a few decades ago.

And the ads almost always use language that is meant to get older parents fired up. One commercial claims, "You don't even need your kids' permission to apply!" That kind of line is aimed at older folks who are dealing with losing some of their own autonomy, and, of course, they react by getting a little mad. "Darn right I don't need my kids' permission! I'm a grown man, and I'll do what I want! Now what is that number?" I'm not joking about this. I believe those ads are designed to get an emotional response so that people become more willing to make stupid decisions.

Plus, the rules related to reverse mortgages are so complicated that homeowners must go through some counseling before they are able to get any money with some of the loans. The Consumer Financial Protection Bureau describes reverse mortgages as "complex" and "hard to understand." They also warn about the risk of fraud and scams with this type of mortgage lending.[4] Too many seniors are still taking out reverse mortgages without understanding all of the ramifications simply because former senator and current pitchman Fred Thompson said it was a good idea. You see, the ads often say that there is no catch. That's not exactly true.

Here's the catch: If health issues cause you to move out of your home and into an assisted living facility or nursing home, the mortgage immediately becomes due. Unless you pay up, you lose the home. And if you, as the homeowner, die, then your heirs have to pay off the loan or surrender the house to the lender. This debt can oftentimes be more than the house is even worth.

If all of these things don't convince you, how about this: I met a really nice lady from Chicago who was in her eighties and had taken out a reverse mortgage on her family home years ago. She was distraught and in a horrible financial situation. Why? Because she had actually outlived the terms of that reverse mortgage! So there she was in her eighties, and the lender came to collect what was *theirs*—her house!

But wait; it gets worse. She didn't really understand the fine print of the agreement she had signed years earlier. Not only did she lose her home, but she also owed the reverse mortgage company $21,000 in fees that were a part of the contract. She was now in debt with no assets and no home, and she had to move into a tiny apartment with her sister and try to figure out a way to earn income to pay back that new debt. It was a terrible situation and one of the reasons I get so upset at this kind of predatory lending.

Here's the bottom line: If you have a paid-for home but need cash that badly, then just sell the house and either rent or dramatically downsize. Then work with your investment professional to find a way to invest the equity you have and use it to manage your retirement.

ASSEMBLING YOUR DREAM TEAM

Throughout this chapter, I've talked about building your dream team of advisors to help you navigate through the legal, tax, estate planning, insurance, and real estate issues that surround the subject of retirement. Now let me tell you what the concept of a dream team means to me.

In 1988, our country sent a group of the best college basketball players to compete in the Olympics. However, there was a problem with this group of young men. It's not that they didn't compete hard; it's that, as good as they were, they were still amateurs. The greatest professional basketball players from around the world defeated these young guys. It was no contest. The US finished with a bronze medal in the game that they invented!

When the US reentered the Olympic basketball competition four years later, they played with a new strategy. The 1992 US Olympic basketball team was made up of the greatest *professional* players in the country. I'm talking about Larry Bird, Magic Johnson, Charles Barkley, Patrick Ewing, David Robinson, and, oh yeah, this other guy named Michael Jordan. We didn't send student-athletes as players this time; we sent the best players on the planet. Together, they quickly became known as the Dream Team, and that Olympic season became the stuff of legend.

Many people remember those days or have at least heard stories about it. What's often surprising, though, is the fact that these pros had to compete just to make it onto the Olympic team. The US coaches sent invitations to the greatest players in the National Basketball Association (NBA), and many of them were cut during tryouts. That wasn't because they weren't immensely talented; instead, they were left off the roster because the Hall of Fame basketball coaches involved in the process were more concerned with building a great *team* than they were in just assembling great *individual* players.

There was one player chosen for that team who made some news because he wasn't a professional. In fact, he wasn't nearly as talented as many of the players who didn't get invited. The college player of the year in 1992, a senior from Duke University by the name of Christian Laettner, was placed on the team. He made it not because of his talent but because he would fit perfectly into his role as twelfth man, or the reserve player. You see, being selected as a backup player was a role that many of the other NBA players would not have willingly accepted.

Team chemistry is important no matter what you are trying to accomplish. When it comes to retirement, I think that keeping in mind how these different professionals will fit with you, your situation, and your personality is as important as how talented they seem to be.

Choose Your Players Wisely

We have covered a lot of important information in this chapter about protecting your wealth. But the truth is, I can't tell you exactly what you should do in your specific situation because I don't *know* your specific situation. That is where your dream team comes in.

You need to assemble a team of people who can help guide you down these paths of protecting your wealth that I have introduced in this chapter. I recommend that you go out and find a specific advisor for each of the following areas that we have covered:

- Investments
- Insurance, including:
  - Homeowners or Renters
  - Automobile
  - Health
  - Term Life
  - Disability
  - Long-Term Care
  - Identity Theft Protection
- Estate Planning
- Taxes
- Real Estate

With these world-class, handpicked players in place, you'll be ready to bring home the gold!

CHAPTER TEN

YOU'RE THE CEO

Managing Your Family and Financial Business

W here does your retirement begin? That should be no mystery at this point: it all begins with one person—you! Why? Because we are talking about *your* budget, *your* plans, *your* goals, *your* effort, *your* sacrifices, *your* commitment, and, yes, even *your* boundaries. You, my friend, are the *catalyst,* and all of the tactical information I have provided throughout this book has been meant to inspire you and help you avoid the pitfalls that can set you back from the retirement of your dreams.

While your retirement begins and ends with you, we have also touched on the fact that you cannot do this alone. Living life well requires relationships. You are the catalyst but, without healthy relationships, you will never achieve your goals. If you do, those achievements certainly won't be as satisfying.

In my years as a financial coach, I've seen how relationships can often make or break someone's retirement. I have witnessed the impact of good relationships in retirement, and I have watched the hopelessness of dysfunctional relationships wreak havoc on high-definition dreams. What makes the difference? It all comes down to how you manage your relationships.

Here is a truth more far-reaching than anything else we have talked about in this book: your family and relationships are the most important investments in life, and if you do not manage those precious investments the right way, then all of your retirement planning will be pointless.

It's true that most of the things that will make your *retirement* a success will also make your *relationships* a success: patience, hard work, investing, and having a plan! Your relationships demand close attention if you are going to achieve your high-definition dreams. We need to spend some time focusing on how to manage those relationships the right way. If you are going to have the healthy relationships your dream requires, you must be intentional about investing in your loved ones, you have to communicate clearly with them, and you must also learn to set boundaries.

Nobody dreams about retiring rich and miserable. You want to be able to actually *enjoy* the fruit of all the hard work you're putting into your retirement dream. And if you really want to enjoy it, you have to make sure your relationships are maturing right along with your investments.

RELATIONSHIPS: THE GOOD, THE BAD, AND THE DYSFUNCTIONAL

As a financial coach, I have witnessed the impact of relationships on my clients' retirements over the years. I have seen the good, the bad, and the ugly. But I want to start by showing you what a healthy retirement can look like if you have handled your relationships in the right way by being intentional, communicating, and setting well-defined boundaries.

The Good Relationships

In the beginning of the book, I told you about the couple from Texas who had retired in their fifties and were meeting with me to figure out the best ways to give their money away to great causes. They had worked incredibly hard. Their visions, goals, and dreams were in sync. As I sat down to counsel them, they were both open and honest about their desires as well as the things causing them confusion. They were intentional about their communication with one another.

But, like all couples, they had different personalities. He liked to travel a lot and she was kind of a homebody who wanted to spend most of her time around the grandkids. Knowing they each had different goals, they had worked together to map out each quarter of the year and how and where they were going to spend their time and money. Some of it was going to be traveling, and some of it was focused on hanging around their home with family. It was amazing for me as a counselor to watch this husband and wife come together to be flexible and honor each other's expectations about retirement.

They had also communicated clearly with their kids about what they were going to do with their money and, as a result, the children were supportive of their decisions. They had also set clear boundaries with their own children, extended family, and the people around them. And, as I listened to them talk, I was impressed with the level of respect they had for each other and their shared passion to give generously in their community.

Looking back on that coaching session, I wonder if they realized how much more wisdom and insight they were giving me than I was giving them. But I sat back and watched them interact with one another and thought, *That is how you want to live your golden years.* If you're married, you want to spend the best years of your life working together with your spouse, being respectful of each other's dreams, and doing the things you always dreamed of doing. They were a wonderful model of what an inspired retirement could look like if we handle our finances and our relationships the right way.

And if you're not married or if, heaven forbid, one of you doesn't make it to retirement, you want to experience that same sense of joy and togetherness in your other relationships, whether it's with your adult kids, close friends, or other family members. You want your hard work and wealth to be a source of joy and opportunity! That's what good, quality, mature relationships add to your retirement dream.

The Bad and the Ugly of Relationships

I have also counseled folks on the other side of the retirement scenario. I've sat kneecap-to-kneecap with couples and families who seemed to be waging war with each other. I've talked with people nearing retirement who had not done their relationship work, and it left a tension in the air so thick that it was uncomfortable to sit in the same room with them. These relationships had been neglected, boundaries were never set, communication was ignored, and the result was the farthest thing from a high-definition dream. Even though many of these families had done all of the financial work—sometimes with incredible success—they weren't able to enjoy their retirements.

Unfortunately, the dysfunctional side is not that uncommon. It often begins with one of the people in the relationship believing they should get their way all of the time. Living like this gets tiresome for the person who never gets their way, the one who always has to give in to make the other person happy. These are the couples I have counseled who were financial millionaires and were relationally bankrupt. These types of situations always break my heart.

I've sat with couples who weren't even friends. They may have raised kids together, but they had basically become business partners in this thing called life and had completely neglected their marriage. After decades of ignoring their relationship, what do you think happens at retirement when neither spouse heads off to work every morning? They end up sitting there, sometimes in a luxurious home with the finest decor, completely miserable. They finally have the two things they've never had at the same time before: time and money. But, because they're relationally bankrupt, the time feels more like an obstacle than an opportunity, and the money just becomes one more thing to fight over.

And this doesn't just happen in marriages. Even if you are married and have maintained a great relationship with your spouse, the other relationships in your life can turn sour and eat away at your retirement dream if you don't set (and enforce) clear boundaries with the people around you. I've also sat with adult children whose parents didn't communicate clearly with them and, instead of leaving them a lasting legacy, left them with pain and misunderstanding.

These scenarios are painfully common, and the results tend to be both financially and emotionally destructive to you, your spouse, your children, your circle of friends, and sometimes even your entire community. That's a terrible retirement! The goal should not just be to cross the retirement finish line; the goal should be to cross the finish line arm in arm with your partner, surrounded by loving family and friends cheering you on!

A Dream Retirement Starts with You . . .
Investing in Your Spouse

We are going to address many of these relationship issues in this chapter, but I want to start with the most important one. If you're married, you and your spouse have to work at your relationship. You have to clearly communicate with one another. A big, fat 401(k) won't mean much if your marriage falls apart before you can enjoy it. Now, I'm from Kentucky, so I'll put it like this: if you're married, your retirement begins with *y'all*. That means working together with your spouse, putting in the effort, and making that relationship what it is meant to be.

Neglecting your marriage is one big way to ruin your high-definition retirement dream. I'll say this: My dreams for retirement include my bride, the mother of my children. We are in this together, and it wouldn't be my *dream* retirement without her there with me. So we work at it. We actually *date.* Can you believe that? Dating your wife. What a crazy idea! But if you have a house full of kids like I do, you have to set aside time for just you and your spouse to get away and talk and laugh and dream. I want you to focus on your relationship with your significant other with the same patience, planning, and care that you are giving the financial aspects of your retirement.

HEALTHY RELATIONSHIPS
REQUIRE BOUNDARIES

In order to have a healthy, long-term retirement plan, we have to take ownership of it. We've talked a lot about personal responsibility in this book, but the area of relationships is one of the most often forgotten, yet most important, areas in which personal responsibility is absolutely crucial. This is serious! You're in charge of your retirement, so any success or failure you have on the financial side or the relationship side will largely fall on your shoulders. With that in mind, I want you to write this on a piece of paper and post it somewhere around your house or office so you can see it and be reminded of it every day: "I am the CEO of my retirement."

What does this mean? It means that you are in charge. It means that you do not let others dictate your retirement. It means that you do not let others steal your dreams. It also means that you put in the work and that you're always looking for ways to improve not only your own life, but also the lives of others. That's what a good executive does, right? They make a lot of people's lives better while still keeping an eye on the bottom line—without letting other people make their decisions. That's the mindset I want you to take with your retirement.

Fencing Your Own Yard

When I tell you to set boundaries, I want you to imagine yourself building a fence around your goals. You want to keep them safe, and that means putting some separation between your retirement dream and all the crazy (and not-so-crazy) demands that your family and friends can put on you. Now, notice I didn't say you're building a wall. A wall shuts people out forever; a fence simply provides a barrier, but it's easy enough to let someone through the gate if you choose to.

I want you to take care of what is inside your fence—your yard—and to not get sidetracked by what is happening in someone else's yard. That's not your business or your responsibility. But that also means you can't allow someone else to move in and build their house in your yard. And people do that, don't they? They try to bring their problems inside of your fence and expect you to take care of them.

Let's get real for a minute. I love my three boys, and I am working hard to provide a good life for them. But that doesn't mean I'm going to run a free bed and breakfast for them when they're adults. Even as young as they are, those little guys know that's not what my wife and I have planned for our golden years. I want my boys to grow up to be strong, responsible men, and that means they can't pitch a tent inside my boundaries and expect to stay there long.

So you don't want your children to mess with your boundaries.

But guess what? Neither do your parents. Chances are your aging parents still look at you the same way I look at my boys. That means you cannot set or impose boundaries for your parents. Of course, you can suggest some of the ideas that you have learned in this book, but you should always keep in mind that it is ultimately their "yard." The same goes for your own adult children and relatives or extended family. Focus on your own boundaries, and leave everyone else's boundaries to them. Be helpful and offer advice, but don't try to take ownership of someone else's fence.

Clear Communication Is Key

Rule number one with healthy boundaries in retirement is clear and open communication. That begins with total agreement and partnership between you and your spouse if you're married, but it also requires clear communication of boundaries to family members. This sets the parameters of the playing field. It basically establishes the "out of bounds" areas of your financial life and relationships. That means your children or relatives clearly understand that there are things you might help with financially and there are definitely things that you will not support.

Clear communication shows others exactly where the lines are for you and your spouse. This prevents family members from asking for money, or it at least sets the expectation for them if they go ahead and ask anyway. It also provides some protection for you because the boundaries you set will keep you from straying too far from your dream goals. For example, if you get an invitation to an expensive, impulsive vacation, you already know the answer: "No. It sounds like fun, but it's just not in the budget right now. We're focused on other goals this year." In a sense, setting clear boundaries enables you to communicate with that future version of you who may be inclined to make a rash decision. It's your way of telling "future you" no!

Boundaries Establish and Protect Values

Boundaries also help establish a life value system. If something goes against your boundaries, it's easy to say no because you've already decided what is truly important to you. Boundaries also help you say yes to the things that really matter if you have already decided in advance where the lines are.

If you've never read Dr. Henry Cloud and Dr. John Townsend's book *Boundaries: When to Say Yes, How to Say No to Take Control of Your Life*, you should. They explain the power of boundaries this way: "Boundaries define us. They define *what is me* and *what is not me*. A boundary shows me where I end and someone else begins, leading me to a sense of ownership. Knowing what I am to own and take responsibility for gives me freedom."[1]

Too many people take a negative view of boundaries, as if they're just a list of things you refuse to do. That's not at all how I see them. Boundaries clarify what is important to me and my wife, show me what I am willing to do and how far I am willing to go to accomplish my dreams, and define what I'll do to protect the dreams we've agreed to. Boundaries aren't about saying *no* to everything; boundaries are about saying *yes* to what really matters—whether or not your family and friends understand or agree.

FAMILY ISSUES IN RETIREMENT

I hate to say this, but, in my financial counseling experience, I have found that your family can be a big threat to your retirement. In fact, your own family can actually be as much a danger as debt!

Raise Adults, Not Leeches

There are plenty of dysfunctional family trends, and one that I have seen more and more these past few years is adult children leeching off of their parents. Yes, there is a portion of the current generation whom I basically call "leeches" because they are taking advantage of their parents and refusing to grow up. I want to be clear, though, that I absolutely think parents should be there for their adult kids when they've had a drastic life change like an illness, divorce, or significant loss. I'm fine with parents even letting an adult child move back in for a little while after a job loss until they can figure things out. I know I'll never turn my back on my boys!

What I am talking about, though, are the thirty- and forty-year-olds who still live at home and have no real plan or motivation to ever leave. These are the ones who have gotten pretty comfortable in the safety net their parents may have provided, and they've turned that net into a hammock for napping! The truth that you need to understand as parents is that your children have no right to your money. You really need to let this point sink in. Say it out loud: "I have no responsibility or obligation to give my adult children my money."

I know that may make you feel uncomfortable—and maybe a little guilty. I get that. But you are the one who has put in the work and made the sacrifices to get yourself to where you are today (or where you hope to be at retirement). When you allow your children to view your money as their own, it actually creates the very entitlement mentality that is running rampant in today's culture. If your children think it is your duty to support them financially as adults, they will have no drive and no motivation to earn their own success and find their own way. It actually stunts their growth as adults. Plus, it can create tension in the home and delay your own financial progress toward retirement. Money and relationships can get pretty messy if you're not careful, but a healthy relationship is grounded in the understanding that money does not equal love. Never forget that you can love your kids well without sabotaging your own financial future.

Giving Out of Guilt and Regret

Sometimes, when retirees have extra resources, they may feel regret for the things they were not able to give their kids when they were young and, as a result, they may dote on the grandkids a bit too much. But the thing to remember as parents and as grandparents is that the greatest expression of true love is actually time and attention—not cash and prizes. What does that mean? For starters, it means that love doesn't require the grandparents to drop $1,000 to $2,000 per month to pay for their grandchild's private school!

If your parents are funding things like this for your children, it is important for you to not just take the money but to consider the impact on your parents' retirement and their own financial obligations. Take a look at what their financial needs are right now. Consider their needs related to health care and housing as they continue to age. As you think about it, your response to your parents' generous spending might need to be, "Mom and Dad, is this really the best use of your money?" Your aging parents may think you *want* them to give such lavish gifts. However, I think any good son or daughter would prefer that their parents actually enjoy their golden years. I know I'd never expect Mama Hogan to cut her lifestyle to the bone just to give big gifts to my sons.

And I would also ask you to think about the impact this type of financial support will have on the development of your own children. Are they really learning how to make their own way in the world financially? Are they growing up with a healthy expectation about money and retirement, or are they growing up with an entitlement mentality that makes them think other people will always be there to pay for whatever they want?

I know these types of conversations can be difficult, but these are important boundaries to set. It may mean that you will have to demonstrate the courage to help your parents help themselves. Help them sit down and look at a budget. Their gifts to you could actually be a curse to them—or for *you* later in life when you find that you have to care for them.

Playing with Enabling

I've also seen a disturbing trend in aging parents who continue to support their adult children, even if they live somewhere else. I find them making car payments, helping with credit card payments, or paying the bill on other debts for their children who are adults and perfectly capable of caring for themselves. The rule is that you cannot sacrifice your retirement plan for your children. Remember my friends James and Judy from earlier in the book? They were hitting retirement with absolutely nothing in savings, and they were still paying their adult child's car payment!

Or maybe you are the responsible adult child, and you have a sibling who is taking advantage of your parents' big spending. If that's you, I've got news, and it won't be a surprise: you'll be seen as the villain if you try to step in and convince your parents to cut off that flow of money. Once an adult gets used to receiving that kind of income from their aging parents, they take on a serious entitlement mentality. Your interference could potentially hurt your sibling relationships for years to come. I'm not saying it's a battle to walk away from; I'm just saying it's one you need to approach carefully.

Of course, enabling is a two-way street. We tend to think about wealthy, retired couples giving a pile of money to their adult kids and young grandkids, but what about when those roles are reversed? I have counseled older couples who fully expected their children to take care of them in retirement because, in their minds, they took care of their children for eighteen to twenty-five years. Now they believe it is their children's turn to return the favor—like the cost of raising their own children was a debt that had to be repaid!

The heartbreaking truth is that setting boundaries may include telling your own parents no when they ask you for money. Entitlement is ugly and destructive no matter which way it's going. I have actually been in counseling sessions where older parents said things like: "What do you mean you won't buy me a house? I clothed and fed you for eighteen years! Now it's your turn to take care of me."

This scenario is one of the toughest situations I've had to help clients through because there is so much guilt attached. So here's a little tip: if the chief motivator for helping someone—anyone from a grown child to a parent to a stranger down the street—is guilt, you need to stop and rethink the situation. It's like the Proverb says, "The blessing of the LORD makes one rich, and He adds no sorrow with it."[2] Pretty much every example of guilt-based spending I've ever seen is full of sorrow. That tells me it's not a blessing at all, but a curse. Don't play that game.

Dealing with Your Family's Expectations

I do a lot of work with professional athletes and have plenty of stories about athletes and their families. I'm talking about young guys from humble homes who became millionaires practically overnight. The stories of how their families reacted and some of the toxic attitudes that appeared out of nowhere would make you sick. One of the best examples of this sad situation is captured perfectly in a book by first-round NFL draft pick Phillip Buchanon titled *New Money: Staying Rich*. Buchanon gets painfully honest in the book about the problem of NFL players becoming instant millionaires and not knowing how to handle their money.

Buchanon was picked seventeenth by the Oakland Raiders in the 2002 NFL draft. When he signed, he received a guaranteed $4.9 million plus bonuses and incentives. But after he signed the contract, Buchanon writes that his mom told him—actually, she demanded—that he owed her $1 million for raising him for eighteen years. Can you imagine? He explains:

I eventually learned how to deal with the numerous "family emergencies." Early on, I found myself in too many situations where some relative would come to me and claim they needed something fixed. So I'd write them a check; of course, the problem never got fixed. The check, however, always got cashed. By trying to fix a problem, I created an additional one for myself.[3]

This reminds me of an NFL athlete I worked with several years ago. He was also a first-round draft pick. This young man had four uncles and three aunts, and when he received his signing bonus, he decided that he wanted to write each of them a check for $20,000. You can do the math. This was an incredibly kind and generous thing to do. He had grown up in his mom and dad's home and had a brother and a sister. He wasn't doing this for his aunts and uncles for any reason other than that he wanted to be a blessing to them and thank them for showing up at his games on occasion to support him. He obviously was planning to do some really nice stuff for his immediate family as well.

But when we sat down to talk a couple of months later, he seemed really bothered. You see, the majority of his aunts and uncles were really appreciative and grateful, but several of them were actually upset with him about the gift because they thought it should have been more. And the crazy part was that they were not shy at all about telling him that. Now, keep in mind, he didn't owe anyone anything; he was just doing this out of the kindness of his heart. He didn't grow up in their homes. They had never financially supported him. They not only had the nerve to *feel* ungrateful for the gift, but to *act* outwardly ungrateful about it too. He was legitimately hurt and said, "Chris, I feel bad, but I think I need to let them know that I didn't have to do anything for them." I wholeheartedly agreed with him.

You see, too often people who work hard and achieve success will have folks around them who bring this unspoken level of expectation to the relationship. They seem to believe that you need to do something for them because you have had success. But you have to be really careful how you handle this type of thing. You must set clear boundaries and be careful of the people you surround yourself with. You have to stay focused, stick to a plan, and make sure everyone else knows what they should or shouldn't expect—and what they do or don't deserve. You probably won't get signed in the NFL draft as you near retirement, but, if you do the things we're talking about throughout this book, you could very well end up a millionaire. That gives you a ton of opportunity, but, the sad fact remains, it will also make you a target for people seeking a handout. And sometimes, those hands can even be the same ones that raised you.

Of course, I am definitely not saying it is always a bad thing to help your family if you genuinely want to bless them and it's a reasonable part of your retirement plan. If you have your boundaries set and your financial house in order, then you are free to help others if you choose to do so. If you have worked hard and are living your high-definition retirement the way you have dreamed, then you don't have to wait until your retirement is fully funded before you bless your family. But you have to have those boundaries set and use wisdom to know when to adjust the throttle on giving and helping out your family.

Some Tips Related to Aging Parents

When it comes to helping aging family members, I first want to suggest that you go back and review some of the material in Chapter Nine and help your parents with those types of issues. Make sure that you or a sibling is a joint signer on their bank accounts so you can access their funds to assist them as needed. Consider getting a power of attorney so you can better assist them with their business affairs. And, of course, you want to make sure your parents have a properly executed will. There's just no excuse for not having these things in place! As always, work with your (or your parents') estate planning professional to get these things squared away as quickly as possible.

If your parents are in or near retirement and have nothing saved to live on, then you and your siblings definitely need to discuss what you are going to do to help your parents. Do you, the financially responsible one, become the caretaker of all of these things? Talk openly with your siblings about your parents' game plan to ensure that everyone understands their wishes. Doing this might actually help your siblings understand that they need a game plan too!

So how should you approach your parents to talk about retirement? First of all, remember that it is always about loving your parents and never about what you think you might get in inheritance. Caring for aging parents should be an act of love, not a runaround to beef up what they might leave you one day.

Second, you should remember to take a supportive, friendly, and conversational approach when talking about retirement with your parents. Never, under any circumstances, treat your parents like children. We're talking about the people who raised, fed, and clothed you. They deserve your love, time, patience, attention, and, most of all, respect.

However, before you're inclined to jump in and pay all their bills and send them on a celebration cruise around the world, let's remember that you've got your own family to care for. The bottom line is that you cannot effectively help anyone else until you first have placed yourself on solid financial ground. Once your financial house is in order, and only if you feel no pressure or guilt to do so, then by all means, treat your aging parents like royalty.

REDEFINING INHERITANCE

I believe it is important to redefine what we mean by inheritance. Despite what people may think, an inheritance is much more than just money. A true inheritance—or *legacy*—includes anything you leave those you love. Money may or may not be part of that. And, as we talk about how our relationships are impacted by our retirement and specifically our wealth in retirement, we need to take a good look at what it means to pass on an inheritance to the next generation.

What If You Can't Leave Money?

We've talked a lot about personal responsibility already, but it's worth bringing up again right here. It is not your obligation to leave a pile of money to your kids or anyone else. As an adult, you take care of you. If your kids are adults, they should take care of themselves. If your retirement planning and preparation provides you enough income to live your dream retirement until the day you die, guess what? You won! Great job! If there's anything left over after that then, of course, it can be a wonderful thing to leave it in the hands of the next generation. If that's passed down generation after generation, just imagine what your great-great-grandkids could accomplish with the wealth you started.

However, I don't want you to worry if you have no money or investments to leave your children or grandchildren as an inheritance. The reality is, if you are already at retirement age and haven't saved much toward retirement, you don't have time to build the kind of wealth to really leave them with a financial blessing. But you certainly want to focus on something that is just as important—building memories with them. The truth is that memories are going to be more lasting and important than any of the financial blessings you might leave them anyway! So I want you to let go of any guilt you may have if you have reached retirement and don't have money to leave to your children or your grandchildren.

I like to look at it this way: Your greatest gift will be what you leave *in* them, not what you leave *to* them. That will be their greatest inheritance. This includes things such as your faith, values, and integrity. It includes tender moments you shared and a heart full of memories. Your greatest investment in your kids and the next generation isn't your money; it's passing down *who you are* and making an investment in *who they are becoming*. That's what really lasts generationally.

I started this book by talking about my grandparents. As I think about the issue of inheritance and legacy, I can't help but think of my incredible grandfather. When I was a kid, he and I would talk and sometimes walk. We'd discuss everything on those walks. He poured his life into me, sharing his wisdom and his heart. The time I spent with my grandfather changed me. It made me more and more into the man I am today.

When my grandfather died, he didn't leave me a pile of money. There was no mansion or a fleet of luxury cars for all the kids and grandkids to split up. Instead, he left me the most valuable and precious thing I have ever owned to this day: his cane. The cane reminds me of the stories and life lessons I heard growing up. The same cane now goes out on walks with my boys and me as I try to pour into them the way my grandfather poured into me.

I love that cane because, as my grandfather got older and needed the cane more and more, it represented to me his lasting faith and how he had always leaned on Jesus throughout his life. I keep that cane to remind me of the symbol of a strong man, a man who would do whatever it took to serve and protect his family. It's also a powerful reminder to me of how, when you can't stand on your own, you can always lean on your faith to keep you moving forward. Those are the lessons my grandfather taught me in our times together.

He understood that his presence with me was an investment, and there's no doubt my life is richer for it.

So Why Leave an Inheritance?

We've spent a whole book together, so I hope you'll let me explain what drives me to do what I do and why I believe the things I believe. I am deeply convicted that we are called to be good managers of what we have, and I also believe that we have a spiritual obligation to leave a legacy. I am a person of faith, and I believe that the Bible is full of truths that can help you live a remarkable life. Whether you are a Christian or not, I think you can agree that the Bible is full of some wonderful wisdom for life.

Proverbs says, "A good man leaves an inheritance to his children's children."[4] What that means to me is that an inheritance will help carry on the good works that you have done in your own life, not only for your kids but also for everyone else you invested in throughout your life. I read a wonderful story that reminded me of the blessings of inheritance. Dean Smith, the Hall of Fame basketball coach from the University of North Carolina, had recently passed away. To call Coach Smith a basketball genius would be selling him short. He was also a civil rights activist, a humanitarian, a person of deep faith, and a second father and lifelong mentor to the men who both played for him and coached under him. It is said that Dean Smith kept in contact with every young man who had ever played basketball for him at North Carolina whether they went on to be an accountant, a schoolteacher, or an NBA star.

At his passing, Smith had prearranged for personal notes and checks in the amount of $200 to be mailed to every player who had ever played for him at North Carolina. His wish was that they would use that money to take their families out to dinner and remember their time with him. He even sent out the $200 check to former NBA stars like Michael Jordan who clearly didn't need the cash to buy a nice dinner. Smith's gesture simply brightened an already beautiful legacy, and when I read this story, I couldn't help but imagine the entire North Carolina basketball family all across the country remembering their Coach over a nice meal. What a legacy to leave for those men whom he had poured his life into serving!

Because I'm a person of faith, the whole idea of inheritance is especially important to me. It's a reminder that this world is not our home. We only get to be here for a little while, and all these blessings we have accumulated throughout our lives will not be able to make the trip with us when we leave. As the old saying goes, I have never seen a hearse pulling a U-Haul trailer behind it!

Make Your Inheritance a Blessing, Not a Curse

How do we leave a financial inheritance? We've already covered the logistics of this in our conversation about wills and estate planning in the last chapter. Now let's talk about the side that does not involve wealth. We need to discuss how to deal with the people and emotions involved in receiving an inheritance.

I had a friend who recently lost his father, and he told me all about how his dad intentionally walked him and the rest of the family through all the details of the will and estate plan. It was a tough conversation, but his father was intent on communicating the plan clearly so that everyone would know what to do when he passed away. He didn't want his children arguing with each other if they had a problem with how things were divided. So he laid everything out in front of them and gave them the opportunity to hear directly from him, in his own words, what his wishes were. That kind of intentionality may be uncomfortable, but it is an incredible kindness to the people you love. It helps prevent the kind of divisive arguments that too often creep into our most important relationships, driving wedges between people in the middle of their grief.

This type of candid communication can actually free your heirs and loved ones from the burden of not knowing your wishes. It also ensures that your legacy will be carried out in the way that you intend. If you are going to leave things to certain people in your family, then you need to communicate that clearly. My friend's father gave him permission to sell some of his stuff. He also explained which of the possessions, like the family Bible, he wanted to be kept in the family and passed down. The thing that stood out to me as my friend told me about his father's plans was that there actually wasn't a lot of wealth involved. The plan centered more around the things that had an emotional impact on the family members. Remember, those are often the things that cause the biggest rifts between people after you're gone.

However, if you are planning to leave money to your heirs, you need to work with your spouse (if you're married) to determine exactly how much will go to each person. Don't assume every heir—even children—will get the same amount. Everyone's life situation is different. An adult child who is raising a child with special needs will have different expenses than a single child with no kids. Or an adult child with a drug problem can't be trusted with money as much as their siblings. These conversations can definitely be awkward, but, remember, you want your inheritance to be a blessing. Simply pouring good money into a broken situation won't bless anyone; it'll just be a curse.

When and Why to Use a Trust

Keep in mind when you are making these decisions that being *fair* does not always mean being *equal*. There are a lot of factors at play here, and you need to consider all of them. You need to be honest about who you can trust with your money. You need to identify who may need more help. And, whether or not you leave equal amounts, you should always work with your estate planning professional to set up a trust to help manage the distributions. If you do your estate plan correctly, you can still make sure the money is handled wisely, even after you are gone.

An older lady came to see me several years back for a kind of wealth tune-up session. At that time, she had a paid-for home, her kids were in college, and she and her husband had really done everything the right way. He had recently passed away, but she had remained focused. As we were talking, she told me that she was working to set up a trust. She had about $3 million in her estate and wanted to pass it on to her children. She needed to bounce some of her ideas off of me before she met with her estate planning attorney. I will never forget the moment when she explained, "Chris, my husband and I worked very hard to establish this nest egg, and I want it to be a blessing to my kids, but I also want to make sure that they are aware of what it took for us to get there. I want them to understand that we were intentional and that we had to make sacrifices to accomplish that goal."

Now, the great thing about setting up a trust is that it can allow some safeguards. She had three sons to whom she wanted to pass on a set amount of money, but she had decided that, in order for them to get that money, they would have to attend *Financial Peace University* at least once a year. She thought it was important for them to go through the course each year so that they could learn how to stay on track and handle their finances effectively. She even planned it so that if her boys did not attend the yearly FPU, their money would be diverted to a local charity that she had preselected! This was honestly one of the most well-thought-out arrangements I have ever discussed with a client. The inheritance she was leaving her boys was far more than money; she was leaving them with a clear statement and reminder of her values.

Of course, you should also work now to raise your children in a way that they will handle money responsibly. You can only trust well if you have trained well. If your kids are still young and in your home, you should pick up a copy of *Smart Money Smart Kids* by Dave Ramsey and his daughter Rachel Cruze. It is the manual for how to raise money-smart kids. Or, if your children are already grown and gone, why not give them a copy of Dave's *The Total Money Makeover* or send them to our *Financial Peace University* class? It's never too late to get your financial act together, and you want to set your children up to win long after you're gone.

Receiving an Inheritance

We have talked about *leaving* an inheritance, but how do we handle *receiving* one? After all, as many of us near retirement age ourselves, our own parents are wrapping up their retirement years. What's the best way to handle an inheritance that's passed down to us?

If you receive this type of money, consider it a blessing. It is a legacy that was passed to you with love. First and foremost, you want to honor that, not squander it. I would tell you to go back to Chapter Three and review our lessons on budgeting. It's okay to have a little fun with the money, but it should primarily go right into your own financial plan. If you're following the Baby Steps, then you should already know what to do with any new money. Don't get distracted by a windfall mentality or the impulse to spend that money just to numb your grief. Put that money to work as part of your plan.

But I also don't want you to ever base your personal retirement plan on the *possibility* of inheriting some amount of cash or property. We've already talked about that earlier in the book. Let that inheritance money be a surprise. Treat it like I told you to treat Social Security—as the icing on the cake. You need to take control of your own retirement and your own financial future without relying on the hope of an inheritance. If your retirement plan is based on someone else dying first, you've got a bad plan!

What About Charity?

There's a big movement out in the world today that says you should give all of your money away to charity and nonprofits. I think there's definitely a place for charitable giving throughout your life, but I don't buy the notion that "good" people "give it all away." Giving has always been and will always be a part of my financial plan, but so is raising my kids to handle money. If I've done my job well as a parent, my children will grow into men whom I can trust with my wealth. By leaving a significant portion to them, I will not only bless them, but also I will give that money time to continue to grow. Then the fruit of my hard work will survive over several generations, always growing and always being there to bless more people than I can bless today.

Now, that said, I always encourage people to find worthy causes through which they can make a big difference. That may mean balancing what you leave to your heirs with what you leave to charity. Of course, you need to do due diligence to make sure the charity is run well and that you can trust it with your money. I've seen too many nonprofits that are run so poorly that a $1 million gift could outright tear the place apart.

But, if you do it right, you can impact your community in a way no one would ever expect. I recently heard the story of a humble, unassuming ninety-two-year-old man who completely shocked his local community with his generosity after his death. A man named Ronald Read, born in 1921, had been the first in his family to graduate from high school. After serving in the military during World War II, he returned to his hometown and worked at a gas station for twenty-five years, followed by seventeen years as a janitor at the local J. C. Penney. He worked for blue-collar wages his entire career. Yet, after his death, this gas station attendant and janitor left over $6 million to his local hospital and library in his small Vermont town! The great part of the story is that no one really knew he had a fortune. The locals said he always wore a flannel shirt with safety pins in place of buttons, and he usually parked far away so he wouldn't have to pay for parking. The only inkling that he had anything in investments was the fact that he would sometimes be seen reading *The Wall Street Journal* during breakfast. I love that story!

What a great story and legacy this man left his community! Charity can be a great part of your plan. But, if you have a family, I don't think it should be *the whole* plan. Find the balance between blessing your family and blessing your favorite charities, and then communicate those wishes to everyone involved!

YOUR RETIREMENT ACTION AGREEMENT

The thing I desperately want you to remember if you are going to retire inspired is that it all begins and ends with you. You must focus on *your* dreams, *your* budget, *your* ability to stay out of debt, *your* investing strategy, and *your* boundaries. Your job now is to stay on track, get the right kind of help when you need it, and stick to your plan.

Hopefully you have learned a lot of new things, laughed at yourself (or maybe someone else), and been encouraged and inspired to get your own retirement plan together. But now comes the most important part. Now, you're getting ready to close this book and go about your life. But before you do, before you set this book aside, I want you to take a moment to consider what you're going to do with all of this information. No matter how much this book taught you, it won't make a difference if you don't apply that knowledge to your life. If you're not motivated to do something, then we've both wasted our time.

I want this to be the moment you look back on fifteen, twenty, or thirty years from now as the time when you made a decision that changed not only your life, but also the whole direction of your family. I want you to remember that you made the decision to work your money and not let it work you. I want you to be able to look back at retirement and know that the time you spent working counted for something.

I usually end my talks by giving the audience a specific call to action—a plea to actually *do something*. I do that to help them take ownership of the information I've shared with them, to put action to the information. I want to do that with you right now. Let's call it our Retirement Action Agreement. The terms of our agreement are simple. In exchange for the information I've shared with you, I want you to agree to go and put this stuff into action! I've shown you the plan; now put it to work!

Like Mama Hogan always told me, "If it is to be, it's up to me!" Your retirement is *your* job, and you can do this! You've seen by now that there's no magic formula, no secret sauce to a healthy retirement. It's the wonderfully predictable result of years and decades of wise decisions and hard work. It's the result of focus. It's the result of dreaming. It's the result of careful planning and occasional course corrections. It's the result of building and working with a dream team of professionals to help keep you moving in the right direction. It's the result of conversation after conversation with your spouse, kids, and other close people in your life.

Remember, retirement isn't just about boring math, and it's not just about working as long as your body can physically stand it. If it were, I would have named this book *Retire Tired*! That's not the kind of retirement I want for myself, and it's not the kind of retirement I want for you. I don't want you to retire broke, stressed, guilty, ashamed, or tired. I want you to retire inspired!

I've shown you how.

Now go do it!

AFTERWORD

When I think of my friends Russ and Joy who retired in their sixties and now spend their days working to support a number of different charities, or my client who retired as a millionaire in his forties after working a blue-collar nine-to-five job, or when I sit kneecap-to-kneecap with folks who have hit their retirement goals and are living out their dreams, only one word comes to mind: *inspired*.

That's how I want you to approach your retirement. In my experience, inspired people have the energy to change. Inspired folks are the ones who have a vision and the determination to see it through. I want you to picture in your mind those want-to moments that really motivate you. Imagine them in your mind. Can you see them? Those, my friend, are your dreams. And that is the beginning of inspiration.

When I hear the word *inspired*, I'm reminded of what so many people have taught me over the years as I have walked with them toward their retirement journey. You know, the truth is that there are a lot of folks—your neighbors, friends, and family—who may retire *well*. There are still way too many who won't retire *at all*. And then there are a few—the precious few—who will retire *inspired*.

If you look closely at the definition, you'll discover the word *inspired* has some deep meanings. It carries a sense of being animated, or moved to do something. Inspired means you are moved to action, and that is exactly how I want you to feel as you close this book!

But that is not all. The definition says that to be inspired means to be animated "by a divine or supernatural influence."[1] I love that part because the inspiration that drives me forward comes from these deep wells outside of myself: my faith, my love of family, my mission to help others. Remember, an inspired retirement needs to *start* with you, but it is about way more than just you!

There is also an interesting secondary meaning listed in the definition for *inspired* that I think we need to talk about for just a moment: "inhaled." Now, when I hear that word, I am not thinking of something silly or destructive. No. I am thinking about how you take that first full breath of ocean air when you get out of your car at the beach, or how you stop to breathe in when you walk into your grandma's kitchen while she is baking a cake. I want your retirement dream to be something that you inhale. I want it to be as second nature as breathing. I want you to think of it in those busy or stressful moments of life when you only have a moment to take a deep breath. Inspired means that you have permission to fully embrace and enjoy your retirement experience. Once you've put in the years of hard work, the planning, the budgeting, the saving, I want you to savor that experience and breathe it all in when you get there!

When Life Punches You in the Mouth

We have spent the entire book working out our dreams and defining our plans, but I must tell you as certain as the sunrise that life is going to punch you in the mouth at some point. Life is going to hit you and leave you wondering if your plans still matter. I can easily get emotional thinking of the folks I have counseled through the years who faced this type of adversity. Your spouse, whom you have planned, sweated, sacrificed, prayed, and dreamed with for twenty years, is diagnosed with a terminal cancer. Maybe a car wreck in your fifties leaves you unable to do the things you hoped to do in retirement. It may be that your business folds or you are unexpectedly let go after thirty years of working at your job. Life is going to happen. I have seen these things rain down on the best, brightest, and most faithful of people. But let me tell you a little secret: your plan still matters. That's right—even when life hits you with something difficult—your plan still matters.

Throughout this book, I've shared a few stories about my former clients and a few about myself. There's one story I've held back up to this point, though, because it's incredibly personal. However, I think it'll help demonstrate my point.

My wife and I were working toward an inspired retirement when life punched us in a devastating way. I shouldn't say punched though. Honestly, it felt more like getting hit by a freight train. Several years ago, our youngest son, Case, was diagnosed with Hunter syndrome, a very rare genetic disorder. There are fewer than three thousand cases worldwide, and my baby is one of them. We were told at the time that our two-year-old son might not live to see his fifteenth birthday. It was a crushing moment.

This blow made us step back and question everything we had planned. I have to be honest: I spent a couple of years handling it the wrong way until I got back on my feet. I was like that fighter in the ring who has just taken a huge hit. I was facedown on the canvas listening to the ten count with no energy or ability to get moving. But through the help of my faith, family, and friends, I began to see that I had a choice. I could either get up and continue to fight or

I could stay down and give up on life. I took a good look at all the people around me who needed me to pick myself up off the canvas to keep fighting. It gave me a different perspective on what it means to live inspired. Your struggle may not look just like ours, but life will happen to you. And when it does, I need you to understand that you have three things that you can control: your attitude, your outlook, and your responses.

You and you alone control your attitude. Your attitude is how you choose to look at the world. I want you to remember that your attitude is leading the way toward your legacy. Other people, including your friends, your family, and your community, are watching how you handle tragedy and adversity in your life and will be lifted up by how you choose to deal with it. You must also be deeply rooted in your faith because that is the place where you are able to plug into something bigger than yourself and truly recharge. Even in the face of adversity, you can still choose to have a grateful heart. It's hard to be hateful when you're grateful.

You also need to control your outlook. When bad things happen, people can often react by expecting more bad things. That's a trap! You should expect positive things in your life. Surround yourself with positive people. Negative folks can pass on their negativity like the common cold, so try to avoid them. But I also want you to be careful of the words that you are telling yourself. If you speak kindly to yourself, it will be easier to speak kindly to others.

Finally, I want you to remember that *you can control your responses.* Tragedy and adversity can be another opportunity for you to invest in the people who really need you. One of the fastest ways to learn to live inspired through tough times is to reach out to others, to extend the wisdom of your experience to others, and to find ways to help people who are going through similar times.

My wife and I began to do this with a foundation we created, SavingCase.com, and a global fundraising effort for research,

ProjectAlive.org, to help other children who have been diagnosed with Hunter syndrome. It is amazing how much clearer things become when you take the focus off of yourself and work to help others. We are holding on to our hope and our faith that everything will be okay.

Most of all, I want to tell you that tragedy is another way to embrace an inspired life. The work and the plan that you have put in place will not go away. It may seem hopeless at the time, but that plan will also help carry you through. Stay positive and don't abandon your dreams. You will honor your family and the people around you who were a part of that plan by continuing to work toward your dreams!

Speaking of retirement dreams, I want to tell you a little more about mine.

My High-Definition Retirement Dream: "Big Pop"

I've explained to you how much of an impact my grandparents had on my life. I keep my granddad's cane, one of grandmother's quilts, and a few other mementos in my office to remind myself from time to time that I have an opportunity to leave a legacy for my children, their children, my community, and people in need.

I've even come up with a name for myself when I cross that finish line to my high-definition dream. Everyone needs a retirement name. For many people, it comes from the lips of a two-year-old grandchild, and it might be "Gramps" or "Poppy" or "Grandfather." I decided a while ago that I am not having any of that! If I am going to live the dream that *I want*, then I sure as heck am going to name the guy who is living in that dream!

So, even though my boys are still young, I've already made it clear to them and to my wife what my grandparent name is going to be. And picking that name is a big deal! It's a name and title you'll carry with you the rest of your life. So, after much thought (and, yes, even prayer), I have decided to go with "Big Pop." If one of my future grandkids tries to call me something else, well, I will bring them back to Big Pop. Lord willing, that's a badge I'll proudly wear for decades in my future!

Big Pop will be the kind of grandfather who is supportive to his three boys and their wives, families, and children. But I'll tell you something else about Big Pop: he won't have any grown Hogan boys living in his house when they are thirty! There's no room for that in his plan; he's got big things to do with his wife and grandkids!

I want to be able to be there when they need me. I want to be free to offer them my presence, my undivided attention, and my love. I want to be able to take my grandkids on trips, give them some adventures, and help them fall in love with the wonder of life. I want to teach them the importance of faith and what it means to help the people in their community.

I still remember going on adventures with my grandparents. That meant anything from rides in the car to driving to church revivals, or even just hanging out in their backyard. Those days left a mark on my life. My grandparents planted spiritual and relational seeds that grew in me and are now reaching people they never even had the chance to meet.

Every time I walk into my home office and see my grandfather's cane or my grandmother's quilt, I think of my grandpa working on a neighbor's car, and I realize now that it was always less about the problem with the car or the truck and more about spending moments with those people in need. He wasn't just fixing broken cars; he was investing in his neighbors.

When I am out speaking, I have some fun with the name "Big Pop," but the truth is that name is significant to me. It is the reminder that I want to grow old like my grandparents did and have the time and the financial stability to be able to love and support people, charities, and causes. You remember, the foundational belief that drives everything I do is that *people matter*. And they do; people matter more than anything. Having the freedom to spend quality time with the people whom you love is what it is all about. If you truly believe that people matter, then you have an obligation to retire inspired.

PRESS ON TOWARD THAT
HIGH-DEFINITION DREAM

Remember that your retirement is up to you. However, none of us can do this retirement thing alone! I want to make sure you connect with other people on the journey, keep your motivation, and learn about other resources available to help you retire inspired. Be sure to stay connected with me at chrishogan360.com and @ChrisHogan360 on Twitter.

While you're there, drop me a line and tell me your story. I want to hear from you. I am inspired by the stories of people who do the work and achieve the retirement of their dreams. Tell me all about it! You could even tell me what retirement name you've picked out for yourself.

Remember, a dream without a plan is called a wish!

So dream it. Plan it. Work it.

Then achieve it!

NOTES

Introduction

1. Nanci Hellmich, "Retirement: A Third Have Less Than $1,000 Put Away," *USA Today*, April 1, 2014, http://www.usatoday.com/story/money/personalfinance/2014/03/18/retirement-confidence-survey-savings/6432241.
2. Proverbs 21:5, NIV.

Chapter One

1. Guinness Storehouse, Archive Fact Sheet: Employee Welfare at Guinness, http://www.guinness-storehouse.com/en/docs/Employee_Welfare_At_Guinness.pdf.
2. Jeanne Meister, "Job Hopping Is the 'New Normal' for Millennials: Three Ways to Prevent a Human Resource Nightmare," *Forbes*, August 14, 2012, http://www.forbes.com/sites/jeannemeister/2012/08/14/job-hopping-is-the-new-normal-for-millennials-three-ways-to-prevent-a-human-resource-nightmare.
3. Ibid.
4. Mary-Lou Weisman, "The History of Retirement, from Early Man to A.A.R.P.," *The New York Times*, March 21, 1999, http://www.nytimes.com/1999/03/21/jobs/the-history-of-retirement-from-early-man-to-aarp.html.
5. "Social Security Monthly Statistical Snapshot," May 2015 (released June 2015), http://www.ssa.gov/policy/docs/quickfacts/stat_snapshot.
6. "2015 Poverty Guidelines," US Department of Health and Human Services, http://aspe.hhs.gov/poverty/15poverty.cfm.

7. "The Crisis in Pensions and Retirement Plans," *Accounting Degree Review*, http://www.accounting-degree.org/retirement.
8. Rob Portman, "Heading Off the Entitlement Meltdown," *The Wall Street Journal*, July 21, 2014, http://www.wsj.com/articles/rob-portman-heading-off-the-entitlement-meltdown-1405983479.
9. "Nearly Half of All Workers Have Less Than $10K in Savings," *Financial Planning*, http://www.financial-planning.com/news/retirement-ebri-savings-2672600-1.html.
10. Angela Johnson, "76% of Americans Are Living Paycheck-to-Paycheck," *CNN Money* (New York), June 24, 2013, http://money.cnn.com/2013/06/24/pf/emergency-savings.
11. Christina Lavingia, "Why Are More People Afraid of Going Broke Than Dying?" GOBankingRates, January 8, 2015, http://www.gobankingrates.com/personal-finance/people-afraid-going-broke-dying.

Chapter Two

1. Rebecca Riffkin, "Average U.S. Retirement Age Rises to 62," *Gallup*, April 28, 2014, http://www.gallup.com/poll/168707/average-retirement-age-rises.aspx.
2. Dee Lee, "My Social Security Benefit Will Be Enough for Retirement," CBS Boston, May 28, 2014, http://boston.cbslocal.com/2014/05/28/my-social-security-benefit-will-be-enough-for-retirement.
3. Ibid.
4. Mandi Woodruff, "Americans Are Deluded About When They Will Retire," Yahoo Finance, April 21, 2015, http://finance.yahoo.com/news/when-americans-think-they-will-retire-ebri-162344633.html.

Chapter Three

1. Gretchen Rubin, "Stop Expecting to Change Your Habit in 21 Days," *Psychology Today*, October 21, 2009, in The Happiness Project, http://www.psychologytoday.com/blog/the-happiness-project/200910/stop-expecting-change-your-habit-in-21-days.
2. "What Could Happen to You: Tales of Big Lottery Winners," NBC News, May 17, 2013, http://usnews.nbcnews.com/_news/2013/05/17/18323470-what-could-happen-to-you-tales-of-big-lottery-winners.
3. Robert Powell, "How to Retire Early While Everyone Else Toils at Work," *USA Today*, August, 7, 2014, http://www.usatoday.com/story/experience/whow%20to%20retire%20early/weekend/lifestyle/2014/08/06/how-to-retire-early/13678931.

Chapter Four

1. Charisse Jones, "60% of Americans Have to Retire Sooner Than They'd Planned," *USA Today*, June 3, 2015, http://www.usatoday.com/story/money /2015/06/02/majority-of-americans-have-to-retire-sooner-than-theyd-planned /28371099.
2. Proverbs 13:12a, NKJV.
3. United States Census Bureau, salary information: http://www.census.gov /hhes/www/income/. Debt statistics: http://useconomy.about.com/b/2013 /05/09/consumer-credit-up-3-4-in-march.htm.
4. Caitlin Johnson, "Cutting Through Advertising Clutter," *CBS Sunday Morning*, September 17, 2006, http://www.cbsnews.com/news/cutting -through-advertising-clutter.
5. "Amex Centurion Cardmember Agreement: Part 1 of 2," https://web.aexp -static.com/us/content/pdf/cardmember-agreements/centurion/Centurion AECB.pdf.
6. Brian Kelly, "Is the Amex Centurion Card Worth the $2,500 Annual Fee?," The Points Guy, May 22, 2014, http://thepointsguy.com/2014/05/is-the -amex-centurion-card-worth-the-2500-annual-fee.

Chapter Five

1. Samuel R. Avro, "How High Have Gas Prices Risen Over the Years?" *Energy Trends Insider*, February 27, 2012, http://www.energytrendsinsider .com/2012/02/27/how-high-have-gas-prices-risen-over-the-years.

Chapter Six

1. "401(k) Fast Facts," American Benefits Council, 401(k) Fast Facts, updated April 2014, http://www.americanbenefitscouncil.org/documents2013/401k _stats.pdf. PSCA Plan Sponsor Council of America, 55th Annual Survey Highlights, http://www.psca.org/55th-annual-survey-highlights.
2. Ibid.

Chapter Seven

1. Teresa Mears, "How Seriously Should You Take Retirement Savings Calculators?," *U.S. News & World Report*, October 31, 2014, http: //money.usnews.com/money/personal-finance/articles/2014/10/31 /how-seriously-should-you-take-retirement-savings-calculators.
2. "Trends in 401(k) Plans and Retirement Rewards," WorldatWork, March 2013, http://www.worldatwork.org/waw/adimLink?id=71489.

Chapter Eight

1. I often use a 10 percent rate of return in my examples because the math is usually easier for people to understand. If you're more comfortable using a different figure, go ahead! My job is to just get you thinking about the power of compound interest when you save diligently over a long period of time.
2. "College Enrollment and Work Activity of 2014 High School Graduates," United States Department of Labor Bureau of Labor Statistics, April 16, 2015, http://www.bls.gov/news.release/hsgec.nr0.htm.
3. Charisse Jones, "For Many Parents, Paying Tuition Tops Retirement," *USA Today*, March 18, 2015, http://www.usatoday.com/story/money/personal finance/2015/03/17/paying-tuition-outweighs-saving-for-retirement/70152912.

Chapter Nine

1. "The Basics of Short-Term Disability Insurance," Insure.com, November 12, 2014, http://www.insure.com/disability-insurance/short-term-disability.html.
2. Penelope Wang, "Here's a New Reason to Think Twice Before Buying Long-Term Care Insurance," Time.com, November 11, 2014, http://time.com/money/3578466/long-term-care-insurance-study.
3. Blake Ellis, "Identity Fraud Hits New Victim Every Two Seconds," *CNN Money (New York)*, February 6, 2014, http://money.cnn.com/2014/02/06/pf/identity-fraud.
4. "CFPB Report Finds Confusion in Reverse Mortgage Market," Consumer Financial Protection Bureau, June 28, 2012, http://www.consumerfinance.gov/newsroom/consumer-financial-protection-bureau-report-finds-confusion-in-reverse-mortgage-market.

Chapter Ten

1. Dr. Henry Cloud and Dr. John Townsend, *Boundaries: When to Say Yes, How to Say No to Take Control of Your Life* (Nashville: Thomas Nelson, 1992), 31.
2. Proverbs 10:22, NKJV.
3. Aaron Torres, "Family, Money and Other Pitfalls of a Professional Athlete," FOX Sports, Outkick the Coverage: College Football Blog, April 2, 2015, http://www.foxsports.com/college-football/outkick-the-coverage/family-money-and-other-pitfalls-of-a-professional-athlete-040215.
4. Proverbs 13:22a, NKJV.

Afterword

1. Dictionary.com, s.v. "inspire," dictionary.reference.com/browse/inspire.

Retire Inspired
ENDORSEMENTS

Chris Hogan has done the impossible—written a book on investing for retirement without losing his audience in a fog of boring jargon. He explains the concepts using concrete and practical examples, and he shows how everyone can enjoy a great retirement, not just the wizards of Wall Street. No matter where you are on the retirement journey, this book could drastically improve your future.

—Art Laffer, chairman of Laffer Associates
and founder of the Laffer Curve

Too many people are bringing debt and regret into their retirement years. That's a tragedy that could—and should—be avoided. *Retire Inspired* can show anyone, at any age and any income, the steps to achieve their retirement dreams.

—Robert Herjavec, co-host of *Shark Tank*
and CEO of Herjavec Group

Here's what Chris Hogan gets about retirement that other people miss: your wishes will remain wishes until you put a plan in place to attack them. Hogan learned from his mentor Dave Ramsey how to do just that. In this book, he passes that wisdom on to you.

—Jean Chatzky, best-selling author
and AARP Financial Ambassador

This book not only provides useful information on retirement, but it also tackles subjects that all of us need to address as we near that stage of life, like estate planning, living trusts, changing your investment portfolio, and talking to your aging parents about money. This is simply the best book for anyone who wants to make the most of their retirement years.

—John C. Maxwell, *New York Times* best-selling author

If you're dreaming of being at peace with your finances and looking for inspiration and a well-rounded plan, *Retire Inspired* will get you there. With practical guidance, motivating stories, and solid advice, this book will propel you toward a financially secure future.

—Craig Groeschel, pastor of Life.Church and author of
#Struggles—Following Jesus in a Selfie-Centered World

As president of an investment firm that has helped thousands of families over the years, I truly believe this is the only book you should consider as your guide to retirement. Chris Hogan takes Dave Ramsey's timeless wisdom on money and digs further into the specifics of retiring well and leaving a legacy. He guides you step-by-step in how to comfortably and confidently make the enormous life transition into retirement. This book is a gold mine of resources and advice that I would recommend to anyone!

—Jeff Dobyns, president, Southwestern Investment Group

Chris Hogan nails it! Retirement might have been about grabbing a rocking chair and being put out to pasture in the past, but soon the average American will live to age one hundred. Retirement should be the time you really live life, and this book has all the tools to make that happen. The great news is anyone can position themselves for truly golden years.

—Charles Payne, host of *Making Money
with Charles Payne*

Knowing how to secure your financial future and following through with discipline and determination are two separate things. Chris Hogan teaches you the first and inspires you to do the second. Bring this man onto your team by placing this book on your shelf and its contents into your heart.

—Rabbi Daniel Lapin, author of *Thou Shall Prosper*
and *Business Secrets from the Bible*

Chris Hogan is extraordinarily gifted at communicating through stories and numbers the reality of a financial life. For years I have preached a message that if you aim at nothing you'll hit it every time. Chris has made this point extraordinarily clear and compelling. I heartily recommend this book for anyone at any age. It is applicable to all of us. Thanks, Chris, for this much-needed book on a sorely misunderstood subject.

—Ron Blue, author and founding director
of Kingdom Advisors

Chris Hogan has one of the most amazing voices on the planet; however, it's not his voice but rather his pen that has impacted me in a profound way! In 2008 I saw people in their late fifties and early sixties watch as their financial lives fell apart because they had worked all of their lives but had never adequately planned for retirement. So when the one thing they had semi-invested in for years crashed, so did their dreams. I remember thinking, *I don't want that for myself and Lucretia*, but I struggled with knowing how to prepare for something that seems so far away. Chris Hogan has filled that need with his book *Retire Inspired*. It is the go-to guide on how to prepare for the inevitable. It's not only a book you will want to read yourself but also one you will want to give to friends.

—Perry Noble, founding and senior pastor
of NewSpring Church

Retire Inspired by Chris Hogan is a must-read because it addresses the number-one, fundamental issue we all face concerning our retirement: we need a clear vision of our retirement and a plan to get there! Inspiration is the key to starting the journey, and this book is the best first step you can take!

—Tom Ziglar, CEO, Ziglar, Inc.

I don't believe in retirement, but I do believe in living the kind of life you dream about. In *Retire Inspired* Chris Hogan says they're really the same thing. Retiring inspired isn't about checking out. It's about plugging into your potential right now so you can have the life you want in the future— and maybe sooner than you think.

—Michael Hyatt, *New York Times* best-selling author
and blogger, MichaelHyatt.com

It's good to think about the future. In fact, the Bible says, "Where there is no vision, the people perish" (Proverbs 29:18a KJV). Sadly, you may retire with nothing if you don't start investing toward your future today. In Chris Hogan's book, *Retire Inspired*, you'll find strategies and concepts to help you start saving for the retirement you've always dreamed you could have. Filled with engaging and empowering information, this book explains how to make solid decisions about your financial future.

—Robert Morris, founding senior pastor, Gateway
Church, Dallas/Fort Worth, Texas, and best-selling
author of *The Blessed Life*, *From Dream to Destiny*,
The God I Never Knew, and *Truly Free*

Retire Inspired is a well-written, comprehensive, gentle wake-up call about retirement, but it's not just about money! Whether you're twenty-one, seventy-one, or somewhere in between, enjoy this book as a blessing.

—Patrick Lencioni, president of The Table Group
and author of *The Five Dysfunctions of a Team*
and *The Advantage*

HOW MUCH WILL YOU NEED IN RETIREMENT?

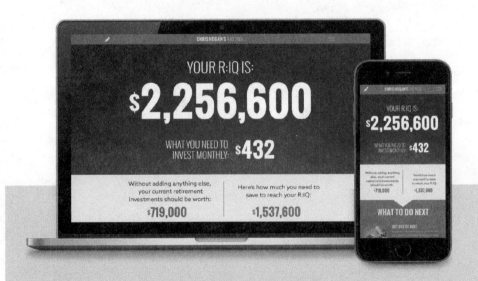

Get your *FREE* Retire Inspired Quotient (R:IQ) assessment at:

ChrisHogan360.com